PREJUDICE IN THE PRESS?

PREJUDICE IN THE PRESS?

PREJUDICE IN THE PRESS?

Investigating Bias in Coverage
of Race, Gender, Sexuality and Religion

George Yancey *and*
Alicia L. Brunson

McFarland & Company, Inc., Publishers
Jefferson, North Carolina

Library of Congress Cataloguing-in-Publication Data

Names: Yancey, George A., 1962– author. | Brunson, Alicia L., author.
Title: Prejudice in the press? : investigating bias in coverage of race, gender, sexuality and religion / George Yancey and Alicia L. Brunson.
Description: Jefferson, North Carolina : McFarland & Company, Inc., Publishers, 2019. | Includes bibliographical references and index.
Identifiers: LCCN 2018048541 | ISBN 9781476671482 (softcover : acid free paper) ∞
Subjects: LCSH: Journalism—Objectivity—United States. | Journalism—Political aspects—United States.
Classification: LCC PN4888.O25 Y35 2019 | DDC 071/.3—dc23
LC record available at https://lccn.loc.gov/2018048541

British Library cataloguing data are available

ISBN (print) 978-1-4766-7148-2
ISBN (ebook) 978-1-4766-3382-4

Front cover image by Igor Stevanovic (iStock)

Printed in the United States of America

*McFarland & Company, Inc., Publishers
Box 611, Jefferson, North Carolina 28640
www.mcfarlandpub.com*

Table of Contents

Preface

Even as we finish this book President Donald Trump is preparing to deliver "fake news awards." However the term fake news first emerged from progressive organizations frustrated with conservative partisan news outlets. Throughout our society charges of media corruption are commonplace. Media bias has become an important political and social football used to further the interest of many distinct vested interest groups. Little wonder a great deal of research has been used to investigate the possible existence and nature of this bias.

So why do we need yet another study of media bias? We believe that an important voice has been lost in the efforts to discover media bias. That voice is the voice of the reporters and editors who report on the various media stories. This research will endeavor to bring that voice to the forefront of understanding media bias. In their own voices we will allow those media personnel to tell us why they use a given story. The experimental audit methodology we use in this research will also let us see if they provide a different story when we alter key demographic and/or social variables in the stories. In this way we see our work as a natural step in determining the possible extent and nature of media bias in that we allow media personnel to explain their rational for the treatment of their subject matter in their own words.

The term fake news was never very useful for understanding how the media manifests itself in our society. With the exception of overtly partisan news outlets, there is too much on the line for media personnel to intentionally deceive their readers. Intentional deception by non-partisan media outlets would destroy the level of trust they need from their audience if they are going to perform their roles as disseminators of news. However, subtle biases are much more possible since reporters and editors may be just as vulnerable to social biases as the rest of us. Thus we see our work getting beyond the "less than" useful charges of fake news to a more nuanced understanding of the possibility of media bias.

Often when individuals think about media bias they tend to tie it to certain media outlets such as FOX news or Breitbart on the right and MSNBC or Huffington Post on the left. However we are not looking at organizations such as these, as much as the individuals in our media institutions. Indeed, most of our respondents do not work for the larger media organizations and thus we have limited information about how politically slanted media organizations may shape the overall delivery of news. We believe that our findings reflect on the entire institution of media, and that the bias of a particular media organization, no matter how powerful it may be, will not dramatically impact our overall findings.

We come at this question as sociologists but as sociologists with slightly different research interests. Both of us have an expertise on issues of race and ethnicity, but Brunson has focused directly on issues concerning the impact to the media in our society. On the other hand, Yancey has previously done little in the way of media analysis, but his work on anti-religion attitudes in the United States help to provide context for some of our findings. Thus each of us brings strengths to this work that will help us to fully flesh out our results.

The work in the book will be presented in seven chapters. In the first chapter we will discuss the controversies tied to social arguments about media bias. This topic generates a great deal of debate due to the powerful influence media can have in society. We briefly look at the social actors debating the fairness or unfairness of the media. Complaints about the media being racist, sexist, and/or bias towards liberals and anti–Christian come from many quarters in society and we explore those claims. Then we make the case for the importance of understanding the nature of potential bias existing in the media.

In the second chapter we theorize about how media bias may manifest itself in the United States. It is possible that it is merely a feature of powerful interests that dominate social institutions. This news ideology suggests that those with racial, sexual, or gender majority group status have the political power to use the media to improve the status of those in their social groups. Another possibility is that media bias is situated in a culture war atmosphere. The progressive political attitudes of the media personnel would predict the presence of a news ideology supportive of progressive elements in that culture war. However, it may be that occupational training in media makes it unlikely for any real bias to develop. Thus, there are three potential news ideologies—Majority Group Power, Culture War and No Bias—to explore with our data. Next, we look at previous literature on media bias in the United States. Previous literature produces mixed findings about the prospect of media bias in a variety of social dimensions. However, there are serious limitations in previous research on media bias. The vast majority of research on media bias utilizes observations of how media respond to outside stimulus. This methodology is vulnerable to problems of subjective bias since the researcher must make assessments of the primary materials generated by the media. Research that directly asks media personnel about why they make decisions about which social events to report and what is important about a given topic provides important undiscovered insights into how media bias does or does not operate in the United States. Finally, we look at some preliminary quantitative results of our research. We largely find that the placement and use of stories is not heavily dependent upon the characteristics of the actors in the story. However, our preliminary examination will still set the stage for the future chapters as we will explore important qualitative contrasts that emerged from our respondents.

In Chapter 3 we discuss three scenarios directly dealing with issues of race and ethnicity. Using these scenarios, we are able to assess whether the majority group racial status has much weight in the construction of a news ideology. Several respondents overtly note that the racial identity of the principles in the stories does not matter, and we find that often to be the case among our respondents. This was particularly the case in a scenario where a man robs another man near an airport. We switched the race of the robber and victim from white to black (but the race of the robber was always different than that of the victim). There was relatively little difference in how the respondents treated the story regardless of the race of the robber or victim, but the differences that did exist tend to protect the minority racial group from stigma. In a race-based kidnapping scenario, where a child is kidnapped and we switched out the race of the child, we could not find quantitative or qualitative differences. However, in the last scenario, we asked about peer review research in which one racial group (half the time the group is white and half the time the group is Hispanic) is documented to be harder working than other racial groups. We found differential treatment as the respondents minimize achievements of whites, but not of Hispanics. Ultimately we find little, if any, systematic evidence of a desire to support those with majority group racial status.

In Chapter 4, we used two scenarios to examine gender differences. We used a scenario in which a businessperson becomes a millionaire, interchanging the sex of that businessperson. We also altered the sex of a parent in a scenario of a parent who sold his/her child into slavery. We did not find a great deal of difference in the treatment of stories based upon the sex of the parent. There is some reinforcement of gender stereotyping in that a male businessman received more attention for his work ethic than a female businesswoman. Respondents also made less overt claims that gender does not matter in a story as compared to the examination of the race-based scenarios. However, there was not a large-scale systematic difference that one would expect if the media were being used as a patriarchal tool to disempower women. We find limited evidence of a theory of majority group support in that certain gender stereotypes may be promulgated by media personnel.

In Chapter 5, we used three scenarios to assess the potential nature of religious coverage by media personnel. All three of the scenarios include Christians, the numerically dominant religious group in the United States. In one scenario, we tested a university questioning the registration of a Christian organization versus a feminist organization. We found that the Christian group's claim was more subject to a need for verification and more likely to be seen in the context of conflict of the group to the university. The scenario with the feminist organization was more likely to touch on larger social issues such as sexism. In another scenario, we contrast a shooting at a Baptist church to a Muslim mosque. We found that respondents were more inclined to see the mosque as an example of a hate crime or discrimination. However, the story of the church shooting was more likely to emphasize the motivations of the shooter and issues of gun access. Finally, we used a scenario where a college professor engages in hate speech against either gays/lesbians or against Christians. We found that respondents were more likely to question how the university was going to handle the situation and to see the professor as a bigot if the professor insulted gays/lesbians, but they were less likely to see this as a big story or to see it as a story of free speech if the professor insulted Christians. These findings suggest merit in the Culture War News Ideology in that Christians are often seen as conservative combatants in that war and media personnel tend to dismiss the potential that Christians are victimized in a given social event.

Chapter 6 is an examination of whether the Majority Group Power or Culture War News Ideology is more powerful as an examination of treatment of homosexuality. Same-sex sexuality can be seen as a minority status or as an important issue in a culture war. In one scenario, we compare the treatment of a rally of gay/lesbian activists to ex-gays/lesbians, finding that more attention is paid to the gay/lesbian rally, and media personnel are more skeptical of the rally by ex-gays/lesbians. We also had a scenario in which either an interracial couple or same-sex couple is shot in a drive-by. The same-sex couple shooting was more likely to be seen as a potential hate crime. As mentioned in the previous chapter, we compared hate speech based on sexuality to that based on religion by a college professor. This scenario also reinforced the notion of the LGBT community being more likely to be victims of hate speech and that homophobia is an issue that requires the interest of media personnel. Treatment of sexuality issues decisively reinforces Culture War News Ideology rather than majority group status power since it paints a progressive participant in that war as victims needing help from the larger culture.

Chapter 7 is the concluding chapter. This work produces valuable information about how media bias can operate in the United States. There is evidence of bias, although it is difficult to determine just how strong this bias may be. We also found that social media personnel have distinct differences from other media personnel and discuss these differences in terms of what they mean about the possibility of overarching news ideologies that impact all facets of media. While there are elements of a majority group status bias, the stronger evidence supports a Cultural War News Ideology. This research also suggests how media bias may be reduced. There have been past efforts to help media personnel be sensitive to race and gender issues. This emphasis, and the occupational socialization that undoubtedly accompanies it, may account for the lack of Majority Group Power News Ideology. If a Culture War News Ideology is problematic to accurate reporting, then a similar effort at socializing media personnel may also serve to reduce this bias. We close the book by exploring shortcomings of this research effort and suggesting possible empirical extensions.

Although both of us worked hard on this research endeavor, we recognize that research is done in a larger community. Without the help of key individuals this research would not have been completed. Professionally we like to thank Dr. Tracy Everbach for looking over initial drafts of our survey and helping us to find media individuals on whom we could pretest the instrument. We also like to thank Dr. David Williamson who transferred money from his research accounts to us and thus provided some of the funding for this work. We are grateful for the reviewers of this work who provided us with insight on how to improve this work. Last, but certainly not least, we thank our respective spouses—Andromeda Yancey and Darin Brunson—who looked over various drafts of this work and gave us invaluable feedback. And of course we also thank them for putting up with us and providing us the space needed to complete this important project.

Introduction

To say that Hillary Clinton is a controversial figure is an understatement. While just about anybody who runs for president of the United States will attract supporters and detractors, the former secretary of state and first lady seems to be one of the more polarizing figures in our current political environment. Perhaps her association with her husband, a president so controversial that he was impeached, has generated these positive and negative passions. Perhaps it is her inability to connect with the public despite her overall skills as a public official. Perhaps Whitewater, Benghazi, or other controversies from her past generate arguments by both those who appreciate her and those who hate her. Whatever the reason for it, this type of polarization may have contributed to her 2016 presidential defeat at the hands of Donald Trump.

Polarizing public figures create strong positive and negative advocacy. Interpretations of these figures' actions are often filtered through that advocacy. One way those interpretations manifest themselves is through the media. Detractors of controversial figures will generally interpret the media as not being harsh enough with that individual, while supporters will interpret the media as being too harsh. Examples of this can be seen in the reaction to the media coverage of the controversies surrounding Clinton. Brittany Stalsburg, a Democrat pollster, complains that the media has overblown her difficulties (Stalsburg 2015), while Don Irvine, chairman of Accuracy in Media (a conservative media watchdog group), argues that CNN failed to tell its audience that an op-ed writer is a major fundraiser for Clinton (Irvine 2015). Such divergent interpretations of the media's treatment of controversial figures are hardly limited to Clinton. Individuals of differing political stripes tend to see in the media the reality that supports their presuppositions.

But is there anything to viewers' claims that the media are left leaning and liberal? Or that they are right leaning and conservative? If, as some journalists point out, they are trained to be objective, are they truly bias-free? Or do they exhibit preferences toward certain groups and prejudice towards others? It is possible Stalsburg is correct that the media is downplaying the strength of Clinton's candidacy. This may be due to the potential discomfort media personnel have towards a female leader. It is as easily conceivable that Irvine is right, and the media has a progressive bias in favor of Clinton. The bias detected by viewers, in other words, is not always or necessarily in their heads: News coverage may in fact be influenced, in ways large or small, by the attitudes and beliefs of those who deliver it.

The saying goes that just because you are paranoid does not mean that they are not out to get you. Certain groups—racial and ethnic minorities, for instance, or conservative Christians—have little faith in media fairness. Sociological theories of group interest (Kaufmann 1998; Visser et al. 2014) and social psychological theories of confirmation bias (Nickerson 1998; Rodenberg 2011; Iyengar and Hahn 2009) suggest that individuals in these groups have an incentive to perceive bias against them whether it exists or not. By painting the media as unfair, they gain a victim image that, at least theoretically, can be leveraged for social power (Campbell and Manning 2014). There is a real possibility, however, that media bias does exist against these or other social groups. Before we dismiss the concern of special interest groups that often complain about this bias, we would do well either to confirm or refute the notion that bias does not exist in any large measure.

To that end, we have conducted research allowing us to address the question of media bias, using a methodology that goes beyond what is merely reported in media primary documents by allowing media personnel to speak for themselves about their approaches towards certain social groups. We do more than simply illustrate the possibility of media bias; we explore how such bias may be reflected in media coverage of social issues. To be specific, we looked at reporters and editors working on the staffs of newspapers; and we assessed their decisions on story inclusion and placement, hoping to determine whether and to what degree they are shaped by the racial, sexual, gender, and political or religious characteristics of the principles in the stories. We utilized an experimental audit technique that allowed us to control for factors other than the experimental variables we investigated.

Experimental Audit Study and Potential Media Bias

A generous amount of research has investigated the possibility of media bias. Econometric models have been used to predict whether media bias would occur and why (Baron 2005; Bernhardt, Krasa and Polborn 2008; Gentzkow and Shapiro 2006). Other research generally has relied upon content analysis of video (Aday 2010; Groeling 2008; Kuklinski and Sigelman 1992; Lowry 2008) or print (Eisinger, Veenstra and Koehn 2007; Ho and Quinn 2008; Schiffer 2006) media. Innovative methodologies such as examining think tanks cited in media (Groseclose and Milyo 2005) or surveys of media individuals (Patterson and Donsbach 1996) have been used to investigate this research question. As we will see in the following chapter, the results of this research are mixed. However, none of the previous work adequately assesses the intent of media personnel as it concerns how they will cover stories containing certain social groups. We believe that we have put together a strategy that can meet this very important need— experimental audit study.

To understand the value of the experimental audit design, we have to ask about the importance of the characteristics of the actors in a media story. Interest groups have shown sensitivity to how they are portrayed in the media. For example, in 2016 Omar Mateen killed 49 individuals at a gay nightclub called Pulse. Immediately after the shooting there was speculation about who the shooter was and why he engaged in such a horrifying act. Given the nature of the nightclub it was easy to speculate that the shooter had religious motivations for his actions. Watching television and following social media of the event brought out interesting reactions from Christians and Muslims. Both were waiting in anticipation, fearful that the shooter would be someone who claimed their faith. Naturally, members of each group wanted to avoid having the distinction that the shooter may have regularly attended a church or mosque. At the end of the day it was Muslims who were left in the awful position of defending their religion from charges of violence and homophobia.

It makes sense that members of these religious groups will react differently to the story of a club shooting depending on the religious identity of the shooter. Those religious groups have a good deal at stake concerning their image and ability to protect their cultural position. But in theory the same story of the shooting should be presented by the media regardless of the religious identity of the shooter. We can never be certain that the stories of the shooting at the Pulse nightclub would have been the same had the shooter been a Christian. But this story illustrates a possible way to think about news coverage in that we should consider whether the characteristics of the principles in the stories matter in whether the story is covered, the prominence of where it is placed and how it is covered.

To this end, the value of experimental audit design can be appreciated. With this design we can investigate the question of how different characteristics potentially shape a media story. To do this we present a possible story to media personnel and ask them questions about whether they would run the story and where they would place the story. We also ask them about factors that led them to the decision they made. But what we do not tell them is that we have altered some of the characteristics of the possible story and sent it to other media personnel. Sometimes the individual is white and sometimes black. Sometimes the group is Christian and other times the group is Muslim. Sometimes we are talking about a man and sometimes a woman. The question is whether members of the media answer our inquiries about the use of the story depending on the characteristics of the principles of the stories.

We do not rely on the answers from a single media personnel to investigate the possibility of bias. By sending out the stories with differences to half of our sample, we are in a position to systematically compare media personnel who are told about one characteristic with those who are told about another. If there are consistent differences in how members with a certain characteristic or from a given group are treated by the media then we have some confidence that this is a pattern that will hold up in general. The real stories that media personnel cover will undoubtedly differ from the hypothetical scenarios we send them through this research, but we are gaining some insight as to how they may cover those with certain characteristics. Those tendencies are unlikely to greatly change when they cover actual stories.

For example, if we find that when we present stories about men who become millionaires that the media personnel are more willing to credit toughness and wits for his success while attributing luck for the success of women who become millionaires then we can reasonably assert that media presentations are more likely to give men credit for their efforts than women. We would expect such a difference to hold up in other stories about successful individuals whether that success is economically, politically, socially or academically based. This would indicate that men are more likely to get favorable media coverage relative to women. It also reveals an important potential bias that helps explain how men may benefit from the way they are portrayed in the larger media. Thus, our technique is well positioned to discover potential media bias as well as the type of narratives that are attractive to media personnel.

In this book we will rely on the information gained by our audit analysis to make assertions about the way social and demographic characteristics impact potential media personnel's decisions about stories. In Table 1-1 we present the eleven scenarios that we will use in this research. By changing certain demographic or social factors we hope to see whether media personnel react differently to the question of whether, and how, they would use a given story in their publication. For example in the first scenario we switch the race of the robber and the victim. We hope to see if reporting on interracial crime differs depending of the race of the participants in that event. In similar ways we will use the other ten scenarios to assess how reporters and editors may change their stories, or not cover a story, based on the characteristics of the principles in that story.[1]

TABLE 1-1
SCENARIOS USED IN SURVEY

Changes to the "B" form of the survey are in *italics*.

1. Rodger Jones, a black *white* man, was robbed at gunpoint two blocks from the local airport. Concern has been raised since the place of his robbery is supposed to be secure due to its proximity to the airport. Mr. Jones states that the robber was tall, slender and white *black*. Local civil rights organizations have complained that the robbery was racially motivated. They have made a spokesperson available for interview. The police are currently looking for witnesses to this crime. (Interracial Airport Crime)

2. A political rally today was held by about 150 members of PFLAG (Parents Friends and Families of Lesbians and Gays) *PFOX (Parents and Friends of Ex-Gays and Gays)* an interest group serving the LGBT *ex-gay* community. The purpose of the rally was to protest a law allowing *forbidding* reparative therapy—which is therapy where the goal is to help a gay or lesbian become straight. The group perceives this law as a threat to their community since if it goes into effect there may be fewer members who are part of PFLAG *PFOX*. A spokesperson describes the group's concerns in detail. (Political Rally)

11

3. Pat Young was once homeless. Now he *she* is a multimillionaire. He *She* became wealthy by starting a small business selling clothes. Over time he *she* invested the profits into larger business endeavors and now he *she* enjoys his *her* current financial success. The paper wants to do a feature on him *her*. (Homeless to Millionaire)

4. The Baptist Student Association *Feminist Majority* has complained that State University's administration is putting unnecessary barriers keeping them from being recognized at the university. The leaders of this organization have noted that while the college usually takes 2 weeks to recognize new campus leaders, it took 5 weeks for the leaders of the Baptist Student Association *Feminist Majority* to be recognized. Furthermore, the administration is demanding changes in the campus organization's charter claiming that the charter as it is currently written unfairly excludes non–Christians *men* from leadership positions. A spokesperson from that group and the university is available for interview. (Campus Organization)

5. A research study indicates that whites *Hispanics* tend to work harder than those of other races. This research is an experimental design where people of different races were given routine tasks and then evaluated to see who put in the most effort into those tasks. Consistently, whites *Hispanics* scored higher than other racial groups. A researcher from this project is available to discuss how the results were generated and a spokesperson from a civil rights organization is available to be interviewed on the implications of this research. (Research Study)

6. An interracial *A same-sex* couple, Sam House and Jackie O'Hare, were shot while walking down the street. They were shot by approximately three men who drove by them in a car. Witnesses state that the shooters yelled racist *homophobic* epitaphs at the couple. Neither of the victims died and both are in stable condition at the hospital. Neither victim is immediately available for an interview, but there is a police report that can be used for the story. Also a spokesperson for a local civil rights organization is willing to comment on the incident. (Couple Shooting)

7. Richard Smith (R) *(D)*, a congressman in a different part of your state, was arrested last night for soliciting prostitution. He is accused of approaching an undercover female police officer and requesting sexual favors. He was quickly arrested but did not spend the night in jail due to bail. The rest of the details of the event are vague as the police will not release further information. But a spokesperson from the congressman's office is available for interview. (Congressman and Prostitute)

8. Candy Evans, a 9 year old white *black* girl, was abducted from her front porch last night. Reports are that she was approached by a man asking her for directions. When she got close he grabbed her and forced her into his car. So far her whereabouts are not known and her distraught single mother is available to be interviewed. (Kidnapped Girl)

9. This morning the Springfield Baptist Church *Islamic Center of Springfield* was shot up by a man named Jessie Ferguson, who killed himself before being caught. Two other people died. One is a Larry Johnson, a thirty-six year old man, and the other is Vanessa Harris, a seventeen year old girl. Three other worshippers were shot but none of those injuries are serious. The church *mosque* is located in a city on the other side of the country so all the paper has access to is an AP report of these events. (Religious Institution Shooting)

10. Sarah Henderson, a female professor at a university in a neighboring state is recorded making hateful comments. She is reported saying that LGBT individuals *conservative Christians* are immoral, hateful people. She commented that LGBT individuals *Christians* are trying to take over the country by making unreasonable demands on the rest of us. The student, Ben Long, making the recording is gay *a conservative Christian* and was especially disturbed that her diatribe was punctuated by the epitaph of "fags" *"Bible thumpers"* during her rant. Mr. Long is available for interview by telephone for this story. Ms. Henderson will not make herself available for an interview. (Hate Speech)
11. Taylor Parker has been accused of selling her *his* daughter to a modern sexual slavery ring. Miss *Mr.* Parker is a single parent who was struggling financially. She *He* reported the child missing six months ago. Yet the police have come to suspect that her *his* child was sold into a slavery ring. The police have indicted her *him* on the charges of kidnapping. This is a local case and the police report is available for this story. (Daughter into Slavery)

We will look at the quantitative results in the next chapter. These results give us an overview of possible differences connected to demographic characteristics of the principles of a story. But the real value of our work may come from our assessment of the open-ended questions asked of each scenario. We refer to answers of those questions in Chapters 3–7. Our open-ended questions will provide our respondents with a voice to express their attitudes towards certain potential stories. This voice and the tone that emerges from it will provide important nuance to the answers of potential media bias. Indeed, this technique will allow us to document the possibility of this bias with the very words of our respondents. Such expressions are something that has not been featured in any other research design on this subject.

Forms of Media—Newspaper, Television and Social Media

As we investigate the possibility of media bias, it is important to note that there are a variety of media forms that can have specific social functions. For instance, it has been suggested (Katz, Haas and Gurevitch 1973) that newspaper media best integrate into the sociopolitical order. Hanson (1997) argues that many Americans believe that newspapers are used to disseminate knowledge. Newspaper journalists are trained to report information on daily happenings from the local to the global. News journalists go to the scene of the action, observe their surroundings and interview individuals pertinent to the event in order to shed light on the causes or implications of the event. The purpose of this type of journalism is to give readers the information necessary to make an informed opinion of the event.

Newspapers are one of the oldest forms of media in the United States, though there is evidence that newspapers are losing influence in our society (Hagan 2005; Seelye 2007). In some ways we still look at newspapers as the foundational source of American media. It is likely that newspaper media personnel reflect general attitudes among media personnel. Historically, newspaper consumers were characterized as being older, better educated and of a higher socioeconomic status (Burgoon and Burgoon 1980; De Waal, Schönbach and Lauf 2005; Grabe, Kamhawi and Yegiyan 2009). Consumers viewed the purposes of newspapers as providing information. Consumers did not consider newspapers as biased. In the present era, consumers of newspapers perceive their function as not only providing information but also entertainment. Newspapers need to "sell stories." Today, consumers perceive newspapers as being biased. This might be the case because news journalism is in a niche market that targets specific consumers to increase readership.

Television as a form of media has not been around as long as newspapers, but it has become an important part of our media tradition. Broadcast news journalists base their programming decisions upon the interest, importance, and visual impact of the stories (Berkowitz 1990). Generally, television is used for entertainment purposes; however, television news media can be used to strengthen already established political views and antagonism towards political out-groups (Bolce and De Maio 2008; Eveland and Shah 2003; Lee 2012). Groeling (2013) contests that television news is overtly partisan and that consumers only watch programming that confirms their political leanings. Generally, individuals who receive their news via television are characterized as having lower levels of education (Grabe, Kamhawi and Yegiyan 2009).

Dowler (2002) proposes that television has different effects than print media. He found that those who get their primary crime news from television are more likely to disagree with easy access to concealed fire arms than those who get their primary crime news from newspapers. Individuals who are exposed to more television news about crime are more likely to fear victimization and have more support for hard crime policies than those who receive crime news via the Internet (Roche, Pickett and Gertz 2016).

By using an actual person for consumers to see and relate to, it is possible that television has more of an impact on social attitudes than even newspapers. Indeed, some research documents the power of television news to impact social attitudes rather than the other way around (Behr and Iyengar 1985). For example, evidence indicates that the type of crime stories on television news has increased the fear individuals have of criminals (Gilliam Jr. and Iyengar 2000; Romer, Jamieson and Aday 2003). Understanding the perspectives of those in television media is important for helping us to understand the presentation of the media to the general population.

Finally, in recent years we have seen the development of social media. Social media attracts a distinct audience (Correa, Hinsley and De Zuniga 2010; Duggan and Brenner 2013; Lenhart et al. 2010). More Americans are using online sources of news than traditional forms of news (Roche, Pickett and Gertz 2016). Consumers of online newspapers tend to be educated and young (De Waal, Schönbach and Lauf 2005). Consumers of online news also tend to expose themselves to information that is consistent with their political views (Roche, Pickett and Gertz 2016).

Being a relatively new media outlet, it is reasonable to argue that social media outlets are not has powerful as traditional outlets such as newspapers and television. However, it is a media form that is reaching those who no longer look to newspapers and television as their source of information. Online journalism is different from traditional forms of journalism because it is interactive (Deuze 2003). Because of the many news options that the Internet provides, consumers may not perceive the media as being hostile against one's political party (Groeling 2013; Lin, Haridakis and Hanson 2016). Unlike people who get their news primarily from television, people who get their news from online sources tend to be more educated (Grabe, Kamhawi and Yegiyan 2009). In addition, Sundar (1999) suggests that individuals who use online news sources use the same criteria for evaluating news from different media. These criteria are credibility, liking, quality, and representativeness. Consumers use the Internet to get their news out of convenience. Individuals are able to choose when, where, and how they get their information (Roche, Pickett and Gertz 2016; Tewksbury 2003). In addition, online news may be replacing traditional forms of news media because it provides gratification by providing solutions to individuals' needs (Dimmick, Chen and Li 2004).

Although online sources are being used more frequently than in the past, consumers view Internet news as only moderately credible. However, online news is rated as more credible than broadcast news (Johnson and Kaye 2010). Newspapers are viewed as the best form of media to receive information from (De Waal, Schönbach and Lauf 2005). Hauke Riesch (2011) cautions that research about online news consumption has a major limitation. Published news consistently changes or may be removed all together. There is no service that provides an archive for all original published news stories. Because of this, there may be different results concerning content, ideology, and use among research endeavors. As such if there is an overarching media bias that transcends all types of media then it is reasonable to consider whether such a bias reaches into the type of new media emerging in our society. However, since newspapers are seen as the most credible news source, bias among newspaper reporters and editors should be seen as being particularly impactful.

Obviously these three media outlets are not exhaustive of all types of media reflected in our society. Most notably we are not dealing with radio media, which has emerged as a force in, and some argue as a counterbalance to,[2] traditional media. However, we contend that if there is a generalized media bias then it should show up in all three of the media outlets used in this current research endeavor. To be sure, we were more successful at obtaining participation from newspaper personnel than television or social media personnel. Thus, we will be able to say more about newspaper media than any of the other types of media. Yet, the increased respect given to information from newspapers, relative to other media sources, indicates that we can most fully examine media bias in the venue where it can have its greatest effect. Furthermore, many media personnel tend to attend the same academic programs and likely share similar social networks. Thus, we have confidence that learning about the social attitudes of this data set will provide valuable insight into the attitudes of media personnel in general, even though the data is heavily influenced by newspaper media personnel.

News Reporting—Objectivity, Bias and News Ideologies

A major concern within journalism and the dissemination of news is objectivity. Many believe that what is presented in the press should be "objective, fair, balanced, and detached" (Hanson 1997). The goal of objectivity is to be unbiased or neutral, with a story being fair since it presents both sides equitably. Hansen explains that objectivity is used to make it easier to gather and assemble information to report as news under tight deadlines and editor expectations. An objectivity norm is also used to persuade consumers that news journalists depict trustworthy and legitimate portrayals of reality (Skovsgaard et al. 2012). However, the journalist's perception of his or her role plays a large part in how the norm is implemented.

There is a long-held journalistic norm of objectivity (Skovsgaard et al. 2012; Vos 2012). Donsbach and Klett (1993) define objectivity as a "valid and true description and explanation of reality." Researchers who fail to find evidence of bias have suggested that occupational training in the maintenance of objectivity may play an important role in such a finding (Black, Steele and Barney 1999; Dennis 1997; Fishman 1988; Schudson 1981). Journalists started describing their work as objective in the 1920s (Streckfuss 1990). Objectivity is used to compensate for the realization that a "true reality" cannot be completely represented in an accurate manner (Skovsgaard et al. 2012). Thus, it became important to make every effort to get as close to an accurate representation as possible. To do this, news media personnel are encouraged to subject themselves to the rigors of the scientific method so that they can make their work appear objective. Of course in the process of making such an effort, journalists may indeed create stories that are more accurate than one would normally expect.

Objectivity is based upon factual accuracy and justified interpretation. "To be factually accurate is to contain objectively verified facts. To provide justified interpretation is to frame a story based on objective editorial judgments" (Figdor 2010). Balance, fairness, accuracy, and transparency are other journalistic norms (Losey and Kurthen 1995; Skovsgaard et al. 2012). Objectivity has three aims: (1) separating facts from opinion, (2) presenting an emotionally detached view of the news, and (3) striving for fairness and balance, giving both sides an opportunity to reply in a way that provides full information to the audience (Donsbach and Klett 1993). Thus, if news media personnel are striving to remain objective, then they will approach media stories with a focus on verifying all of the facts and make sure that the perspectives of all of the principles in the story are represented. The social and demographic characteristics of those principles should not influence these sorts of choices. If they do influence those choices, then one will not obtain the objectivity sought. Thus, majority or disempowered groups should not be treated worse, nor should they be treated better, if objectivity is the value that determines which news stories are written.

Introduction

Efforts towards objectivity have been criticized with arguments that journalists cannot present reality, but rather an interpretation of their perception of reality (Skovsgaard et al. 2012). What is considered news is not the event, but rather an interpretation of the event. Because of this subjective interpretative element, journalists are encouraged to be fair, accurate, balanced, and/or transparent in their work (Skovsgaard et al. 2012). However, we cannot expect the journalist to be objective. Furthermore, objectivity may be used as a tool to delegitimize opposing ideologies. Ribeiro (2012) claims that objectivity as a value became prominent during World War I, when English newspaper journalists claimed objectivity to attack German "toxic propaganda." Toxic propaganda is described as the dissemination of lies by the enemy. English journalism, on the other hand, was considered truth. Ribeiro cites John Hartley and his claim that objectivity is not about coming closer to the truth, but rather "trust between the addresser and the addressee" (p. 277). Just as claims of objectivity were used to promote the English cause in World War I, they can also be used to promote other causes media personnel deem to be important. This use of objectivity to undermine a deviant perspective has likely been utilized by a variety of media personnel at different times of our history.

However, Schudson (2001) distinguishes objectivity journalism from partisan journalism. Objectivity journalism aims and claims to report unemotionally and fairly without commenting, slanting, or shaping of the event. Conversely, partisan journalists are viewed as allies or agents of political parties. Groeling (2013) posits that partisan news is quite evident in modern times. In modern society, partisan journalists may be seen as allies of certain social or cultural movements. Here we can see a modern adherence to objectivity and rejection of journalists expressing their personal views. Partisan journalists may not be seen as real journalists by their peers, in part, because they make their social and political perspectives clear to potential consumers of media. Nevertheless, the question remains whether objective journalists also impart their perspectives to media consumers, only in a less obvious manner.

The other side of objectivity is bias. Lee (2010) reports that many Americans believe that news media are biased and should not be trusted. Lee argues that this belief stands although it is not supported scientifically. Some misunderstanding of bias may stem from the conflation of trust and media bias. Trust can be seen in whether the audience perceives a source as trustworthy, while bias is due to the actual media content. Lee found that components that influence consumers' perception of bias within news are their political perspectives, political affiliations, trust of the government and fellow citizens, and their view of the economy. Unsurprisingly, conservatives attest that journalists tend to be liberal and biased in their reporting, while liberals argue that news is biased in a conservative direction. In particular, liberals contend that news media are controlled by large corporations that only allow the voices of the political elite to be heard, making mass media a tool used to maintain the status quo (Glynn and Huge 2014; Lin, Haridakis and Hanson 2016). On the other hand, politically conservative activists (Coulter 2002; Goldberg 2014; Shapiro 2011; Stossel 2004) argue that the media is ran by political progressives who push an agenda sympathetic to progressive ideals. Some contend that the only way conservatives can get a fair hearing within the media is to set up their own conservative partisan media (Anderson 2013; Grossmann 2017). Glynn and Huge (2014) contend that perception of media bias is equivalent to political ideology. Partisan individuals assume heightened media bias when they are greatly involved in the issue presented within the media message.

Appiah, Knobloch-Westerwick and Alter (2013) argue that bias is also tied to a consumer's social identity. Media consumers are attracted to and use media that promote their social identity and self-esteem (Appiah, Knobloch-Westerwick and Alter 2013; Lin, Haridakis and Hanson 2016). Social identity and self-esteem are connected to in-group experiences and beliefs about one's own group. Media messages can positively or negatively impact an individual's perception of his or her social identity and self-esteem (Appiah, Knobloch-Westerwick and Alter 2013). Other factors that increase perception of bias include political cynicism, group status, inter-group bias, and political ideology (Lin, Haridakis and Hanson 2016). Thus, consumers may be creating the media results they desire and in doing so help to facilitate biased media presentations.

Consumers' perceptions of bias may come from the belief that journalists write according to their political beliefs. Others argue that bias is due to the constraints journalists face by working for news organizations with their own political standpoints (An et al. 2012; Skovsgaard et al. 2012). In particular, journalists are characterized as liberal while media corporations are characterized as conservative (Kperogi 2013; Lee 2012; Skovsgaard et al. 2012). Eveland and Shah (2003) argue that perception of news biases are not actually due to media ownership or journalists' political beliefs but rather environmental factors. Another factor that increases the perception of bias is communication that confirms an already held belief (McNerney 2011). For instance, Eveland and Shah (2003) suggest Republican partisans are more likely to believe that media are biased in a liberal direction when they consume other media that agree with their already held ideologies.

Yet, bias and objectivity may not be the best way to look at how the media cover news events. Figdor (2010) argues that objectivity is not possible. Many factors make it very difficult for an individual to report objectively. Journalists report from their point-of-view, and all observations are subjective. Figdor does not push for subjectivity to be regarded as bias. Rather, reporting must include factual accuracy and justified interpretation. His assertion on the impossibility of objectivity is supported by epistemological arguments that challenge the notion that any human can be truly objective (Becker, Niehaves and Klose 2005; Campbell and Wasco 2000; Kuhn, Cheney and Weinstock 2000; Megill 1994; Roszak 1958).

If objectivity is not possible, then we have to consider what subcultural mechanisms may influence choices made by media personnel. A good deal of previous research has explored different aspects of journalism culture (Bohrmann, Klaus and Machill 2007; Frith and Meech 2007; Hanitzsch 2007; Mellado et al. 2012; Nolan 2009; Stamper and Brants 2011; Vine 2006). Hanitzsch (2007) argues that culture can be conceptualized as the ideas, practices and artifacts within a given community. Journalism culture can thus be seen in the way journalists act and think. At one level, certain ideas and values are very specific to accomplishing the task of reporting on news events. Certain operational cultural norms, such as adhering to deadlines, are necessary for simply accomplishing the task of reporting the news in a timely manner. However, Hanitzsch points out that the terms culture and ideology are often used interchangeably. A dominant ideology in journalism would help shape the values and orientations that journalists possess. For example, Hanizsch argues that ethical ideologies are specific to the unique cultural context within the media. Thus, ideological perspectives can inform media personnel how to navigate the ethical decisions they have to make to do their jobs.

But ideologies are not necessarily limited to the practical issues about how to perform one's occupation. Westerstahl and Johansson (1986) discuss what they term "news ideologies." News ideologies are tied to the other ideologies of media personnel, such as those based in their political and media values. They are also ways in which media personnel not only inform the audience, but also attempt to influence them. For example, they note that in the mid–60s, news ideologies changed from an emphasis on a traditional reporting of what the public wants to a focus on critically examining news events. These news ideologies can also help motivate media personnel to promote certain social and political activities. As such, Caspari (1982) points out that black media had specific goals of attempting to change their society. Black media clearly exhibited news ideologies focused less on objectivity and other traditional values that we tend to tie to media but instead on societal transformation. News ideologies can represent the underlying social and political assumptions that media personnel bring into their reporting of news events.

Theories of confirmation bias (Klayman 1995; Nickerson 1998) indicate that our overconfidence in our previous beliefs interferes with our attempts to develop objective opinions. Due to such influences, individuals develop an intellectual framework shaping how they will interpret social reality. With such a framework, individuals tend to emphasize evidence supporting their presuppositions and de-emphasize evidence challenging their presuppositions (Klayman 1995). If this is accurate for other individuals, then it is likely true for media personnel. News ideologies can be an important mechanism by which journalists also filter social facts and evidence to support their social and psychological presuppositions.

Despite these natural tendencies to focus on information that supports one's presuppositions and/or social position, there is a powerful attempt within the media to neutralize such efforts. Hanitzsch (2007) identifies the tension in the institutional roles of journalists between being an objective gatekeeper and a participatory advocate. If most media personnel attempt to fulfill the role of a gatekeeper then they would work towards an objective presentation of news events. Much of the training and socialization among media personnel can be oriented towards enabling them to accomplish this objectivity. If that training is effective, then media personnel may gain the ability to shape a news ideology that is based upon objective presentation of the news rather than the social and political presuppositions of the media personnel.

Have media personnel been successful in neutralizing their social and political biases? That is the major question this book will attempt to answer. To that end we have chosen a methodology that will inform us of the informal ideologies that influence the media community. By not focusing on individual instances that may, or may not, reflect an example of a news bias, we will look at the larger ideological decisions made in the construction of news stories. This will allow us to make sense of the way news ideologies impact the type of media we receive. While our book is not the final word on the question of media bias (Can research ever deliver the "final word" on such a complicated topic?), we assert that we will come closer to determining how media personnel actually think differently about a story based on the characteristics of the actors. This book will take the study of media bias into a new realm, where the respondents will actually discuss their potential bias in their own words.

1

News Ideologies

Media has the ability to set the national agenda and shape public policy (Losey and Kurthen 1995). News stories, in particular, have social, economic, and political consequences (Meyers 2004). Because of this tremendous influence, it is not surprising that activists and scholars from a variety of different special interest groups consistently complain about the problem of media bias (Bullock and Jafri 2000; Goldberg 2014; Lawrence and Rose 2010; Savali 2015). These groups have motivation to paint themselves as the victims of a media that they argue is hostile towards them, either because they do not like members in their group (Anderson 2013; Huston 2011; Olasky and Smith 2013) or because the media is serving corporate interests (Alterman 2008; Cromwell and Edwards 2006). However, such motivated claims are not the best way to assess why media bias may exist.

Understanding the potential origin of media bias is important if we are going to have an informed investigation of the presence and nature of such bias. If media bias is driven by antipathy towards out-groups, then evidence of which groups face negative bias would be insightful in determining who the media perceive as out-group members. For example, if class issues are a major way in which media members define who is in their out-groups, then one may expect a positive bias towards those in the middle and upper classes. Thus, the origin of media bias would be the protection of the capitalist system that operates to the benefit of media personnel. On the other hand, if political identity is how media members define their out-groups, then, given the progressive beliefs of those in the media (Dautrich and Hartley 1999; Weaver and Wilhoit 1996), there should be a negative bias towards political conservatives. An origin of media bias based on political and cultural struggle would produce evidence of bias in support of a progressive political agenda.

We have identified two potential areas of social conflict that may lead to the construction of news ideologies that could shape the type of media coverage we see in the United States. One possibility is based on the reality that media personnel generally have a fair amount of social power. Therefore, these members may be highly supportive of those in the majority group as it concerns race, gender, religion, sexuality etc. This support does not have to be overt, and few would assert that media personnel are rank racists, sexists or homophobes. Instead, they may be relatively unaware of how majority group members have gained institutional advantages in our society and the subtle stereotypes that feed those advantages. Media personnel may inadvertently, but firmly, reinforce norms that support majority group members in our society. We call this Majority Group Power News Ideology. It reflects the larger majority/minority conflict in our society.

On the other hand, media personnel may react to what has been termed the culture war (Hunter 1991). This "war" has focused on issues, such as abortion and same-sex marriage, that cultural conservatives and progressives find to be important. This conflict may represent more than different notions of what should be the cultural norms of our society, but also may emerge in ways to allow certain cultural groups to protect their social interests. For example, Christian groups may experience a loss of prestige with an increase of a modern sexuality norm that challenges the legitimacy of their traditional moral values. Research (Ranly 1979; Underwood and Stamm 2001) suggests that media personnel tend to have lower levels of the religious identities that support cultural conservatives. Furthermore, education is inversely related to support of cultural conservative ideology (Legge Jr. 1983; Loftus 2001; Ohlander, Batalova and Treas 2005). If media personnel are more likely to be well educated and relatively irreligious, then one would predict that they would be supportive of a cultural progressive viewpoint in the culture war. The potential of this possibility to shape the way the media influences our society can be called Culture War News Ideology.

"News ideologies" is a useful term that helps us understand the dominant perspectives likely influencing decisions in the newsroom. Given previous research on media bias and the nature of social attitudes in the United States, we have identified three news ideologies—Majority Group Power,

Cultural War, and No Bias—that we argue are useful for understanding potential origins of media bias.

Previous Work on News Bias

Generally, discussions of such bias rest on contentions of whether liberal or conservative preferences are favored by our media institutions (Bagdikian 2014; Eisinger, Veenstra and Koehn 2007; Groseclose 2012; Losey and Kurthen 1995). Historically there was some evidence of anti-conservative media bias (Baum and Groeling 2008; Groeling 2008; Groseclose and Milyo 2005; Lichter, Rothman and Lichter 1986; Lowry and Shidler 1995). McCombs and Shaw (1972) argue that the media has great power to frame issues in ways that draw attention to concerns they find important. Kuypers (2002) builds on this observation to argue that the media uses this agenda-setting potential to promote a liberal bias. But other research suggests pro-conservative media coverage (Kenney and Simpson 1993; Morris and Francia 2010).

What is quite interesting is the possible explanations of potential political bias. Alterman (2008) argues that there is a lack of liberal media bias, he focuses on potential ways the media serve the interests of corporations rather than the government. He defines political bias as favoring corporate interests by silencing the masses and de-emphasizing the advantages of, and the dysfunctions caused by, powerful conservative interests. Furthermore, progressive activists argue that media is misrepresenting oppressed groups (Funt 2015; Savali 2015). They contend that in order to accomplish this goal, conservatives insist media is biased to divert our attention from the reality that the media has helped maintain a society working against minority group interests (Alterman 2008; Bagdikian 2014; Parenti 1996).

On the other hand, Olasky and Smith's (2013) complaints about progressive bias focus on what they see as the mistreatment of Christians. They tie media bias to cultural issues. These divergent focuses make narrow discussions of conservative or progressive media bias to be inadequate. Moreover, Losey and Kurthen (1995) argue that one major media bias issue is political correctness. Conservatives contend that the media is silencing views that are not progressive. These conservatives complain that free speech is being attacked and that truth is being muddled by progressive propaganda (Berkowitz 2015; Fields 2015; Goldberg 2014). They also assert that American values and institutions are being lost, in part because progressives control media.

Either side of the debate sees themselves as the victim and the other side as the oppressor. This is not surprising since individuals have a tendency to perceive media coverage as negative to their own in-group, no matter in what group they had their membership (Dalton, Beck and Huckfeldt 1998; Gunther 1992). Yet, how this bias manifests itself can differ depending on whether conservative or progressive activists are making the complaint. Kperogi (2013) argues that journalists are liberal, but that the press and news corporations are conservative. This suggests that whether newspapers have a conservative or progressive bias depends on whether journalists or news corporations have more influence on the finished articles. If journalists have the interest of the progressive organizations, then they will attempt to promote a positive bias for underrepresented groups. Thus, we would find more than merely a bias that supports progressive public policies; instead, we would see a bias against groups perceived as harming disadvantaged groups and a positive bias towards those disadvantaged groups. On the other hand, if there is a conservative bias, there is a desire to protect the general status quo in our society and to ignore the plight of the underrepresented. Such a bias would lead to either ignoring the problems disempowered groups face because of how they can be mistreated or even finding ways to blame them for their circumstances. Such actions would reinforce the position of the majority group members who tend to run news corporations.

This analysis suggests that rather than looking at an overview of conservative or progressive ideology, we can explore potential media bias by looking at how the media treats disadvantaged groups and/or those perceived to maintain our traditional cultural norms. It may be better to focus on explorations of how the media covers different social groups than to examine an overall conservative or progressive bias. As such other research has documented the potential of bias from the perspective of different social groups. For example, feminist activists have argued that the media de-emphasizes the reporting of patriarchy in our society (Douglas 1995; Smith, Choueiti and Gall 2011). Previous empirical work has found evidence that there may be a media bias against women (Gershon 2012; Kahn 1994; Miller 1996; Niven 2002; Sreberny-Mohammadi and Ross 1996). Race and ethnic activists and academics discuss a media that perpetuates the racialized nature of our culture (Amaya 2013; Balkaran 1999; Giroux 1998). This fear has also been empirically substantiated (Entman and Rojecki 2001; Gershon 2013; Niven 2002; Pitt Jr. 2006; Schaffner and Gadson 2004; Zilber and Niven 2000). Finally, conservative Christians have also expressed concern about the way they are portrayed in the media (Chapman 2015; Dempsey 2013; Olasky and Smith 2013; Viguerie 2012), a charge with at least some empirical support (Kerr 2003).

On the other hand, some research (Covert and Wasburn 2007; D'Alessio and Allen 2000; Domke et al. 1997; Lee 2010; Stempel III and Windhauser 1984; Watts et al. 1999) has found evidence that media bias is not as big a problem as many people fear that it might be. It is possible that media personnel are able to maintain some degree of objectivity in their work. While clearly there will occasionally be egregious examples of overall political bias or bias against specific groups, generally the institution itself is fairly balanced in coverage of news events.

News Ideologies

As we discussed in the first chapter the concept of news ideologies can be used to conceptualize how a journalistic culture can influence the larger media institution. News ideologies are part of the general practices and values of the media. However, they can also impact the values and expectations that determine how stories may be presented. Often such values can be taken for granted, and there is no need for a reporter or editor to have an explicit desire to shape a story to fit a particular agenda. However, such taken-for-granted perspectives can be quite powerful mechanisms in shaping media bias.

Previous discussions about political bias suggest that corporate interests may directly and indirectly shape the attitudes of media personnel. This may generate a taken-for-granted cultural expectation to downplay the dysfunctions connected to those with social power. This is generally seen as serving those in the corporate class. However, the arguments concerning media bias against racial/ethnic minorities and/or women also suggest that those in the majority group also may gain from the willingness of the media to cater to more powerful elements in our society. Thus, we envision a potential Majority Group Power News Ideology.

On the other hand, media personnel tend to have progressive political and religious values (Lichter, Rothman and Lichter 1986; Patterson and Donsbach 1996; Ranly 1979; Underwood and Stamm 2001). One could expect to find them supportive of those who share those values. It is plausible that part of our political conflict is driven by a culture war that pits cultural progressives against cultural conservatives. In such a war one can reasonably expect political and religious progressives to more easily accept narratives that support cultural progressives than ones that support cultural conservatives. Such a difference could explain the findings of some of the previous studies that political and religious conservatives may be negatively represented by the media (Groeling 2008; Groseclose and Milyo 2005; Kerr 2003; Lichter, Rothman and Lichter 1986; Lowry and Shidler 1995). Such findings allow for the possibility of a Culture War News Ideology.

Finally, some research suggests that the notion of media bias is a myth. As such, it is plausible that the training of media personnel is such that the values and practices in modern media culture minimize the chances that there is systematic media bias. This allows for the possibility of a No Bias News Ideology. We will now take a more in-depth look at the possibility of each of these news ideologies.

Majority Group Power News Ideology

The premise of the Majority Group Power News Ideology is that media is controlled by dominant groups (i.e., white Protestant heteronormative elite males) who seek to maintain their social, and perhaps economic, power (Losey and Kurthen 1995; Meyers 2004).[1] From this perspective, the media is seen not necessarily as a tool to circulate information, but rather as a capitalist enterprise. The interests of the owners, shareholders, and advertisers are more of a concern for the media than informing the public (Alterman 2008; Branton and Dunaway 2009). The media, and in this case print media, is not used to criticize and challenge dominant views; but instead, pressure from the conservative institutional interest discourages journalists from reporting on news stories in ways that discourage media consumers from challenging the current social reality. Conforming to the perspective of the dominant group may be envisioned as a way the media helps to perpetuate the power of majority group members in an effort to placate those members. This placation may arise due to the societal power of the majority group or simply because the majority group tends to be, although it is not always, numerically larger than disempowered groups.

To identify those in media positions of institutional leadership as conservative is not necessarily referring to conservative cultural values. Their conservatism is not the same as those promoting a pro-life or anti–same sex marriage agenda. Rather, it is a conservativism in the larger sense in that there is a desire to maintain the current configuration of our social patterns. It is not hard to consider why those vested in the institutional power of the media would have an interest in maintaining the status quo. Having control of the media provides individuals with a great deal of social power. Societal shifts are more likely to decrease, rather than increase, such power. While this is clearly true in an economic sense, such power may also be threatened by social progressive movements that clamor for the rights of disadvantaged groups. Furthermore, although those with such institutional power may not have any animus against these marginalized groups, any efforts to help those groups can lead to a replacement of those with power and thus, at least indirectly, threaten individuals with current institutionalized media power. Often such social movements are tied together with calls to radically alter our cultural and economic system in ways that may not serve the interests of those in powerful media positions.

One of the ways the institutional structure perpetuates the status quo is through the notion that the dominant view is synonymous with objective reality (Meyers 2004, Niven 2002). The news is portrayed as neutral to mask the conservative, institutional ideological roots in the stories. This neutrality is accomplished by using specifically chosen words, limiting the presentation of opponent's arguments to suppress their views, and presenting stories so that they seem not to be ideological. Indeed, the belief journalists may have that they are presenting their stories in an objective manner can be used to keep them from questioning alternative perspectives on the stories of the day. The value of objectivity becomes a weapon used to insure that the status quo faces limited resistance.

Whether the media is truly objective may depend on whom you ask. As previously mentioned, feminist activists have argued that the media de-emphasizes the reporting of patriarchy in our society (Douglas 1995; Smith, Choueiti and Gall 2011). Race and ethnic activists and academics discuss a media that perpetuates the racialized nature of our culture (Amaya 2013; Balkaran 1999; Giroux 1998). According to such activists, the media is less about an objective assessment of social reality and more of a mechanism that projects majority group power by reinforcing the stereotypes and beliefs that support a status quo that works to their advantage. There is little evidence that individuals in powerful media positions are especially intolerant of others based on race, gender or sexuality. However, one of the major complaints of progressives concerning media is that minority groups are not represented realistically if they are represented at all (Akbarzadeh and Smith 2005; Dixon and Linz 2000; Gershon 2012; Len-Rios et al. 2005; Meyers 2004). Instead, disadvantaged groups are painted as a problem or threat to communities and to society as a whole. It is less likely that media elites have intolerant attitudes but more plausible that they, even if only indirectly, prefer to support a narrative that legitimates the lower status of disempowered groups by perceptions that such individuals do not have the same type of work ethic or innate abilities as those who succeed in our society. The perpetuation of these stereotypical images and messages of these groups influences how the majority of society thinks and interacts with these groups. But such images also shape how these groups view themselves (Johnson 1991; Meyers 2004) and the media may contribute to the perpetuation of social and cultural inequality. In doing so, the media justifies the continued dominance of majority group members.

Furthermore, Awad (2011) suggests that minority groups are not represented well because of the type of training journalists receive. Journalistic practices and standards tend to be conservative. The standards of journalism demand a homogeneity that opposes valuing cultural differences. Once again, the demand to be objective can be used to reinforce support for the current institutional reality. For example, it may be argued that this training leads to the notion that "bureaucratic sources" are seen as legitimate while other sources are considered "soft." Such a notion persuades reporters to find bureaucratic sources in order to be perceived as objective. This limits the perspectives that challenge our current social reality from being introduced into the news.

Beyond projecting an image of objectivity, there are other important ways the conservative infrastructure of the media maintains the current social and cultural reality. For example, although multiculturalism may be a stated goal of print news, Rodriguez (2009) argues that this value does not consistently emerge from our media. Multiculturalism can be seen as a way of bringing together differing social and cultural groups so that we have a society that benefits individuals across the cultural spectrum. However, while print news media may desire this type of national integration, the reality is that it often reinforces European-American values. This occurs when European-American culture and values are seen as the normative culture and the standard to which all other cultures are compared. Thus, it has become commonplace for individuals to envision our current race relations as being post-racial. The idea that our country is now in a post-racial era can be argued as supporting a form of color-blind racism. Bonilla-Silva (2003) argues that color-blind racism is comprised of four central frames—abstract liberalism, naturalization, cultural racism and minimization of racism. For our purposes the minimization of racism is salient since by downplaying the role of racism in our society, racial majority group members can legitimate the status quo. Efforts to prematurely promote the idea that racial issues no longer have great import in our society can be seen as promoting a color-blind racism that prevents proactive efforts to address systematic, institutionalized racism. Indeed, scholars (Doane and Bonilla-Silva 2003; Twine 1996; Winant 2004) have talked about a white racial identity that values efforts to maintain the status quo with claims of colorblindness and individualism. Efforts to conceptualize the United States as being post-racial play an important role in supporting color-blind racism.

Even as there is a narrative that racial issues have little importance in our society, evidence suggests that the opposite may be true as it concerns media coverage. Johnson (1991) reports that there is a pattern of troubling biases and misinformation within major national print and broadcast media in that whites and blacks are portrayed differently. White reporters tend to seek out white experts for comments even on issues that are pertinent to the black community. These actions remove the ability of African-Americans to speak for their own issues and to bring their own interpretation of social reality into media stories. If Majority Group Power News Ideology is an overarching philosophy that determines media coverage, one should expect a similar silencing of voices from the African-American community as well as from other people of color.

While understanding the plight of racial and ethnic minority groups is an important way of indicating how Majority Group Power News Ideology may shape stories that impact disadvantaged social groups, clearly these will not be the only groups affected by this perspective. For example, feminist values and concerns may also not be represented in print media in a positive manner. Mendes (2012) asserts that there is even an erasure of feminist activism from newspapers. Thus, when feminist concerns are present in media, they are often trivialized or attacked. Indeed, North (2009) asserts that feminism is the new "F-word" to be stigmatized and rejected. Thus, affiliation with feminism has halted careers, and this type of institutional pressure may account for journalists' reluctance to write about feminist concerns. Instead, a neoliberal post-feminist sentiment is apparent in print media. Women are pressured to confine their activity to the home and concern themselves with their appearance rather than with politics, public culture, or work outside of the home. Another component of neoliberal post-feminism is that women now have equal standing with men. The major struggles that women had are over, and any woman who complains is responsible for her own failures (Mendes 2012). Such a perspective is similar to notions of a post-racial society and just as that notion supports modern forms of racism, a post-feminist sentiment may be valuable for helping to maintain the institutional sexism that inhibits the opportunities of women.

Furthermore, post-feminism does not take into account the realities of women who are not white, middle-class, able-bodied, and heterosexual. While some middle class white feminists have been criticized by women of color for their inability to help women marginalized in ways other than gender (Lorde 2003; McEwan 2001; Oyewumi 2001), there is a movement within feminism to address these particular women's issues. The rejection of feminism is often linked to rejecting marginalized groups and negating their interests. While we will not explore marginalized groups that feminism may protect, such as lesbians and disabled women, it is clear that a similar pattern of rejection of the marginalized develops through the Majority Group Power News Ideology. Rather than overt intolerance, the focus is on ignoring the concerns of marginalized groups. This ignoring is justified as an attempt at objectivity or to support a generalized American culture. No matter how it is legitimated, the end result is a perspective that dismisses the concerns of the marginalized and bolsters the social system that serves the conservative interests in control of the media. Thus, the Majority Group Power News Ideology is one whereby the desires of more progressive journalists are trumped by the conservative institutional powers signing their paycheck.

Cultural War News Ideology

In contrast to the notion that journalists are beholden to a conservative corporate interest is the possibility that their progressive inclinations are major drivers of news content and presentation. This may particularly be the case if the more progressive political and cultural beliefs of journalists are the major factors in shaping the way news stories are presented. So a different perspective asserts that liberals have control of the media and that conservative voices are silenced, resulting in an attack on American culture (Anderson 2013). Specifically, conservatives are threatened that their control of major institutions such as the media is weakening (Losey and Kurthen 1995), and this perception is part of a new social reality. While there are many political issues with a progressive bias, much of the current political polarization is tied to debate over cultural issues such as abortion and same-sex marriage. In Hunter's (1991) analysis, he reinforces this perspective with what he terms a "culture war." This war is being fought for the right to determine which cultural mores and values will be widely accepted in our society. Progressives support values that reflect modernist ideas of flexibility of family structure and sexuality. Traditionalists idealize historical family structures and sexual mores. The contestation of these two groups in the cultural, political and educational dimensions in our society reveals the effects of this culture war.

Previous work (Berger 1986; Ehrenreich and Ehrenreich 1977; Gouldner 1978; Kristol 1979) has suggested that we are seeing the development of a "new class" of professionals who are shaping social attitudes. This theory implies that professionals in industries that produce culture or are affiliated with government work are part of the knowledge class. These individuals tend to accept modernist cultural ideals emphasizing individualism and diversity of family structures. Research (Yancey and Williamson 2012) indicates that such progressives have little confidence that those with culturally conservative values have the education and/or critical thinking skills that allow them to move society forward. This lack of confidence may lead such progressives to gain an interest in controlling the information consumed by the general public. If media personnel perceive themselves as part of the knowledge class that produces the cultural knowledge necessary to support a progressive cultural morality, then they may shape media stories to provide that support. This indicates that a notion of a culture war is the major factor determining how media stories are covered describing what we call the Culture War News Ideology. With this ideology, media personnel have chosen the progressive side of the culture war and shape their coverage to support their side.

In the context of a culture war, there is not simply a blanket expectation about how disempowered minority groups will be treated by the media.

For example, there are not strong connections between minority racial identity and progressive culture war issues. In fact, some research indicates that racial minority groups have relatively traditional attitudes on some cultural issues (Abrajano 2010; Sherkat, De Vries and Creek 2010). Male and female societal roles are factors in the culture war since traditionalists are theoretically less supportive of the flexibility within modern gender roles. There are also possible gender implications concerning abortion. Issues connected to sexuality are where there may be a great deal of culture war impact. Conflict over the desirability of homosexuality is often at the heart of cultural arguments today. If media personnel have a distinct desire to promote a progressive cultural agenda, then assessing whether they provide favorable treatment to sexual minorities is a key issue.

To fully investigate a possible Culture War News Ideology, it is not merely important to determine if media personnel are favorable to gender and sexuality minority groups but to see if there is a bias against cultural conservatives. Previous empirical research indicates that progressive political media bias may not be a myth. There is work documenting that conservatives (Baum and Groeling 2008; Groeling 2008; Groseclose and Milyo 2005; Lichter, Rothman and Lichter 1986; Lowry and Shidler 1995) tend to receive negative media attention. On the other hand, some researchers claim that there is a positive bias for political conservatives (Kenney and Simpson 1993; Morris and Francia 2010). However, political conservatism is not identical to cultural conservatism. A better gauge may be an assessment of how the media treats conservative Christians, who tend to be conceptually linked to cultural conservatism. To this end, Yancey and Williamson (2012) suggest that religious conservatives, especially those who are Christian, are typically seen as members of the out-group for cultural progressive activists. If media personnel envision themselves as part of the knowledge class that supports a progressive interpretation of cultural values, then they can be acting as cultural progressive activists and likely share some of the attitudes shown in their work. Those activists possess a variety of negative images of politically and theologically conservative Christians, including a fear that such Christians are seeking to take over society and to impose a negative set of values such as intolerance, bigotry, irrationality and sexual repression. If media personnel share these sentiments, then they can be more likely to frame a news story in ways to reinforce these negative characteristics of conservative Christians. Furthermore, since this is seen as a war, media personnel would be less likely to create stories that provide "comfort" for the enemy. Thus, we would expect coverage of events that may create sympathy for conservative Christians or the causes they support to be framed in ways to minimize this sympathy.

Yet, while there is ample research investigating the possibility of political bias, there is scant research assessing the possibility of positive or negative bias concerning conservative Christians. The one exception is Kerr (2003) who found evidence of negativity towards Christian fundamentalists. However, it is not clear how news media may define Christian fundamentalism. Is it merely a few individuals, such as those in the Westboro Baptist Church, who are marginalized by most other Christians or Christians with a more basic belief, such as biblical inerrancy?[2] Such a distinction is important since, if Kerr is correct, we are to determine whether the media is engaging in a pitch battle with a segment of society or with just a few outliers. If a Culture War News Ideology accurately predicts that culture-war concerns drive news coverage, then it is more important to assess negative coverage of conservative Christians than negative coverage of political conservatives in general. It is also important to comprehend the social situations that can activate potential bias against this religious out-group.

However, Fiorina, Abrams, and Pope (2006) contend that there is not a culture war. They argue that claims of a culture war are a strategy to raise money and make normally occurring events seem more exciting. If a culture war is occurring, it is not among the general population who tend to be centrists or moderates. The polarization between cultural conservative and progressive elites determines what issues are important. But while those elites fight it out, news media personnel may have a large concern developing stories more relevant and useful to the moderates who make up a majority of our society. These arguments suggest that news media personnel are not likely to be motivated by culture war concerns. Furthermore, it has been argued that the media may have a strong anti–P.C. bias (Losey and Kurthen 1995) and may not be supportive of a progressive cultural agenda. Thus, it is not clear whether news media personnel do actually play an important role in supporting the causes of cultural progressives. Even if they do possess more progressive attitudes than others in our society, they may engage in powerful efforts to control those biases and to report fairly on the day's events. This possibility produces the last news ideology that we will test in this research.

The Cultural War News Ideology contrasts with the Majority Group Power News Ideology in the determination of which group is hypothetically protected by media personal. The Cultural War News Ideology asserts that cultural progressives are the group that deserves protection. On the other hand, the Majority Group Power News Ideology asserts protection for groups traditionally seen as having disproportionate societal power—whites, males and heterosexuals. In key ways cultural progressives and those in the majority share key characteristics. For example, wealthy, highly educated whites are more likely to support cultural progressive political goals than the poor, the less educated or people of color (Baunach 2012; Ellison, Echevarria and Smith 2005; Herek 2002; Ohlander, Batalova and Treas 2005). There is the possibility that some of our results will reflect the merging of these interests. This is one of the reasons why we find value in the actual manner by which our respondents attempt to justify their publication's decisions. In that justification we can assess whether they may operate out of a Cultural War or Majority Group Power News Ideology. Furthermore, a key group we will examine, conservative Christians, also will be a useful bellwether for us. Since Christians have often been seen as part of the majority group (Blumenfeld 2006; Nadal et al. 2010; Schlosser 2003), but hostile to the interest of cultural progressives (Yancey 2013; Yancey and Williamson 2012), this becomes a group that should be favored by a Majority Group Power News Ideology, but disfavored in a Cultural War News Ideology.

No Bias News Ideology

It is quite possible that journalists do not include their personal beliefs and politics into their media presentations. Thus, news personnel neither endorse the conservative corporate values desired by those in elite media institutional positions nor their own progressive proclivities. Instead, they rely on their journalistic training that helps them to remove such biases in stories. This is the No Bias News Ideology. The premise of this news ideology is that the powerful culture of remaining objective in the media overcomes the natural tendencies we have to allow our biases to shape the way we report events. If there is a subcultural value that focuses on recognizing and controlling our biases, then it should shape the sort of news stories we receive.

A journalist's understanding of his or her role determines his or her interpretation of objectivity (Donsbach and Klett 1993; Skovsgaard et al. 2012). Some journalists try to remain impartial while others are clear advocates for a given cause or political philosophy. Print media journalists may envision themselves serving citizens as watchdogs who report current events, debates, and possible abuses of power. This would remove their ability to present multiple sides of a given issue; however, such media personnel may rationalize these efforts as a service to the public. On the other hand, some in the press do not intentionally take part in any debate of controversial issues (Losey and Kurthen 1995). This would provide them the freedom to allow for multiple perspectives and to approach all interest groups in an egalitarian manner. Roles in the media include everything from passive mirror to public mobilizer (Skovsgaard et al. 2012). Thus, representing a variety of perspectives on the role objectivity is to play in the presentation of news stories.

There is a historical tradition of arguing that the objectivity norm should be abandoned. As early as 1935, the original meaning of objectivity was diluted. Textbooks described objectivity as a way reporters write to keep themselves and their opinions out of their stories (Skovsgaard et al. 2012). However, some had come to recognize that the media is inherently biased because journalists cannot rid themselves of their personal beliefs and experiences (Figdor 2010). Since all observations are subjective, it is difficult to discern between truths that are "objective" from truths that are just an "opinion." Furthermore, the pressure of deadlines contributes to the ineffectiveness of objectivity. Due to time constraints, few journalists conduct independent research and their own investigations. This forces them to rely upon special interest sources that may have their own political and social agenda. Even if a journalist is truly objective in his or her presentation of the news, these sources may provide only information selected to further a cultural or political goal and thus can eliminate the possibility of an objective presentation of social events. It is not merely the sources connected to special interest groups that make it difficult, if not impossible, for objectivity to result in bias-free news, it also must be noted that journalists are more likely to use elite and/or official sources. The perspectives of the elite are more likely to be presented in print media than the perspectives of a person from the general public (Donsbach and Klett 1993). Thus, attempts at objectivity can result in the reliance of elite official sources that can reinforce a Majority Group Power News Ideology or special interest group sources which can reinforce a Culture War News Ideology.

Finally, objectivity can actually be a hindrance to uncovering the truth. The effort to be objective may provide a journalist with an unwarranted confidence in his or her presentation. Lea Hellmueller, Tim Vos, and Mark Poepsel (2013) argue that transparency is now seen as a better way to unveil the truth than objectivity. Transparency focuses on openness and accountability as well as showing where facts originated. This allows the responsibility to be placed on the source of the fact rather than the journalist's judgment. It also allows the journalist to be checked by others who have potential information that offers a different perspective. In a society where there is nearly instantaneous news and the ability of individuals from many different subcultures to comment on stories, transparency may be a more reliable mechanism for creating accurate stories than attempts at objectivity.

It is not clear whether objectivity is a powerful value that helps to shape the way media is presented in the United States. It is quite possible that despite the critiques of objectivity featured in the last few paragraphs, it is still the presiding value that dictates how news stories are covered. However, it is also possible that many news media personnel either fail in their attempts to present a balanced, fact-driven presentation of a given story by either favoring conservative or progressive interests, or they might even deliberately promote those interests. Given the central role that treatment of racial, gender, sexuality and religious groups is to the types of news ideologies we have explored, looking at whether all groups are treated equally can provide important insight into the role objectivity plays in media presentations.

Initial Results

Now that we have distilled the three major news ideologies that we intend to investigate in this book, we can turn to our analysis. In the remainder of this chapter we will provide information on the use and placement of media stories. Beyond merely examining whether a story is used, we are also interested in whether the story receives more attention through the placement of a story. Information that supports the biases of media personnel may be more prominently placed than other stories. Thus, this initial examination allows us to see if either of these news ideologies is supported by whether and where media stories are displayed.

Our basic plan for investigating the possibility of our different news ideologies is to learn how news media personnel approach coverage of selected interest groups. The influence of Majority Group Power News

Ideologies suggests either negative or less coverage of racial, gender, sexuality and religious minority groups. Culture War News Ideologies suggests comparatively more favorable coverage for progressive political, sexuality and religious groups. No Bias News Ideologies indicate roughly equal coverage for all social groups. In the following chapters, we will explore our qualitative findings within the different dimensions we are exploring—race, gender, religion, sexuality and political identity. But at this point, we take a preliminary quantitative exploration of the level of attention paid to different scenarios. This attention partially explains whether certain social and demographic characteristics merit differential treatment from such personnel. Understanding the potential differences in the level of coverage groups may receive is a useful starting point for the in-depth analysis we will explore in the next few chapters.

TABLE 2-1
WEIGHTED PERCENT OF RESPONDENTS WHO WILL USE STORY ON FRONT PAGE/FRONT SECTION OF PAPER OR USING THE STORY AT ALL

	Story on Front Page/Section		Story Used at All	
	Survey A	*Survey B*	*Survey A*	*Survey B*
Interracial Airport Crime	54.0%	41.0%[a]	96.5%	88.8%[a]
Political Rally	61.2%	37.4%[b]	92.6%	90.0%
Homeless to Millionaire	76.0%	79.8%	99.0%	97.4%
Campus Organization	46.8%	31.7%[a]	95.0%	86.2%[a]
Research Study	36.6%	48.5%[#]	63.9%	79.0%[a]
Couple Shooting	89.4%	80.7%[##]	99.0%	98.7%
Congressman and Prostitute	57.5%	60.3%	86.9%	89.5%
Kidnapped Girl	88.3%	88.0%	97.9%	96.0%
Religious Institution Shooting	55.4%	66.1%	78.8%	81.8%
Hate Speech	27.6%	20.9%	65.6%	51.7%[a]
Daughter into Slavery	94.6%	91.0%	99.5%	96.0%
N	127	100	127	100

a–p < .<.05; b–p < .001
#–p = .061; ##–p = .062

In Table 2-1, we first looked at the percentage of respondents who indicated that the scenario contained a story that was important enough to either be on the first page or in the first section of the paper. The data were weighed by the circulation of the paper where the respondent works.[3] Differences between the two versions of the survey indicate possible effects due to the social or demographic aspects of the individuals in the scenarios. Since stories considered more important are likely to be placed in a prominent position in a newspaper, we can also assess the priorities of the newspaper personnel by whether a story is placed on the front page or section of the newspaper. Understanding such priorities is a beginning step to understanding the news ideology that possibly drives the decisions of newspaper media personnel.

In table 2-1, there are three scenarios where there is a significant difference (at least to $p < .05$) in the answers of the respondents due to filling out a contrasting survey. Given the differences we designed for the surveys, we now know that respondents were more willing to publish an airport robbery story if the robber was white rather than black, more open to prominently place a story about a rally for gays than for ex-gays, and more open to publishing a story of a student Baptist organization complaining about inclusion than a feminist organization. The first result works against the notion that media personnel are more concerned about the interests of whites than non-whites. This challenges the notion of a Majority Group Power News Ideology. It is likewise the case that more attention to a pro–gay than a pro–ex-gay rally does not comport with arguments of a heterosexualist media but rather seems to support the Culture War News Ideology. However, there is more attention provided to the complaints of conservative Christians than feminists, which does suggest some propensity to support traditional groups over progressive activist groups. However, in all three cases, it is quite possible that the tone of the articles may differ, and these assertions are quite preliminary.

There were two results that barely missed the $p < .05$ level of significance but were so close that they warrant brief mention. Those findings indicate that newspaper media were more willing to publish the research story when it indicated that Hispanics, rather than whites, are more likely to work harder, and they were more likely to publish a story where an interracial couple is shot rather than a same-sex couple. The first finding is not expected if the media drives a Majority Group Power News Ideology. Indeed, the possibility that newspaper media personnel show more interest in the shooting of an interracial couple rather than a same-sex couple is even more evidence that such personnel are quite concerned about the interest of groups of color. Though these results are technically not significant, they are worth observing since we may not have quite enough statistical power to pick up the differences.[4] Furthermore, it is vital to note these potential differences to provide context for the potential contrasts we find with our qualitative data.

We wanted to know if these findings are biased by only looking at whether a newspaper puts a story on the first page or section. So in the third and fourth column of table 2-1 we examine whether the respondent believes the story should be used at all. Thus, even if a story is to be used as a news brief they were included as accepting the story. Our findings were not greatly altered by this change, but there were some notable differences. Once again, there is a greater desire to publish the airport robbery story when the robber is white and to publish the complaints of a Baptist student organization rather than a feminist student organization. One of the two results that barely missed significance in the first two columns (publishing the research story that indicated that Hispanics, and not whites, were harder workers) did reach significance in these latter two columns. There were two differences when we looked at the inclusion of the story in any part of the paper. One is that it is no longer more likely that political rallies headed up by gays were more likely to be covered than those by ex-gays. This suggests a favoring of the interest of the LGBT community, but only in the placement of their rallies, not in whether the events would be covered at all. Second, there was more of an inclination to include the incident of hate speech when that speech was used against sexual minorities than conservative Christians. Thus, one could argue that the urge to feature a story about hate speech on a college campus is not deeply influenced by the potential victim of such speech but whether to include it as a secondary story in a non-prominent portion of the newspaper is shaped by who is the target of the hate.

We also compared the percentage of respondents who would use the story online. Since an online story requires no space to be taken up in a paper, it is reasonable to assert that if the paper offers stories online, that they have little incentive to exclude a story if they envisioned any importance to it. Thus, the use of this variable can be seen as measure of whether a respondent desires to completely ignore a particular story. The results of our comparison can be seen in table 2-2.

In only one scenario did the propensity of the respondents to use the story online change with the details of the scenario. They are significantly more willing to publish the research story when it indicated that Hispanics, rather than whites, are more likely to work harder. This reinforced our earlier assertion that the quantitative data indicates some concern for individuals of color. If we relax our standard to $p < .1$, we find that respondents are slightly more willing to publish an airport robbery story if the robber is white rather than black, which also reinforces the attention to people of color finding in table 2-1.[5] The relatively few significant findings with the online stories may be due to the very high percentage of stories used online regardless of the scenario given.[6] These high percentages reinforce our assertion that newspaper reporters and editors are willing to put many stories online, some of which may have minimal levels of importance. But these percentages also created relatively little variability between the competing scenarios.

TABLE 2-2
COMPARISON OF WEIGHTED PERCENTAGES
OF USING SELECTED SCENARIOS ONLINE

	Survey A *(n = 127)*	*Survey B* *(n = 100)*
Interracial Airport Crime	93.7%	86.3%[#]
Political Rally	89.8%	84.3%
Homeless to Millionaire	96.4%	96.4%
Campus Organization	84.8%	83.0%
Research Study	58.0%	72.1%[a]
Couple Shooting	95.6%	96.0%
Congressman and Prostitute	77.5%	84.5%
Kidnapped Girl	99.4%	96.0%
Religious Institution Shooting	65.6%	64.3%
Hate Speech	56.3%	47.8%
Daughter into Slavery	97.7%	94.1%
N	127	100

a–p <.05
#–p = .06

Our initial quantitative assessment indicates that some concerns about media bias may not be borne out in reality. We see evidence that newspaper media personnel do not forward the Eurocentric approach that ignores the concerns of people of color. At the other end of the political spectrum, they also do not seem to ignore the complaints of conservative Christians relative to the concerns of feminists. However, such conclusions are premature and must be contextualized by exploring the approach that newspaper media personnel take towards these stories.

Assessment of Non-Newspaper Media

In the first two tables, we looked at only the propensity of newspaper personnel to favor certain stories based on different social characteristics of the principles in the stories. But our greater interest is the general media culture and the news ideologies that may emerge from that culture. We calculated t-scores for our other two media groups—television and social. For the television media personnel we asked whether they would air a potential story. Only those who stated that they would definitely air a story were operationalized as accepting the story.[7] We found no significant differences tied to use of either scenario. This was true even at the more generous p < .1 level. The most basic interpretation of the television data is that social and demographic differences have little impact in whether a story is shown. Our analysis of why television personnel make such decisions and how those social and demographic differences may impact those decisions distinctly will be explored with our qualitative data. The results of our analysis of television news personnel can be seen in Table 2-3.

TABLE 2-3
WEIGHTED PERCENT OF TELEVISION RESPONDENTS WHO WILL DEFINITELY USE STORY IN SCENARIO

	Survey A (n = 43)	*Survey B (n = 23)*
Interracial Airport Crime	57.6%	61.6%
Political Rally	52.3%	44.4%
Homeless to Millionaire	45.1%	48.6%
Campus Organization	24.5%	32.6%
Research Study	21.4%	16.0%
Couple Shooting	57.4%	54.4%
Congressman and Prostitute	49.7%	50.2%
Kidnapped Girl	58.2%	54.4%
Religious Institution Shooting	39.0%	44.4%
Hate Speech	14.7%	18.5%
Daughter into Slavery	58.7%	58.2%

In table 2-4 we investigate our quantitative results of social media personnel. With our social media personnel we asked if they would include such a story in their online website. For this group there were no significant differences at p < .05, but there were three significant differences at p < .1. One big surprise is that social media personnel are less likely to accept the research story when Hispanics, relative to whites, are the harder workers (49.7% v. 20.2%: p = .073). This may reflect a higher percentage of social media personnel catering to a more conservative audience than other media personnel. We did not ask newspaper or television media personnel about the political orientation of their shows, but we did do this for social media and found slightly more shows catering to a conservative, as opposed to a progressive, audience (8.33% v. 6.94%).

TABLE 2-4
WEIGHTED PERCENT OF SOCIAL MEDIA RESPONDENTS WHO WILL PLACE STORY IN SCENARIO ONLINE

	Survey A *(n = 26)*	*Survey B* *(n = 14)*
Interracial Airport Crime	54.7%	66.7%
Political Rally	58.6%	53.5%
Homeless to Millionaire	66.2%	46.5%
Campus Organization	61.8%	46.5%
Research Study	49.7%	20.2%*
Couple Shooting	65.0%	36.9%*
Congressman and Prostitute	61.7%	29.1%*
Kidnapped Girl	65.0%	49.3%
Religious Institution Shooting	35.4%	27.4%
Hate Speech	34.4%	23.0%
Daughter into Slavery	58.8%	32.6%

*$-p < .1$

Given our small sample we can only speculate, but we surmise that social media has a much more politically charged atmosphere than newspaper or television media. It does not escape our attention that the research and congressman scenarios (along with the shooting at the church/mosque and hate speech on a college campus) are among those less likely to be used by newspaper respondents. The political polarization in social media outlets may make stories that are normally not very enticing to media personnel of greater interest to media personnel with more explicit political goals. Nevertheless, we found that the shooting of the interracial couple was more newsworthy than of the same-sex couple (65% v. 36.9%: $p = .096$), which did not differ from the general direction found among other media personnel. Thus, similar media forces may impact social media personnel as impact other media personnel. As we look at the results of our research, we will be mindful of the possibility that social media personnel may be an anomaly to the general findings due to their potentially greater desire to engage in the political process. The number of social media personnel who are politically motivated is relatively small ($n = 11$) and so there should be a minimal effect from their inclusion in our sample. However, at times we will check our findings by eliminating the social media personnel from the sample to see if our results hold up.

In table 2-5, we looked at the data concerning all media personnel.

We combined the newspaper personnel's willingness to use the story at all, with the willingness of television media personnel to state that they will definitely use the story and the willingness of the social media personnel to put the story online. With one exception, we found that there was no difference in any of the scenarios as it concerns the different versions of the survey. Even that single difference, the willingness of media personal to prioritize the research of Hispanics as harder workers than whites, was only significant at p < .1. However, it should be noted that when we eliminate the social media personnel, for reasons enunciated in the previous paragraphs, the potential racial effect is eliminated. We did find that the Hispanic worker story is significantly more favored that the white worker story at the more traditional level (67.2% v. 52.3%: p < .05).[8]

TABLE 2-5
**WEIGHTED PERCENT OF ALL MEDIA RESPONDENTS
WHO WOULD DEFINITELY USE STORY IN SCENARIO**

	Survey A	*Survey B*
Interracial Airport Crime	82.5%	82.0%
	(195)	(136)
Political Rally	79.3%	78.6%
	(196)	(137)
Homeless to Millionaire	82.8%	84.0%
	(196)	(137)
Campus Organization	75.1%	73.2%
	(196)	(137)
Research Study	52.7%	62.5%*
	(196)	(137)
Couple Shooting	85.4%	85.0%
	(196)	(137)
Congressman and Prostitute	75.4%	76.8%
	(196)	(137)
Kidnapped Girl	84.8%	84.3%
	(196)	(137)
Religious Institution Shooting	64.4%	70.0%
	(196)	(137)
Hate Speech	50.3%	43.2%
	(196)	(137)
Daughter into Slavery	85.0%	83.3%
	(195)	(137)

\#–p < .1; a–p <.05

We conclude that the social and demographic differences of the principles in our scenarios have relatively little impact on the generalized media

45

culture concerning inclusion of the stories in any capacity. There was some tendency of newspaper media personnel to favor stories painting people of color in a favorable light whether we are exploring stories about crime or research and a lower desire to deal with complaints from a feminist, as opposed to Baptist, student organization. There may be unique cultural aspects among newspaper personnel creating more focus on certain news ideologies in comparison to the general news media culture. Yet, as it concerns the generalized culture and story inclusion there appears to be an overall effect in which the potential biases in certain types of media are balanced by the inclusion, or non-inclusion, of stories in a different type of media. Thus, with uncommon exceptions, stories are not more likely to be excluded when taking into account the totality of contemporary media. This does not mean that all media stories will be treated in a similar manner. Indeed, media personnel may want to include a story to punish a suspected out-group and use the same story to show sympathy to an in-group. In the following chapters, the comments of these respondents will provide us more insight into the general news ideology of the media.

Conclusion

In this chapter, we have looked at three news ideologies that explain possible bias in the shaping of the presentation of news stories. It is possible that the values of a conservative institutional elite, culturally progressive special interest, or objectivity constitute the core subculture value that influences how media stories are written. We do not see these news ideologies as comprehensive. For example, it is quite possible that the media favors conservative social/economic policies or progressive social values for reasons other than those outlined in a Majority Group Power News Ideology. However, these news ideologies do generate mutually exclusive predictions. Either media personnel favor certain disadvantaged groups as suggested by Cultural War News Ideology, disfavor those groups as suggested by Majority Group Power News Ideology, or treat those groups the same as they treat majority groups regardless of the context of the story as suggested by No Bias News Ideology. The exclusive nature of the predictions arising from these particular news ideologies allows us to determine which one is closest to the reality of how bias plays itself out among media personnel.

Our quantitative results do not seem to favor either a Majority Group

Power or Culture War News Ideology. Indeed, our results indicate some evidence for the No Bias News Ideology. This is true even when we explore the area where we found the most potential for media bias—newspapers. Our initial results suggest that there is little difference in the placement of stories based on the social and demographic characteristics of the principles in these stories. These initial results may be tied to the media personnel's desire to remain as objective as possible. Placement of stories may be a viable way to project the importance of objectively.

However, perhaps even more important than the placement of stories is how the stories are written and what tone is set within the stories. In the next few chapters, we will read in the words of our respondents whether their decisions about story inclusion are driven by a desire to be fair and even-handed. The descriptions they provide can help us understand the sort of stories that are likely to come from media personnel. While true objectivity is unlikely to be obtained, it is likely that intentional efforts at objectivity can lessen differential treatment due to the social or demographic characteristics of individuals in a scenario. This may lead to descriptions of stories that are remarkably similar to each other regardless for the social and demographic characteristics of the individuals in the scenarios. However, it is also reasonable to assert that obtaining relative objectivity is easier with certain social or demographic characteristics than with others. It is plausible that producing an objective analysis is easier when considering racial, gender, sexuality, political and religious issues than other issues we are not measuring with our scenarios.

Thus, even though we have little evidence that the position and emphasis given to a story is shaped by these social and demographic differences, news ideologies may emerge due to the way a story is presented. The tone that a reporter or editor utilizes to construct the story might vary depending on the characteristics of the principles in the story. We argue that this difference will not emerge from the quantitative analysis of this chapter, but from the qualitative responses of our respondents. Over the next four chapters we will use the answers of the respondents to our open-ended questions about why they will or will not present a particular story to explore whether the presentation of stories is shaped by social and demographic differences.

2

Racism

In this chapter, and the next, we will look at two important dimensions that arguably are most likely to define stratification in the United States: race and gender. We contend that the examination of these two elements is vital to exploring the possible existence of a Majority Group Power News Ideology. When we have completed our analysis, we will discuss reasons to be skeptical of this news ideology.

Overt racial animosity is no longer accepted by media personnel, nor by most individuals in our society. However modern theories of racism (Bonilla-Silva 2003; McConahay 1986) indicate that racism is no longer overt, but instead now supports institutions that legitimate unequal treatment. The "new right" perpetuates white racial privilege in a seemingly race-neutral way (Lu and Nicholson-Crotty 2010). Members of the dominant group maintain their privileges by choosing not to see racism (Drew 2011). Theories of white racial identity (Doane and Bonilla-Silva 2003; Hughey 2010; Twine 1996) suggest that majority group members have values supporting a status quo, which works to their advantage. It is plausible that the media is hesitant to address racial inequalities due to the promotion of the white racial identity perspectives (Doane and Bonilla-Silva 2003; Twine 1996; Winant 2004) that maintain Eurocentric advantages. Drew (2011) asserts that media perpetuates racism because journalism reproduces the racial status quo. Journalism sets the agenda by directing what readers should think about, how they should think, and how they should perform race relations.

On the other hand, the progressive ideology and crusading spirit of media personnel may motivate them to search for examples of societal racism. If media personnel are seeking a more progressive society, then addressing the tribal aggressions of racism can fit into their preconceived notions about society and their occupational role. Furthermore, media personnel might be motivated to address racism for an economic reason. A story documenting racial abuse may garner a front-page headline. As such, reporters may have an occupational interest in seeking out a big story on racism. On the other hand, if media personnel are influenced by the biases imbedded in a Majority Group Power News Ideology then they should be resistant to reports of the concerns of racial minorities. They may participate in hiding the effects of racism with a focus on colorblindness or attributing responsibilities to people of color.

Focusing on how racially subordinated groups are represented is important because these representations influence policy and how racial groups are perceived and treated (Embrick and Henricks 2013). Stereotypes of racially subordinated groups in media tend to be negative. However, the occasions when representations are positive may lead to pro-social outcomes (Mastro and Tukachinsky 2011). These positive images may push media consumers to challenge their beliefs about the racial group being represented and possibly lead to consumers negating the stereotype altogether. A caution is needed since the positive images should not be so deviant from the typical representation of the racially subordinated group if the news image is going to have an impact on the overall eradication of the negative stereotype.

Racial Scenarios

Our work contains three scenarios directly dealing with issues of race and ethnicity.[1] In the first scenario we described an airport robbery. We switched the race of the robber and victim from white to black (but the race of the robber was always different than that of the victim). Some have argued that the media is quicker to report on crime committed by an African-American than by a European-American (Dixon and Linz 2000; Gilliam Jr. and Iyengar 2000; Romer, Jamieson and De Coteau 1998).

Depictions of criminals and victims matter in various media types. Callanan (2012) argues that television news and crime-based reality shows have an impact on perceptions of neighborhood crime and fear of crime. Specifically, Callanan notes that perceived realism of the content, the actual content portrayed, and how the content is framed influence perceived neighborhood crime and fear of crime. It is particularly important to pay attention to broadcast news because one-third of all television news consists of crime-related content and, specifically, atypical forms of crime (Surette 2014). Callanan (2012) describes broadcast news coverage of crime as lacking content, description, and explanation. Because of this, television news consumers perceive crime as rampant and unmanageable.

This scenario provides a test of that assertion. The second scenario is a race-based kidnapping scenario, where a child is kidnapped and we switched out the race of the child. We hope to test whether the media is more concerned when whites, instead of people of color, are victimized. Finally, we asked about peer-review research in which one racial group (white v. Hispanic) is more productive than others. While the first two scenarios provide "bad news" of a criminal nature, in this scenario we hope to see if the media is quicker to report on good news about a racial group if that group is the majority group.

Airport Robbery Scenario

One reason why people tire of watching the local news is that it always seems to be bad news filled with crime. This seems particularly true when African-Americans are consistently seen as the criminals paraded in the newspaper or on TV. Images of African-Americans as criminals may be partially tied to the media consistently putting a black criminal suspect on the television screen or in the pages of the newspapers. These images are important especially in cases where face-to-face contact with racialized groups does not occur. Callanan (2012) posits that white Americans typically do not have experience with crime on which to base their interpretation of crime-related media. Crime-related media is a substitute for their lack of experience. In addition, media depiction of crime-based reality tends to disproportionately portray white Americans as victims and people of color (i.e., African Americans) as criminals.

We are not directly concerned with whether these images reflect the true reality of crime. Instead, we are concerned with whether there is an implicit racial bias that makes a situation where a black individual, instead of a white one, is the criminal more noteworthy to media personnel. So imagine hearing about a robbery where one person is white and the other black. As far as this robbery being a media story, is it important whether the criminal is white or black?

In our airport robbery scenario the answer is yes, but not in the direction predicted by the Majority Group Power News Ideology. The newspaper reporters were more likely to want the robbery on the front page or first section of the newspaper if the white robber is taking advantage of the black victim than vice versa (54% v. 41%: p < .05)[2] and were more likely to run the story in the paper at all (96.5% v. 88.8%: p < .05). The newspaper personnel are also more likely to run this story online if the robber is white (93.7% v. 86.3%: p < .1). Looking at all media, however, we found that there was no difference in which story was presented (82.5 v. 82.0: ns). One possible reason for this leveling out is the relatively strong propensity of our social media respondents to use the story of the black robber than the white robber (66.7% v. 54.7%: ns).[3] Although the difference is not significant it is great enough that a measure of all the media types indicates no difference between the scenarios.

So why would a white robber gain more attention? To answer this, we now turn to our qualitative data. The statements the respondents provided about their decisions indicate important patterns. In an interesting twist, when the robber is white, the respondents were two and a half times more likely to discuss whether the robbery is racially motivated (26.8% v. 10.1%: p < .001).[4] Here are a few examples of the type of comments provided when discussing the white robber.

> Robbery in a "secure" area, suggestions by credible civil rights group that it may have been racially motivated (Newspaper Reporter, Government beat, circulation over 500,000)

> If a man was held up at gun point, we would cover the story, period. Being close to the airport only adds urgency. We might talk to the civil rights organization but certainly not use them as our only source. Motive is also speculative in a case like this, especially right after the event. (Television Reporter, Crime and Local beat, circulation under 10,000)

> What evidence exists to support contention that race was a factor (Newspaper Editor, News Media beat, circulation 100,000–500,000)

The respondents were not always convinced that the crime was racially motivated; however, the issue of whether the robber had racial intentions was much more likely with the white robber. Respondents were more willing to explore the racial implications when the potential robber was white, even if they were not convinced that race played an important role in the robbery. Thus, one can ask why there is more willingness to explore the racial angle with a white robber. Ascribing racial intentions generally suggests a racist action that would produce additional stigma to the robber. Usually, such arguments are tied to pointing out the race of a person of color, instead of a majority group member. Media personnel are more hesitant to identify the potential effects of race when the robber is white. Thus, this is clearly a finding that differs from what is expected in a Majority Group Power News Ideology, since it is the white robber that is on the receiving end of this stigma.

There was a second important difference between the respondents in the two scenarios. Those who were given the scenarios with the black robber were more likely to state that race is unimportant in their reporting of the story. Respondents given that scenario were much more likely to mention that race is not important (20.2% v. 9.5%: $p < .01$). For example, one respondent stated that "the fact that he was robbed at gunpoint is the most important part. We'd run it in the local section just the same if it were a white man suspected of robbing a black man" (Newspaper Reporter, Crime beat, circulation 100,000–500,000). This was typical of the attempt of the reporters and editors to make sure we knew that they were not emphasizing black criminals. However, this was a finding that was not replicated among our social media respondents. Among only those respondents, there was a relatively equal likelihood to mention that race was unimportant regardless of the race of the robber. Indeed, scenarios with the white robber were slightly more likely to produce a comment about the race of the robber being unimportant, although the difference was far from significant (18.1% v. 17.7%: ns). The difference between the social media personnel and the rest of the sample is the relative higher willingness of social media personnel to dismiss the racialized elements of the scenario with the white robber. This may be driven by a colorblindness perspective of some of the conservative social media personnel.

Theoretically, a colorblind ideology is characterized in a way that institutional racism and discrimination do not occur in contemporary America. Each individual has equal opportunities, and upward mobility is based upon meritocracy (Gallagher 2003). In actuality, colorblindness perpetuates systemic forms of racism, white privilege, and racial inequality. A colorblind perspective is ahistorical. It ignores how contemporary racial inequality is a product of historical institutional inequality and racial prejudice. While individuals may claim that they are colorblind, they tend to notice race when racially subordinated communities organize politically or make group-based grievances. The reaction is often to claim that reverse racism is occurring (Gallagher 2003). Race scholars have argued that claims of reverse racism are often utilized to frame whites as victims and to avoid confronting the reality of the majority group power of European-Americans (Bonilla-Silva, Lewis and Embrick 2004; Cabrera 2014; James 2007).

Combined with our first finding, we argue that media personnel want to de-emphasize the racial nature of the crime when there is a black criminal, but emphasize it when there is a white criminal. This fits with a definite pattern of our first observation in that there is an attention to race when the robber is white that is missing when the robber is black. We suspect that this pattern may emerge because newspaper personnel are sensitive to the charge of mistreating a potential black criminal. Journalists may be sensitive to an individual's alleged criminal behavior when the criminal is black. This may be due to either the journalist's adherence to objectivity or colorblindness. If the journalist is abiding by objectivity, the journalist will wait until as much information considered fact is collected. If the journalist holds a colorblind perspective, the journalist may believe that institutional factors do not account for criminal behavior but rather personal choices. In addition, journalists "know" that it is not politically allowable to label racial groups as being more likely to be criminal. They take extra precautions because they fear being called racist or bigoted. Drew (2011) argues that journalistic objectivity is just another form of colorblindness. By not seeing society as racialized, journalists may not consider expert witnesses who are from racially subordinated groups (Robinson and Culver 2016). In addition, racism is normalized in the workroom when journalists are not self-reflective to know that objectivity silences voices that are not from the racially dominant group (Drew 2011; Robinson and Culver 2016).

This assertion would help explain why they were less likely to see a racial motivation for the black robber. Finally, they are more likely to declare in the open-ended questions, without prompting, a desire to ignore race when asked about a potential black robber. While the propensity to carry this story is somewhat greater if the robber is white, it is also important that how the story will be written is likely to be different depending on the race of the robbery. The story of the black robber will be one relatively sanitized of implied racialized accusations of the assailant. Any concerns from dominant-group organizations about racial motivations are likely to be ignored. The story of the white robber will be one that emphasizes the danger of the robber and/or robbery, and the concerns of black civil rights organizations will be featured. Contrary to the concerns of race scholars, newspaper media treat these crime stories in ways that protect, rather than stigmatize, the image of African-Americans.

Perhaps part of the reason behind this tendency can be found in the answers of nearly one-fifth (18.4%) of our respondents who indicated sensitivity to the racial complaints of civil rights organizations. There was not a significant difference between the two surveys so the tendency to pay attention to civil rights organizations was not shaped by the race of the robber. But how they approached those organizations appears to differ. When the robber was black there was a tendency to note that the civil rights organizations believe that this is a racially motivated robbery.

> That the local civil rights organizations thinks this robbery was racially motivated. (Newspaper Reporter, Multiple Beats, Circulation 10,000–50,000)
>
> Robbery in a "secure" area, suggestions by credible civil rights group that it may have been racially motivated (Newspaper Reporter, Government beat, Circulation over 500,000)

However, there was a great deal more skepticism about the civil rights group when the robber was white. Media personnel were more likely to suspect that the civil rights organization had ulterior motives.

> Airport security concerns. Race issues are more speculative, likely driven by political motives, but they're worth looking into. (Newspaper Editor, multiple beats, Circulation under 10,000)
>
> To dispel notions of racially-motivated, black-on-white crime, when the apparent, obvious motive was robbery. (Social Media Editor, Culture and Local beat, Circulation 100,000–500,000)
>
> That political organizations are ready to start guessing at the motives of a crime before witnesses are found or suspects arrested. (Newspaper Editor and Reporter, Culture and News Media beat, Circulation 100,000–500,000)

While media personnel often questioned whether the crime was racially motivated when discussing a black robber, there was a lack of questioning motivations of the civil rights organizations. This indicates that civil rights organizations tied to African-American causes are taken more seriously than organizations that identify with the concerns of racial majority group members. Thus, concerns about possibly offending minority-oriented civil rights organizations may be a key to why the racial aspect of the robberies is downplayed when the robber is black.

We have our first clue as to how race may play out in newsrooms across the country. That clue indicates an effort to avoid the perpetuation of negative images of a black robber. The story of the airport robbery is likely to be included in the media, regardless of the race of the robber, since a robbery seems to be important news. However, a sensitivity to not stigmatizing African-Americans, and the organizations that serve them, likely shapes how the robbery will be reported.

KIDNAPPING SCENARIO

Our next scenario focuses on the kidnapping of a child. In the first version the child is white and in the other version the child is black. Certain television programs tend to focus on real-life crime stories. However, the media has been criticized for concentrating only on crimes where whites are the victims (Cooper 2006; Everbach 2013; Johnson 2004; Robinson 2005). The implication of such criticism is that black lives are not important to the producers of the shows or to the audience. This scenario allows us to explore whether the race of the victim matters when it comes to newspaper coverage.

Clearly, the quantitative data indicates that the race of the victim does not matter at all. Whether the girl is white or black, about 88 percent of the newspaper reporters and editors see this as a front page or front section story. An overwhelming number of our respondents also want the story to be included somewhere in the paper (97.9% v. 96.0%; ns) and published online (99.4% v. 96.0%; ns). As it concerns the television media (58.2% v. 54.4%: ns) and social media (65.0% v. 49.3%; ns), we also see relatively strong interest, in comparisons to other scenarios, for this story regardless of the race of the child. Thus, it is not too surprising that this scenario was one of the highest accepted for inclusion as a story regardless of the race of the child (84.8% v. 84.3%; ns). We speculate that the story we constructed is too sensational to determine potential differences motivated by the race of the victim. A kidnapping of a girl off the porch of her home is the type of terrifying story almost all reporters will perceive a need to cover. We attempted to calibrate our scenarios so that they are stories that some individuals are motivated to cover while others are not convinced that the story is newsworthy. In this scenario, we likely made the story too newsworthy. Any potential effects due to racial differences are lost in the lack of variability in the responses.

However, our qualitative data allows us to go beyond this limitation to see how the respondents talk about their decision to run the story. Although the story may have been too sensational to detect differential treatment with quantitative analysis, if there are racialized distinctions, then it is likely that they will come out in the comments of the respondents. This may allow us to clarify how white and black victims are seen differently by media personnel. We found a higher tendency of respondents to mention a need to warn the community about a safety issue if the girl is black (29.3% v. 17.9%; $p < .05$). The respondents did not directly bring up the race of the child but simply were more likely to issue a general concern about the safety of the community. For example, one respondent (Newspaper Editor, Local beat, Circulation 10,000–50,000) stated, "Crime is very important to community members, especially when child safety is involved." While we found this tendency with all three types of media, the difference among just the newspaper reporters was not significant (28.5% v. 22.1%: ns), but the difference between the television (32.8% v. 11.4%: $p < .05$) and social media (28.7% v. 7.7%; $p < .1$)[5] were significant. While the general trend of exploring issues of safety when writing about a black girl is present in all the different types of media, it is much stronger in non-newspaper media.

There was no other real distinction between the scenario of the white and black girl. This lack of difference complicates a narrative that the kidnapping story supports the Majority Group Power News Ideology. At least when it comes to a spectacular kidnapping story, there is no real support for that news ideology. However, it is interesting to note that journalists were concerned about the safety of the community in which the black girl resided. Whereas in the case of the kidnapping of the white girl, it was perceived as a tragedy for an individual family.

As was clear in our airport robbery example, several respondents made it clear that race would not be important in the coverage of this story. There was not a significant difference in this sentiment when asked about the white or black girl. This respondent (Newspaper Editor, Multiple beats, Circulation 10,000–50,000) may capture the reluctance to discuss the race of the girl by saying that "don't use race" as the forefront. Nothing in the news industry should be about race, sex, or orientation. There is a concerted effort to downplay the racial implications in a case such as this. Our limited findings may have touched upon a subconscious propensity among our respondents, but they likely do not reflect a concerted effort to observe racial distinctions. In our two criminology scenarios, we have seen a tendency to ignore racial differences. When media personnel are confronted with the potential of people of color as robbers, this tendency may lead them to de-emphasize the racial elements of the crime. Race is more likely to be taken into account when the robber is white. As stated in the gunpoint robbery scenario, we should be cautious to attribute the difference as being due to journalistic adherence to objectivity or to a colorblind ideology. When media personnel are confronted with the stories about people of color as crime victims, this attempt at colorblindness may be so complete that it is quite successful. Thus, either racial differences are ignored, or if they are brought to the attention of our respondents they are done so in a way to minimize the potential stigma of people of color. Our initial exploration of how media are racialized does not easily fit the expectations tied to Majority Group Power News Ideology. But are media personnel more likely to ignore race altogether or do they only do so to avoid providing stigma to people of color? This last scenario provides important information as to whether no bias or protection of racial minorities is more likely to motivate media personnel.

Research Study Scenario

Many complaints about racial media bias are linked to the different ways crime is covered. But concern about the criminal law is not the only area where media bias can play a role in our racialized society. Our final scenario can help us to see if issues not concerned with crime may also have racialized differences. To this end, we envisioned a scenario where a particular racial group gains good news due to a research study. However, the nature of the research story is such that good news for one racial group would entail a more problematic result for other racial groups. Given such a dynamic, the Majority Group Power News Ideology suggests that reporters and editors are more willing to report the good news for majority group members, but ignore this good news for people of color.

The premise of this scenario is straightforward. Research has been published in a peer-review study indicating that one racial group tends to work harder than other racial groups. The peer-review nature of the imaginary study allows the media personnel to accept that this is real scientific work and not the efforts of a biased group. Using the notion of hard work not only allowed us to reward one of the groups but to imply that other groups are not hard workers. Thus, we can explore whether media personnel realize this zero-sum situation and if it makes them less likely to support publication of this story.

This is a scenario where we obtained quantitative consensus from newspaper and television media personnel. The scenario where Hispanics, instead of whites, are more willing to work hard is more likely to be put in the front page or front section of the newspaper (48.5% v. 36.6%: p < .1), to be used in the newspaper at all (79.0% v. 63.9%: p < .05), and to be included in the online version of the newspaper (72.1% v. 58.0%: p < .05). Our television media respondents also are more likely to run a story on the research study favorable to Hispanics (40.0% v. 28.6%: ns). Although not all of these differences are significant, they are all in the same direction, which lends credibility to the assertion that stories of hard-working Hispanics will gain more attention than stories of hard-working whites. However, as we observed in the previous chapter social media personnel were actually more likely to put the story of white workers online (49.7% v. 20.2%: p < .1).[6] We suspect that the politicized nature of social media may be responsible for this counter finding. Nonetheless we recognize that for this scenario, our social media respondents do not likely reflect the culture in the rest of the news media, and we will leave them out of further analysis.

Thus, with the rest of the media, we can now ask why there is favoritism for the scenario with Hispanics. At least part of the motivation to favor the scenario with the Hispanics over the one with the whites is the possibility of furthering the racial interests of Hispanics. The respondents indicated this tendency with their desire to reach out to Hispanic civil rights leaders when discussing the scenario with whites as the harder workers.

> Is the civil rights organization's concern about the way the data was collected or is it about the outcome? And where the results accurately/fairly generated. (Newspaper Other role, Crime beat, circulation under 10,000)
>
> What the civil rights organization says to counter this and whether there have been any other studies whose data supports these same conclusions. (Newspaper Reporter and Editor, Education beat, circulation 50,000–100,000)

If the respondent is going to run the story with results favorable to whites, then sometimes the respondent is careful to make sure that the civil rights organization is available for comment or critique. There was not the same tendency to seek out comment from other political organizations when the story favored Hispanics (8.5% v. 2.2%: p < .05). Similar to the results connected to the airport shooting, media personnel are more sensitive to the desires and concerns of civil rights organizations, but less so to any organizations that advocate for the interest of the majority group. Thus, it is reasonable to assert that a story written for research that favored whites is more likely to contain a segment expressing opposition to the findings than one written for research that favors Hispanics.

The quantitative finding is backed up by the reality that respondents are much less likely to perceive the story to be news if the scenario concerns the working advantages of whites. For example, one respondent (Reporter and Editor, News Current Events beat, circulation under 10,000) commented that "although interesting, what impact would this have on a reader? What can a reader use in such a project?" This blasé attitude was decidedly more likely when the scenario favored the white workers (33.5% v. 18.3%: $p < .01$). But before we can assume that reporters are simply less interested in a story where whites are seen as better workers, we also must take into consideration the context behind the discussion of such a story regardless of who is favored. Some of the respondents discuss the outrage this story may generate.

> Common sense says this story will evoke traditional, cultural "racist" attitudes and emotions that the study may not set out to cause. If anything can be learned from the story it would be a detailed explanation of the implications of the study and what it truly means. (Newspaper Editor, Local and News Current Event beat, circulation over 500,000)

> Although I highly doubt that such an empirical survey would be confected, it would be newsworthy if it existed. It smacks of "Bell Curve" nonsense, which might become the point of the article if peers sought to knock it down. The controversy sells itself. (Newspaper Reporter, multiple beats, 100,000–500,000)

It may be due to the potential controversy in this story that fewer respondents are willing to include it in their media relative to the other scenarios in our survey. Our respondents may feel safer offering the story when Hispanic workers are seen as superior workers since media personnel do not fear organizations that cater to majority group members as much as those serving minority groups. But the controversial nature of the story provides a reason for the story to be avoided.

We have already seen that our respondents are concerned with making overt mentions about race. However, the racial identity of the workers is an intrinsic part of this story. Some of our respondents mentioned a fear of the racial aspect of the story and wanted to avoid the furthering of racism. Even when the results indicated a favorable outcome for Hispanic workers some respondents were nervous about the potential racism in this story. One respondent (Television Reporter, Culture beat, Circulation under 10,000) with the Hispanic worker version of the survey simply said, "race-baiting," while another (Newspaper Reporter, Multiple beats, Circulation 10,000–50,000) stated, "Holy crap, how is this not racist?" In all three scenarios, there is strong evidence that a significant percentage of media personnel tend to minimize the racial implications of news stories. A fear of being labeled racist may account for this propensity.

If there is such a fear of a social backlash or of replicating racism, then why would a reporter or editor run the story of white workers having better work habits? The one explanation given more for running the story of the white workers is the peer-review nature of the research. It is a slight but significant difference between the two versions of this scenario (11.0% v. 3.0%: p < .01). This motivation was clearly the case with some of our respondents.

> I'd put this on the front page because the findings are so controversial, and there is bound to be follow-up. If it wasn't a peer-reviewed, respected journal, I wouldn't use it at all. (Newspaper Editor, Government beat, circulation 10,000–50,000)
>
> Possible land mine here … any comparison of racial performance carries the risk of strong reaction by the runner-up races! Since this is an "experimental design" study, I think that should be stated and explained at or toward the top to clarify that the results may not be generally accepted as scientific. The fact that a "highly respected journal" printed it weighs in favor of printing it, but with some explanation of what constitutes an "experimental design" versus a mainstream design. (Newspaper Editor and Reporter, Local beat, Circulation under 10,000)

There was less of a need to justify use of the story with peer-review findings when the focus was on superior Hispanic workers. But some of the newspaper and television media personnel, perhaps realizing their lack of scientific expertise, are willing to run the story of white workers if the study is peer-reviewed. However, our quantitative findings indicated that this tendency does not override the larger concern of most respondents about the possible racist effects or racial controversy the story of white workers will generate.

Another explanation why stories presenting Hispanics as hard working may be favorable to print is that it offers a positive prototype of an often negatively stereotyped group (Lu and Nicholson-Crotty 2010). Mastro and Tukachinshy (2011) argue that positive exposure to groups lead to positive evaluations of that group. Favorable media representations of Latinos lead to positive evaluations concerning work ethic, intelligence, and criminality. Lu and Nicholson-Crotty (2010) contend that media representations of Latinos and Latinas are important because media representations influence policy, especially immigration policy. When media consumers see positive representations of Latinos and Latinas, they are more likely to favor open immigration. In addition, Embrick and Henricks (2013) argue that, on average, people of color are held to a higher standard and punished more severely when those standards are not met. This suggests that journalists may publish a study of Latin Americans being hard workers as a way to demonstrate when racial minority group have met and surpassed the standards concerning employment.

In light of this third scenario, we can now consider our interpretations of the race-based scenarios. In all three scenarios our respondents showed a willingness to avoid demonizing people of color and perhaps even to put them in a favorable light. Even in the kidnapping scenario, several of our respondents indicated that they wanted to be careful not to treat the story differently due to the race of the girl. We want to be careful not to assume too much out of the information added by this third scenario. Clearly, if we have many more racialized scenarios, we would have more confidence that avoidance of racial stigma towards people of color is a dominant theme motivating the work of media personnel. However, it is evident that an important part of the motivation perceived by media personnel is due to their desires to avoid stigmatizing people of color. How much of their motivation is tied to this desire to not stigmatize people of color in comparison to other possible motivating impulses is a question that needs to be addressed in future research.

Does Activism Matter?

Our research indicates a willingness of media personnel to favor stories that place people of color in a positive light over those that provide whites with a positive image. The qualitative data indicated some of the ways media personnel are able to justify their reluctance to publish work that makes majority group members look good. Questioning whether a study is racist or de-emphasizing an alternative opinion of a study that portrays whites in a favorable manner is not only meaningful as it concerns whether a study is published, but it also provides insight into how the research story will be covered. One can imagine a newspaper reporter reluctantly writing a story on research about the advantages of white workers and adding in concerns about methodology and discussing civil rights implications with leaders from communities of color. On the other hand, the same reporter writing a story on research about the value of Hispanic workers might emphasize the way this study challenges common racial stereotypes and show less concern about the potential shortcomings of the research.

Likewise, when it comes to crime the reporters may have a similar willingness to discuss a criminal enterprise whether the victim or villain is white or not. However, our respondents indicated a desire to make sure that these criminal stories do not reinforce racial stereotypes, making it reasonable to assert that how a media professional approaches a crime story when people of color are involved will differ when people of color are absent. This may mean playing up the heinous nature of a crime if committed by a white person in a way that media personnel would not be comfortable doing if that crime were committed by a person of color. The difference in how the story is covered may be small and even, as in the case of the girl kidnapping, imperceptible. Few believe that any one story will have a major impact on how individuals perceive racial issues; however, these differences in tone can have a cumulative effect in shaping cultural attitudes. Over time and with many stories, the care journalists take to make sure that they are not seen as perpetuating racial inequality will shape how racial stories are reported, and that constant impact would contribute to a larger cultural effect.

We argue that there are two particular reasons why media personnel may be especially hesitant to publish stories that either make people of color look bad or write them in a way that minimizes negative perceptions of people of color. One possibility is that the journalist is sensitive to the nature of our racialized society and therefore takes extra care not to publish stories in ways that reinforce the majority group status of European-Americans. This suggests an internal motivation, which drives the journalist to make decisions that are sensitive to the fears of people of color. The other possibility is that the journalist is sensitive to civil rights organizations and does not want to run afoul of them. This suggests an external force, which limits the ability of journalists to address these stories in ways that may work to the disadvantage of people of color. Our research methodology does not allow us to determine whether internal or external motivation is the more powerful predictor of this propensity to protect the image of people of color. However, answers of our respondents indicate that both internal motivation and external forces are at play in shaping the findings of this research. We do not see this as an either/or question. It is entirely possible that pressure from civil rights organizations produces attitudinal changes within the journalists. Social movements such as Black Lives Matter can motivate media personnel through arguments not previously taken into consideration as well as a fear of protest if a story does not meet the expectations of the group. This would reflect a confirmation bias whereby individuals convince themselves to accept beliefs that make their job easier by avoiding unpleasant confrontation with an activist group. Thus, it may be that both internal and external elements reinforce each other to ensure that stories about people of color are covered in ways that pay attention to the fears of those racial minorities.

Given the likely interactive nature of the internal and external motivations driving journalists, it is worth considering the role of civil rights organizations in the possible shaping of the media. Undoubtedly, some media personnel see such organizations as problematic and react to them in ways to minimize the controversy that such organizations can create. Others are sympathetic to those organizations and convinced by their arguments. Such individuals likely craft stories that media leaders of these organizations find acceptable. Either way, our data suggests that such organizations are helping to shape the agenda created by our media. Given the new push towards colorblindness in our society, traditional civil rights organizations may have a limited ability to directly shape the racial attitudes of Americans. Many Americans, especially majority group members, are likely to dismiss the racialized reforms offered by those civil rights organizations. However, if those activists are able to influence the type of stories covered by our media and how they are covered, then civil rights organizations may have an indirect impact on such attitudes. One of the lessons of our study is that civil rights organizations do have an impact in shaping our society, if we consider their influence in the larger media. Indeed, such organizations may have more impact by indirectly influencing society through the media rather than directly by addressing the general public.

Evidence Concerning Majority Group Power News Ideology

The information in this chapter does bear some light on the possibility of the Majority Group Power News Ideology. Clearly, our findings challenge the idea that this news ideology motivates media personnel. In two of the scenarios, the differences in whether a white or non-white person was included resulted in findings suggesting more attention to the concerns of people of color than whites. In the other scenario, there were not sufficient differences to make any conclusion about whether media personnel are concerned with maintenance of majority group power. However, even in this scenario some respondents explicitly stated their intention to avoid recognition of racial implications. Even though media personnel tend to have majority group status in a variety of ways,[7] we do not have evidence that they intend to use their status to further the racial interests of the majority group.

We briefly note one possible exception to this trend in that social media personnel do exhibit Majority Group Power News Ideology as it concerns the research scenario. In this one instance, we have slight evidence of the Majority Group Power News Ideology. Future work with a larger sample of social media personnel can further clarify whether social media personnel follow a general trend of downplaying racial issues or indicating concern for people of color as seen among newspaper and television personnel, or whether social media personnel deviate from other media personnel on racial issues.

Of course there are other majority group issues beyond race. Another key stratification dimension is gender. Male media personnel may have a propensity to protect their power as a gender majority group more than whites have a propensity to protect their racial majority group. These men may create an occupational atmosphere that generates media gender bias stronger than potential media racial bias. Our examination of majority group power is incomplete until we also investigate the possibility that majority group power works through gender, instead of race, differences. Such an investigation is the focus of the next chapter.

3

Sexism

Another important dynamic for assessing whether journalists are subject to a desire to perpetuate majority group power is to see if stories about men are treated differently from stories about women. Sex differs from race in that often individuals hesitate to connect physical differences to racial distinctions, but they do not have that problem regarding gender differences. There is generally an acknowledgment that men and women physically differ from each other. The perception that these differences play a role in the actions of men and women can buttress our society's general sexism.[1] For example, most Christian groups decry racism and argue that people of all races are equal (Kelsey 1965). As such, there is little, if any, overt effort within Christian congregations to promote different social roles for distinct racial groups. However, many denominations, especially those with conservative Christians, advocate traditional gender roles (Martin et al. 1980; Roof and McKinney 1987) that perpetuate different tasks for men and women.[2] Merely because individuals do not advocate the use of racial distinctions to make social decisions does not mean that they are equally hesitant to use gender differences.

If media personnel are as willing to utilize gender differences and contrasting roles for women as conservative Christians are, then we may see this difference play itself out in our scenarios. However, it is possible that these scenarios provide some insight into the Culture War News Ideology. There are some gender issues, such as abortion, that are often a factor in society's culture wars. We did not use a scenario concerning abortion, but some research indicates that cultural conservatives are less comfortable with women working outside of the home than cultural progressives (Morgan

1987; Wilcox and Jelen 1991). In our scenarios, we have the opportunity to assess traditional gender expectations about women working outside of the home and the notion of an exceptional mother's role in a child's life. As we determine whether news media personnel are supportive of women in non-traditional roles, we can gain a bit of insight into whether the Culture War News Ideology may be at play among our respondents.

GENDER SCENARIOS

We used two scenarios to determine whether media personnel acted differently depending upon the sex of the individuals in the scenarios. The first scenario concerns a business person who is a millionaire, but once was homeless. In one version of this scenario, the person was a man; and in the other version, the person was a woman. The general idea is to see if our respondents will be as happy for the female millionaire as the male. We are also interested in whether respondents mention traditional manifestations of gender roles. The second scenario is about a child being sold into slavery by her parent. In one version, the parent is the father; and in the other, the parent is the mother. Previous research suggests that Americans expect women to be more nurturing than men (Eagly 2013; Lippa 2005). If this expectation is the case for our respondents, then they may be more upset at the mother selling the daughter than the father. This may be reflected in the quantitative assessment of the scenario if the respondents are more likely to use the story of the mother, rather than the father, who sells the child into slavery. But the open-ended responses to our questions will give further insight.

There is a third scenario with some gender implications. That is the scenario whereby we look at the ways two campus groups are treated. One of the campus groups is a Baptist group while the other is a feminist group. The gender issues connected to the feminist group definitely bring with them the possibility of different treatment by gender. However, we contend that the religious nature of the Baptist group of this scenario is more important than the gender dimensions. We could have reconstructed this scenario so that we are comparing a female oriented campus group, like a sorority, to a male oriented campus group, like a fraternity. Such a comparison would have provided a cleaner test about the importance of gender in how a story is shaped. However, we decided to make this a Christian/feminist comparison and will explore this story in more depth in the next chapter.

Homeless to Millionaire Scenario

In recent years we have seen more examples of successful female businesspeople. Indeed, one such individual—Carly Fiorina—made a credible run at gaining the nomination of one of the two major parties for the presidency of our nation. However, the common image of the successful business person still tends to be male. So when we generally think of someone in poverty who has overcome all the barriers, it is not surprising that we usually consider that person to be male. Has our media reinforced this societal assumption? Or perhaps our media is merely expressing the social reality whereby men are still more economically successful than women. Using content analysis of media stories, it is extremely difficult to determine whether the media is merely representing reality or shaping our perception of that reality. Our research offers the opportunity to look at the cognitive processes used to determine whether media personnel are more open to a non-traditional gender perception of a business person.

The quantitative analysis with the newspaper respondents indicates that it does not matter if Pat,[3] the business person in the story, is male or female. There was a strong desire to run this story regardless of the business person's sex. Roughly, the same percentage wanted to put the story on the front page or front section regardless of the sex of Pat (76.0% v. 79.8%: ns), include the story in the paper in any way (99% v. 97.4%; ns) and to run the story online (both 96.4%). The sex of Pat did not matter in the question of whether the story should be included in the newspaper. When we looked at a combination of all media we do not find much of a difference either (82.8% v. 84.0%: ns). However, it is worth noting that there was an insignificant (66.2% v. 46.5%: ns), but notable increase in the willingness of social media personnel to put the story online when Pat is male.[4] As we consider personnel in different media outlets, it is important to explore the exceptional nature of the attitudes of those in social media.

With our qualitative data we also have the ability to see if the way the stories are constructed may differ according to sex. The sex of the business person may indeed shape the way this human interest story could be told, although the differences do not seem to be great. An example is found in the comments on how this story can encourage others when the successful business person is male (32.5% v. 22.0%: p < .05).[5] Such comments talked about how the reporting of Pat's life can encourage others to find success as well.

> Readers will be inspired and educated to learn of this man's path. (Newspaper Editor, multiple beats, circulation under 10,000)

> Hope and inspiration to viewers. Highly teasable. (Television Reporter, News Current Events and News Media beat, circulation under 10,000)

> Ties to the community and how Pat Young managed to proceed with his business ventures. Avenues for other people who would like to do the same thing. (Newspaper Editor, multiple beats, circulation 100,000–500,000)

Thus, we see an image of a businessman who can inspire others that is slightly more accessible to our respondents than an inspirational businesswoman. The media personnel may be tapping into an emotional expectation of how we envision male success as opposed to female success. It could be that gender essentialism explains why there is an expectation that men are successful as opposed to women. Women may go into traditionally female-oriented fields because of gender essentialism or sexism (England 2010). Women's work is not valued or compensated for. Because of this women may fail to go into fields like business. It could be possible that journalists focus more on the success of businessmen because women only make up only 5% of CEOs of S&P 500 companies (Long 2016). Although women are well represented in the S&P workforce, they are not in the top position of CEO (Sola 2016). As of 2016, 27 women held the top positions in S&P 500 companies. Although women have made some gains,[6] it is predicted that it will take at least 45 years to reach equality in the workplace if five new female CEOs were added each year. Berry and Franks (2010) suggest that although women have the skill and credentials to hold positions of leadership in the workplace, they do not necessarily want them because of the loneliness and sexism they face.

This possibility of adhering to gender norms is strengthened when it is coupled with a propensity to see the male's success as an opportunity to feel good. This tendency for the respondent to discuss the story as a feel good story was higher when Pat was a man than a woman, although the difference was not quite significant (16.4% v. 9.9%: $p < .1$).[7] There was an upbeat nature in these comments that showed the hopes of the respondents to put forth a story that produces positive feelings within their consumers.

> Classic rags to riches story. Nice bright for the front if it hasn't been widely reported on. If it has, then maybe it goes on the front of the business section. (Newspaper Reporter, Crime beat, circulation 50,000–100,000)

> This would be a great feature story ... literally rags to riches. Clearly not a lead story, but one that could be teased to later in the newscast. (Television Reporter, Government and Politics beats, circulation under 10,000)

In some ways, the feel good motivations of the respondents is compatible to the desire to encourage others with the male Pat's story. Both of the trends appeal to a desire to inspire those who are not as fortunate as Pat. As one respondent (Television Reporter, multiple beats, Circulation under 10,000) puts it, the story is a "challenge to presumption that homelessness is a dead end." Thus, in the male Pat, we have a story that is meant to help others achieve the same accomplishment of Pat by providing them with emotional support. There is a lesson in the story of the male Pat. The story is that the media consumer can overcome his or her obstacles as well.

We are not arguing that such "lessons" were not offered when considering a woman's success story. However, they were offered significantly less than when talking about a male. The media personnel may have believed that the story will be better received when the business person is a male. Perhaps there is an expectation that a male businessman is more inspiring than a female businesswoman. The higher likelihood of placing the male businessman on the pedestal to generate inspiration increased the chances that men are seen as heroes relative to women in a story of a successful business person. We acknowledge that these differences are not overwhelming. However, as noted in the previous chapter, slight differences in this single story are not likely to have a great deal of impact on social attitudes unless these differences are played out in dozens and even hundreds of stories documenting male and female success, then we may see cultural dialog towards a championing of males as the inspiration for overcoming life's difficulties.

Yet, the respondents were just as likely to run a story with the female business person as they were with the male business person. This leads to the question of what motivates them to run stories of the female business person if they are not as motivated by her work ethic and their eagerness to show her as an example to others. The most important distinction is their willingness to mention some aspect of Pat's gender. The respondents did not make a big deal of the sex of Pat, but we coded whether there was any reference to the gender of Pat.[8] This was significantly more common when discussing the female Pat (63.4% v. 49.7%: $p < .05$). On the one hand, the media personnel are hesitant to call attention to characteristics such as sex and race. As we saw in the last chapter, respondents overtly talked about not wanting to mention the race of the principles, and they were not eager to notice Pat's sex. However, they did refer to some aspect of Pat's sex more often, which suggests that Pat's sex matters to them more when

Pat is female. It is reasonable to assume that if media personnel are more likely to note the sex of Pat when explaining what makes a story important, they are also going to be more likely to note the sex of Pat in their actual news stories.

It is tricky to interpret what this difference indicates. But our interpretation may be situated against our previous observations about the male Pat. If the male Pat is seen as the example of inspiration, then perhaps there is the expectation that males are more likely to provide a motivation of success rather than a female business person. Thus, a story of a female business person is less about inspiration and more about a woman in an unexpected societal position. Respondents may reinforce this angle of the story by making sure that the consumers of media are told, if not directly than indirectly, about the sex of Pat. If this interpretation of these differences is correct, then the respondents may be tapping into a traditional gender notion whereby men are expected to succeed and be inspirational, while there is surprise when a woman gains economic success. If such traditional gender expectations are behind these differences then it is likely that the stories would be written differently, even if slightly differently, when discussing male or female business success. The inspirational male Pat can at least tacitly support common notions of gender distinctions. The difference is subtle, and we do not assert that there is a sexist motivation driving this difference. But if this distinction shows up multiple times in many different stories, then it becomes possible that media reinforces traditional gender norms.

While we have worked hard to assess the possible differences between the two stories of Pat, we do not want to leave the impression that the contrasts in the stories are wildly distinct from each other. Indeed, the stories of the two Pats have much more in common than they have different from each other. Our interpretation is that the basic story offered by the news media personnel is likely to be quite similar with minor tweaks about the inspirational male Pat and a few more mentions of sex with the female Pat. However, the general rags-to-riches emphasis and a focus of what Pat can give to the larger community will remain mostly the same. Thus, our conclusion with the homeless to millionaire scenario is that there is not a tremendous difference between the two stories, but the difference we do find slightly reinforces a general notion of traditional gender expectations.

3. Sexism

Daughter into Slavery Scenario

Our second scenario also is a test of traditional gender notions as we explore how media personnel may interpret the role of father and mother. The story we tell them is clearly horrifying. Selling a child into slavery is the stuff of sensational documentaries and cable news programs. For example, MSNBC runs several series of documentaries about slavery in the United States, such as "Sex Slaves in America," "Trafficked: Slavery in America," "Undercover: Sex Slaves in America" and "Sex Slaves: Vegas Escorts." It is not hard to see the prevalent media interest for stories of local slavery. But the horrifying nature of the story may be worse if the parent is female because we think of a special bond between the mother and the child that the father does not possess. It is quite common to hear a story of a woman who has abused her child and then to have someone comment, "How could a mother do that?," implying that it is not as surprising to find out a man abuses his child.

Some may argue that it is unfathomable for mothers to harm their children because of the natural and biological connection between mother and child. The hormone oxytocin is produced during labor and lactation. Traditionally, mothers serve as the primary caregiver and are usually the first social bond that children establish. Mothers provide a sense of comfort and safety for their children. In addition, Katz-Wise, Priess, and Hyde (2010) contend that the birth of a child changes women more than men. Women become more traditional in their gender roles than men. These differing expectations help to set up the gender roles that limit the economic success of women (Judge and Livingston 2008; Keene and Quadagno 2004). Our scenario will help us explore whether such expectations come into play for media personnel.

The first question is whether the story gets more attention if it concerns a mother than a father. The answer is basically no. The terrifying nature of this story produces almost universal agreement that the story deserves a place in the media regardless of the sex of the parent. There was virtually no difference between newspaper editors and reporters in whether the story should be placed in either the front page or front section (94.6% v. 91.0%: ns), included in the newspaper at all (99.5% v. 96.0%; ns) or as an online article (97.7% v. 94.1%: ns). With such small differences, it almost seems incidental that the version with the mother is used slightly more often than the version with the father. When looking at all media outlets, there is again almost universal agreement that the story needed inclusion (85.0% v. 83.3%: ns). Just as we saw in the last chapter with the kidnapping of a girl, when a child is abused, the media is aggressive in the inclusion of the story regardless of the social/demographic elements of the principles. This aggressiveness creates a lack of variation in our quantitative responses.[9]

Analysis of the open-ended questions did not reveal evidence that the newspaper media personnel were harder on mothers than fathers. In fact, the opposite appears to be true. The newspaper media were more interested in the slavery aspect of the scenario when it was about a father as opposed to the mother (58.8% v. 43.9%: p < .1), although it was not significant at the traditional p < .05. Examples of how slavery is discussed are:

> Sex slavery is alive and well and thriving in Middle America. Who knew? (Newspaper Reporter, Culture beat, circulation 100,000–500,000)

> Is this practice common or uncommon in the community, state and nation? Where does the slavery ring exist, or whom does it serve? How do slavery rings operate? (Social Media Editor, Culture and Local beats, circulation 10,000–50,000)

> Children being sold as sex slaves is a huge story. One that is not reported on often enough as it occurs all over. I would get the police report and attempt to speak with the father, or his attorney. (Newspaper Reporter, Crime beat, circulation 10,000–50,000)

It is not necessary that the respondents specifically connected aspects of slavery to the fact that the parent was male, but somehow the parent being male made it more likely for them to recognize the slavery aspect of the story. The slavery element of the story is arguably the most heinous, controversial aspect of it, and making a stronger connection to this aspect when the father is the parent likely makes the father look worse. How having a father selling a child into slavery motivates reporters and editors to be more willing to recognize the slavery component of this story is not completely clear. But we gain a potential clue when we noted another difference between fathers and mothers selling their children into slavery. There was an even stronger tendency to talk about the parent as a bad parent when the scenario was about the father than the mother (16.3% v. 7.7%: p < .05). Here were some of the comments about this condemnation of the father:

> Some people shouldn't have children.… I know he's only been accused, but what an accusation it is … (Newspaper Reporter and Editor, multiple beats, circulation 10,000–50,000)

> What would possess a man to sell his daughter regardless of financial struggle.
> (Television Reporter and Editor, Local beat, circulation under 10,000)

Media personnel have an easier time seeing the father as a bad parent than the mother. We anticipated that the media personnel would have a harder time, or would be in greater shock, at the notion of the mother selling off her daughter than a father. However, it appears that there is a higher willingness to believe the worst of the male parent as opposed to the female parent. A traditional impression whereby the mother gains more blame than a father is not accurate. The father is more likely to be seen as a bad parent and the presence of the father is more likely to motivate a discussion about slavery. The question becomes why would the presence of a father create more negative impressions than the presence of the mother?

To answer this question, we consider whether a notion of power is relevant for interpretation of these results. Slavery is the ultimate relationship whereby one person abuses power at the expense of someone else. If the media personnel come to this story with an idea of power differentials between men and women in a marriage then they may be more sensitive to the greater power a father may possess relative to a mother. If the father is seen as significantly more powerful than the mother, then he may be in a position to do more damage as a parent. It is not the shock of the mother being willing to sell her child into slavery that is the main shaper of the image in this story, but rather the image of a brutal uncaring male.[10] It is possible that some respondents envision the father selling the child despite the protestations of a woman in a weaker power position. If our speculation is correct, then we would get slightly different stories depending on whether a father or mother is caught selling a child into slavery. The story would be covered just as much regardless of the sex of the parent, but there may be more emphasis on the power differentials when a father is the guilty parent. Such a difference indicates more acknowledgment of patriarchy within our society than reinforcement of traditional gender values.

Whether the consumers of newspaper media would pick up on such a difference in a single story is questionable. However, it is reasonable to assert that over time treating men as more powerful, and perhaps more dangerous, than women would have long standing effects in how each sex is perceived. For example, the reporting of crimes may be seen as more sinister when the crime is committed by a man instead of a woman due to the media treating men as more dangerous than women, even if they commit the same crimes. Whether the story of "men as dangerous" translates into non-criminal wrongdoings, such as sexual affairs of public figures, is a question that may be answered in future research. Nevertheless, the image of men as dangerous could feed into a traditional gender narrative in that it emphasizes women as helpless and needing masculine protection.

However, we are not completely comfortable that this is powerful evidence indicating promotion of traditional gender roles. One of the reasons for our doubt is that when the respondents decided to run the story of the mother, the focus was slightly different. There was a higher propensity to focus on the financial angle with the mother, but it was not significant at the traditional $p < .05$ level (7.1% v. 2.6%; $p < .1$). For example one respondent (Newspaper Editor, Local beat, circulation 10,000–50,000) noted that the story is important to run "to show people still can get that desperate for money and not know where to turn." It is plausible to argue that the media personnel may have considered the weaker financial position of women relative to males when considering a mother selling her child. This type of attitude would not be reinforcement of traditional gender roles, but rather it would challenge the viability of those roles. Thus, we are unconvinced that a reinforcement of traditional gender roles is the most powerful explanation for our results in this scenario.

Indeed, the most plausible interpretations may be that there simply is not much difference between the treatment of fathers and mothers when such a crime has been committed. We suggested a possible "no bias" finding as it concerned racial issues; however, eventually settled on an interpretation that there was a bias in the focus on not stigmatizing people of color. The evidence for a "no bias" finding appears to be perhaps even stronger when exploring possible gender differences. The differences that do exist may be at the extended margins of gender attitudes and the respondents may generally not differentiate between men and women regarding the care of their children. This interpretation suggests that media personnel are comfortable with some degree of an egalitarian understanding of gender notions, although they are willing to explore traditional gender roles in muted ways.[11]

Our findings are unclear about the question of whether the interests of women are being sacrificed for the interests of men. As it concerns the homeless to millionaire scenario, there is limited evidence that a traditional notion of the man as the inspiration for economic achievement is supported. The scenario dealing with notions of parenthood indicates potential support for traditional gender images, if men are seen as dangerous and women are seen as relatively helpless. But the slight focus on the economic deprivation that women may face appears to fly in the face of the notion that these media personnel are seeking to reinforce a traditional patriarchal order. Furthermore, one can argue that making men seem dangerous can also work against the interest of men. For example, the image of men as rapists, rather than the reality of how often rapes actually occurred, may have motivated much of the recent activism on college campuses that appear to have led to some false rape accusations (Cohan 2014; Somaiya 2015). It is not clear that the interpretation of attitudes of the respondents in this project must be interpreted as pejorative to women.

Given that we have one scenario that shows limited support for male achievement and another where we have limited support for male danger, we cannot strongly assert that the media consistently promotes attitudes that reinforce norms supporting men over women. With regards to support for a Majority Group Power News Ideology, at best we can argue that there is weak evidence for the idea of a media bias against women, and at worst it is possible to argue that the attitudes exhibited by our respondents actually support women. Taking both scenarios into account, it is plausible to argue that in either scenario there is a slightly greater focus on how proactive the male is, whether as a productive businessman or a dangerous father, that helps to determine the tone of the article. Media personnel may strive to create an egalitarian presentation, but they still have some proclivity to look towards the actions of the male to determine how the story will be presented. It is plausible that these differences are so small that the best interpretation is that media personnel have obtained a "no bias" stance as it concerns issues of traditional gender norms, except with the assumption that what men do is prioritized. One can speculate about whether there will be enough stories with male and female gender distinctions for the small differences documented in this research to help reinforce or shape current gender attitudes. However, our finding concerning the focus on male activities for shaping the tone of the story can be a guideline by which one can consider how gender expectations shape the stories produced by American media.

Contrast to the Race Scenarios

Given that race and gender are traditionally considered important ways to assess stratification in the United States, we must consider why they are treated differently by media personnel. When we explored race, we detected little, if any, evidence that whites were being favored over non-whites. Indeed, it seemed that the reverse may be true in that the avoidance of stigmatizing non-whites was highly prioritized. There seemed to be incentive among media personnel to protect people of color from potential stigma and less concern about protecting the position of racial majority group members. Lay theories about race are associated with greater prejudice than lay theories about sexual orientation (Jayaratne et al. 2006). We cannot make such a statement as it concerns sex differences. Depending on how we interpret our findings, one can argue that traditional attitudes that favor men are supported by the decisions made by media personnel. These decisions promote attitudes that harm men by painting them as dangerous. Another possibility is that in reality there is little difference between the way men and women are treated by media personnel. We can argue that there may be a focus on the role of men that feeds into a generalized patriarchal notion that the actions of men matter more than the actions of women. Ideally, future research can quantify the importance of male activity in determining the value of a story to reporters. However, it is perhaps more plausible that our respondents generally treat men and women the same in news coverage.

One reason why there may be a difference in the manner by which race and gender is covered is the notion of whether a dimension has an essentialist nature. Essentialism contends that differences are natural rather than social constructions. These differences define an object or person (Richardson 2011) and are perceived to be biological (Jayaratne et al. 2006). Under essentialism, culture is unmalleable. It is important to realize when essentialism is occurring because these ideas impact perception and representation of groups, law, medicine, and other social institutions (Richardson 2011).

Given the push towards a colorblind perspective by racial majority (Bonilla-Silva 2003; Ryan et al. 2007) and even by many racial minority group members (Yancey 2010) it is not surprising that there is a great deal of social pressure to perceive no difference between members of distinct racial groups. It has been established that racial identity is socially constructed (Omi and Winant 2014). Even though we generally use superficial physical elements to designate contrasting racial groups, the reality is that there is very little, if any, actual systematic physical difference between individuals in various racial groups. This reality is often used by many individuals to justify arguments that people of different races are essentially the same. Race matters in significant ways. Smedley and Smedley (2005) argue that until the government assesses racial and ethnic inequality fully, racialized science or scientific racism will explain racial inequality as due to deficiencies in the racially subordinated group rather than institutions and ideologies that maintain a racial hierarchy.

The same notion of being alike is not the case as it concerns sex differences. Beyond sex organs, biologically, men tend to differ from women in their physical stature.[12] Gender essentialism is the belief that men and women are biologically or naturally different in interests and skills (England 2010). Therefore, despite arguments for the perception of gender as a fluid dynamic, most Americans perceive innate differences between men and women. To be sure, our society is at a time where even the idea of biological sex is facing a great deal of challenge. The day may soon come in which sex is seen as socially constructed just as race, but that is not yet true outside of subcultures of progressive activists. To the degree that they pick up on the tendency in the larger society to understand men and women as different, some media personnel may find some justification in some of the traditional gender notions in our society. They may perceive less incentive to protect women than they do people of color. This may not only lead to a more traditionalist interpretation of men and women, but the lack of a willingness to protect women may also motivate media personnel to treat men and women the same in the different scenarios.

There was a second important difference in the manner by which issues of gender were treated differently than issues of race. When we dealt with the race scenarios, there was mention concerning the possible engagement with civil rights, or other external, organizations. Such mentions were missing in these scenarios. Part of this difference may have been the type of scenarios we used for each group. It may be more natural to decide to seek out civil rights organizations when there is an accusation of a racially based crime. However, we did have a criminological situation with one of our gender scenarios and the respondents could well have mentioned feminist organizations as part of the celebration of a woman who obtained wealth after being homeless. Thus, we have to consider if other factors accounted for the failure of any of the respondents to mention external organizations that cater to the interest of women.

In theory, feminist organizations that address the plight of women should be just as powerful as civil rights organizations that address the concerns of people of color. Yet, it is plausible that activism connected to people of color through formal organizations is more recognized than activism connected to women through formal organizations. This may be the case if causes connected to the stated desires of women's organizations, such as reproductive control, are submerged within more general cultural progressive activists groups. Furthermore, there is a proximity that men and women share which does not have to be shared between whites and non-whites. That proximity may enable women to challenge sexism in ways not available for people of color who desire to challenge racism. If both reasons are accurate then women may have less need to have formal organizations to specialize on issues of concern to them than people of color.

However, for reasons that are not clear at this time, it may also be true that media personnel have a lower level of concern about sexism than about racism. The lower level of concern may lead to less desire to bother with feminist organizations relative to ethnic civil rights organizations. It is beyond the scope of this work to explore whether activist organizations based upon race/ethnicity are more effective than those based upon sex. However, if that is the case, then the comparative higher willingness of reporters and editors to accept traditional gender roles as opposed to Euro-centric racial attitudes is tied to the relative effectiveness of activist organizations. The power of special interest groups to shape media products is a subject that should be explored in future research.

Finally, it is worth observing that our respondents indicated a powerful desire to downplay overtly mentioning both gender and racial characteristics of the principles. We assert that the intention to ignore race and gender does not mean that they did not have an influence on the stories written by the media personnel. However, this intention does speak to the possibility of a No Bias News Ideology that the respondents may work to implement in their work. Such a focus may mute the potential ways in which racial and gender characteristics of the principles of the scenarios help to drive the results emerging from our analysis. It also indicates the possibility that social desirability biased the way in which the respondents have answered the questions in our survey. However, we contend that if the respondents are able to lessen the racial and gender differences in their self-presentation for our survey then it is likely that they can also lessen those differences in the stories they produce. This is especially the case if there is a larger media culture that reinforces the values of objectivity and neutrality of producers of media.

3. Sexism

Evidence of Majority Group Power?

The results we found in this, and the previous chapter, cast serious doubts on the possibility that motivation of media personnel is due to a desire to promote the power of the majority group. As it concerns racial issues, there is even evidence for the media attempting to challenge majority group power. We did find some information suggesting that media personnel may be somewhat focused on the activity of males, but this finding was fairly weak. Collins (2011) posits that women are under-represented in media. When women are portrayed, it is usually with suggestive or provocative depictions. In addition, women are represented in traditional, stereotypically feminine ways. When women are depicted in traditionally male ways, they are viewed by both men and women as potentially good role models (Taylor and Setters 2011), suggesting that masculinity is viewed more favorably than femininity.

This indicates the possibility of a mixed result concerning the Majority Group Power News Ideology. It is quite possible that with a different set of scenarios, we would have found more evidence to support this news ideology or perhaps even more findings that there is no evidence for it. We cannot state with complete confidence that support for majority group power plays only a minor role in the motivations of our reporters and editors. However, given the limited evidence of this news ideology in our current set of scenarios, we assert that it is unlikely that this is the most important news ideology motivating media personnel.

To be sure, we are not totally done with testing the Majority Group Power News Ideology. It is quite possible that our examination of sexual minorities will indicate support for the power of this news ideology.[13] Furthermore, Christianity has historically been seen as the majority religion in our society. Thus, our exploration of how this religion is covered can also tell us some idea about the willingness of the media to either support or to criticize majority groups. Yet, issues of race and gender can be seen as core indicators of stratification and power in the United States. Even if we find evidence of support for majority groups in our examination of sexuality and religion, the failure to find powerful results supporting majority group power with these two dimensions shows the relative weakness of this news ideology.

The other news ideology that we are exploring concerns the possibility that a culture war is shaping potential news ideologies. We found some evidence of support for traditional gender roles, but not overwhelming evidence. In a limited way, media personnel may support some cultural conservatism. But, although cultural attitudes are correlated to general political ideology, cultural progressives or cultural conservatives do not tend to focus on political issues surrounding race or gender. It is issues of sexuality and religion that play an important role in shaping those cultural conflicts. Our examinations of those issues in the next two chapters will not only provide minor refutation or confirmation of the Majority Group Power News Ideology but will go a long way to establishing the importance of the Culture War News Ideology.

4

Religion

In the previous two chapters, we looked heavily at traditional issues of stratification to explore whether media personnel are influenced by a willingness to defend majority group interest. However, a second news ideology concerns whether media personnel have chosen sides in the culture war. There is reason to believe, as we expressed in Chapter 2, that they would choose the side of the cultural progressives. We will explore this possibility in the next two chapters. One of the important components of the culture war is religion. Cultural conservatives can be of a variety of faiths, but conservative Christianity is generally seen as the major promulgator of the cultural conservative perspective. Thus, our explanation of the Culture War News Ideology will begin with examining the possibility of a bias against Christians and Christianity.

Previous research suggests that media personnel are less religious and thus less likely to be Christian than the general population (Lichter 1990). This may indicate a lack of influence from contact with Christians,[1] allowing the Culture War News Ideology to motivate media personnel into ignoring the concerns of Christians. It is also possible that some journalists have hostility towards Christians and create an uncomfortable atmosphere for Christian journalists. There is some evidence of a consistently negative media image of conservative Christians (Kerr 2003). Individuals with anti-Christian hostility may have intrinsic motivation to construct a news ideology that supports a negative Christian image. If the Culture War News Ideology is correct, then journalists may perceive part of their duty to demystify Christianity and expose the shortcomings of cultural conservatives. Such motivations would generate less sympathy for the plight of conservative Christians relative to other social groups, especially less than social groups perceived to be culturally progressive.

However, other scholars have argued that Western religious values often provide the context by which media stories are reported. Silk (1998) argues that this process allows religious views to be privileged over secular views. Moore's (2008) work suggests that this religious framework is based on Western religious values, which can be forced upon stories concerning Eastern religions. While the moral system media personnel are tapping into is likely tied to Christian notions of a social gospel (Underwood and Stamm 2001), and thus may not be themes popular among conservative Christians, media personnel may be unlikely to be overtly critical of the general religion due to their loyalty to that tradition. Thus, a Majority Group Power News Ideology may arise from our examination of religious scenarios.

Since journalism training encourages neutrality, it is quite possible that this training has enabled them to overcome their lack of contact or possible hostility toward Christians. This training may create a mindset whereby the journalist perceives him/herself as an impartial referee who refuses to take sides in a cultural debate. Furthermore, although our earlier findings dispute this, if the Majority Group News Ideology is an accurate description of journalists, there may even be a desire to protect the interest of the majority religion. If that is the case, then claims of anti–Christian bias are not well founded. Culture war considerations would matter little in the way Christians, particularly conservative Christians, are treated in the media.

CHRISTIAN SCENARIOS

We wanted to address common arguments put forward as examples of possible anti–Christian media coverage. Our first example concerns an issue that has developed in recent years on some college campuses. At Vanderbilt University and Bowdoin College, as well as the University of California college system, there has been the use of what has been called "all-comers" policy, which mandates that the leadership of student organizations have to be open to those of any faith. This has led to some Christian organizations being kicked off campus for their unwillingness to comply with this rule (Dreher 2014). There has not been a lot of media coverage of this issue beyond what can be found in Christian and conservative media. We wonder whether this lack of coverage is due to relative lack of importance of the issue or due to the rules mainly affecting Christians. Thus, we create a scenario whereby we look at a conflict between a college student organization and the college's administration. We augment the scenario with a complaint about delaying the charter of the organization to help make it a full-blown controversy. In one version, we look at the conflict with a Baptist organization that wants to keep its leadership Christian. In the other version, we discuss a conflict with a feminist organization that wants to keep its leadership female.

In the second and third scenarios, we test other situations whereby Christians may be victimized. Thus we compare Christians to members of a different religion (Muslims) and to those seen on the other side of the culture war (LGBT community). In the second scenario, we look at a religious congregation shooting. Two people died, which clearly indicates a tragedy but perhaps not automatically national news. We placed the story out of the local areas so that the respondents would only consider the issues at play with this particular story, and not be concerned with local security issues, as they decide whether they should pursue it for coverage. In this scenario, we used a Baptist church in one version and focused on a Muslim mosque in the other version. This allows us to assess whether the attention and narrative given to the story is influenced by the identity of the religious group victimized. In the third scenario, we look at an example of possible hate speech. In the first version, a teacher uses derogatory language towards Christians, and a Christian student has recorded the language. In our alternate version, we have the teacher engage in hateful homophobic speech that is recorded by the student. This scenario will allow us to see whether hate speech is equally assigned to the story regardless of which side of the culture war is victimized by this possible hate speech. Given the current argument over same-sex marriage, the LBGT movement is clearly on the progressive side of the culture war debate, which enables us to assess whether journalists equally treat both sides of that war.

CAMPUS ORGANIZATION SCENARIO

Yancey and Williamson (2014) document that individuals with Christianophobia want to preserve an image of religious neutrality and thus support measures that disparately impact Christians to express their hatred and fear of Christians as long as it can be done with non-bigoted justification. One possible way this may happen is with a rule by which all college student organizations are required to allow people of all different faiths to be part of the leadership of that group. While on the surface this type of rule influences all religious groups, conservative Christian groups are generally more particularistic in their theological outlook.[2] For such groups, ideological purity in leadership has a stronger priority than religious groups that are more ecumenical in nature. Consequently, evangelical Christians tend to form groups that are most likely to be removed from campuses that have adopted what has been termed an "all-comers" policy. If there is a problem of anti–Christian attitudes within U.S. media, then ignoring such events can be driven by anti–Christian hostility, and we would not expect this lack of attention if another student group suffers.

However, our evidence indicates that the Christian nature of the student group is not driving the dismissal of all-comers policy. We found that the scenario with the Baptist group was actually more likely to be in the front page or front section of the paper than the feminist group (46.8% v. 31.7%: p < .05), or if the story is used at all (95.0% v. 86.2%; p < .05), although there was no real difference in whether the story would be included in an online story (84.8% v. 83.0%: ns). It is also the case that inclusion of the story in all media was not shaped by the nature of the campus organization (75.1% v. 73.2%: ns).[3] The relative lack of attention all-comers policies receive is not due to the Christian nature of the student group. We argue that the lack of attention indicates that the general media simply is not very interested in college campus issues, or in what professors do, since the three scenarios with the lowest percentages of respondents willing to use the story at all are Student Organization (74.3%), Research Study (56.7%) and Hate Speech (47.4%). The lack of attention to all-comers policy may simply be due to the fact that media personnel are bored with what happens on college campuses. Perhaps those of us who are academics should take offense at this reality more than conservative Christian groups.

However, while the attention given to the story is fairly equal, or slightly higher for the Baptist group, the approach of the respondents to the actual story is rather different. When discussing this story with the feminist group, there was a higher tendency to focus on the larger societal concerns connected to gender, as opposed to larger religious concerns when the story was about the Baptist group (19.9% v. 9.7%: p < .05). For example, one respondent (Newspaper Reporter and Editor, multiple beats, circulation 10,000–50,000) answered, "Women's pay equality is getting a lot of attention right now ... how much progress has really been made?" Another respondent (Social Media Editor, Science beat, circulation 50,000–100,000) remarked "that men still think they're the ruling class." These patterns indicate that respondents writing about a feminist group complaining about being mistreated have a focus on issues larger than the immediate conflict between the group and the university. These media personnel are likely to contextualize the story to the larger issues of sexism that women face in our society. We would expect a story about them to be an examination of not only whether there is actual bias towards the feminist group by the university, but how sexism in general may account for the experiences of the women or motivate university officials to mistreat members of the Feminist Majority.

We envision this finding as an indicator of a possible reason why the respondents are so concerned about examining the evidence and getting the information right about the feminist group. There are larger issues of gender at play, and this event provides an opportunity to examine those issues. This does not mean that reporters and editors are looking to promote the agenda of the feminist group, but they do recognize sexism as a problem, and this story can be a vehicle to address that problem. If the reporter and/ or editor are able to document mistreatment of the student group, then he or she can document a possible way sexism manifests itself in a university setting.

It is likely that it does not occur to the media personnel that the conflict between the Baptist group and university is tied to a larger cultural conflict in the general society. It would be odd for respondents to envision societal mistreatment of Baptists in the same way some of the media personnel would envision societal mistreatment of women. In part this is due to the historical place Christian have enjoyed as majority group members in our society[4] while women have traditionally dealt with minority group status. It is not surprising that some respondents would follow the advice of this newspaper reporter and editor (Culture beat, circulation 10,000–50,000) and engage in "assessing the climate on local campuses regarding gender and sexism." However, it is plausible to think of the event as reflective of the larger culture war that has taken place in the United States. In such a war, it is quite plausible that the way the university officials have approached the Baptist organization is reflective of the animosity that conservative Christian organizations experience from their cultural competitors. Thus, just as a potential conflict between feminist and university officials can be contextualized as part of a larger social struggle based on gender, so too it is possible to contextualize the conflict between the Baptist and university officials in a larger social struggle captured by notions of a culture war. Such insight does not require the ability to envision Baptists as minority group members, but rather it requires a vision of societal conflict that is not trapped by traditional focuses on race, class, gender and sexuality.

However, our quantitative results indicate that the story of the Baptists is more likely to gain the attention of the media personnel than the feminist group. So what aspects of the Baptists' story are worth the attention of our respondents? Instead of exploring the possibilities of general anti–Christian attitudes that may situate the controversy, more attention was paid to the conflict between the university and Baptists. Of particular interest to the respondents is whether the Baptist group was being treated differently than other groups (10.2% v. 0.14%: $p < .01$). Evidence of this focus be seen in these comments:

> What is university policy, how it is exercised, what is justification for treating Baptist group differently, does it differ from other similar groups that have been permitted. (Newspaper Editor, Education beat, circulation over 500,000)

> What's the precedence for allowing Christian groups on state university campuses? Is this typically OK, or does it seem that this university is giving them a harder time? (Newspaper Reporter, Local beat, circulation 10,000–50,000)

This focus appears to suggest that more specific campus issues are at play when discussing Baptists rather than feminists. The evidence from these documented differences indicates concern about this specific group and its relationship with the university. There is also the concern about how Baptists are treated relative to other groups. Media personnel may want information about the other groups to have a baseline by which they can understand the Baptists' complaints. However, it is also plausible that the media personnel want the information about other groups so that they can dispute the Baptists' concerns. So rather than situate the conflict in a situation where we should use societal sexism (relatively few media personnel are likely to question the existence of such sexism) to understand the plight of the feminist group, media personnel may gather information that can potentially discredit the Baptist organization. This suggests that the Christian group is placed in a situation whereby they have a higher burden to show that their concerns are more valid in comparison to the feminist group. With this current data, we cannot determine if the exploration of other groups is to support or refute the claims of the Baptist group. Nevertheless, the drama of the conflict of the university and a specific student group may help to provide the higher motivation to put the Baptist, relative to the feminist, story on the front page.

As stated above, this scenario is based on a real world occurrence with the removal of Christian groups at Vanderbilt University, Bowdoin College and the University of California college system. It is quite probable that some respondents heard of these controversies and formed their opinion about this situation before receiving the survey. This pre-knowledge may have influenced them to conceptualize this scenario as conflict between specific Christian groups and the institution of higher education. We contend that this conflict is not limited to the particular issue of all-comers policy, but to a general sense of science/religion conflict perceived at least by some cultural progressives (Yancey and Williamson 2012). It is not possible for us to disentangle how much of this effect might be tied to a general perception that religious groups, especially Christian groups, are at odds with the larger education system as opposed to previous knowledge about previous all-comers policy controversies. However, both explanations are tied to a general perception that Christian groups are in conflict with the university, which creates a different focus on stories about Christian student groups.

Although the story of the Baptist group is more likely to wind up on the front page, the way the stories are to be written is likely to be substantially different from each other. The story about the feminist group is more likely to envision a conversation about sexism on campus and perhaps the larger university. Such a story may tap into arguments put forth by feminist scholars and explore the possibility of this group's discrimination in light of such sexism. There seems less of a concern about the specific conflict between the feminist group and the university, but more of a concern that sexism in general may have led to an unfortunate result. The story of the Baptist group focuses more on the story of the conflict between that particular group and the university. For many respondents it is quite possible that the Baptist group has been mistreated, perhaps in part due to existing knowledge about previous conflicts over the all-comers policy between Christian groups and the university. Perhaps, there are notions of a generalized religion/science debate that is playing itself out in this particular situation. However, larger issues of potential religious prejudice are likely to be overlooked in favor of a specific concern for a specific group. Thus, there is less likely to be a discussion about anti–Christian attitudes in general in comparison to the respondents' concern with sexism.

There were qualities that were common between both stories of feminist and Christian groups. Several respondents dismissed complaints about delays of organization recognition and others simply did not see this story as big enough to warrant attention. Among those who did see a story, there were similar levels of concern about getting the facts correct. Thus, whether the story is written about a Baptist or feminist group, there is likely to be an investigation of the story to learn what may have happened on campus. These similarities provide a basic framework that would undergird the story no matter the student organization that complained. However, the differences we have noted do indicate distinctive focuses that can provide different interpretations by media consumers.

Our general sense is that attention to the Christian group is distinctive relative to attention to the feminist group. Arguments for a non–Christian bias due to ignoring the concerns of Christian groups are not supported with this scenario. However, when the story of the Baptist organization is covered, the focus will not be on the struggles of Christians in general, but rather on how the organization may have experienced differential treatment. This indicates that media personnel do alter their approach in the story due to the nature of the groups complaining. There are possible interpretations of this exploration as a fair assessment of whether the Baptists are being mistreated. Furthermore, we cannot ignore the fact that our respondents are more likely to feature the story of Baptists in conflict with the university. Thus, we do not have a clear answer as to whether there is a bias against conservative Christians with this scenario. To gain a holistic assessment of the existence of anti–Christian bias, the next two scenarios provide important insight.

Religious Institution Shooting Scenario

Recognition or non-recognition of a student campus group does not appear to stir the interest of journalists. Such an incident has some appeal, but journalists may argue that not much is really lost when a group is unable to obtain recognition on a college campus. The same cannot be said if a crime is committed at a religious institution. This is particularly true if the crime is murder. When we were working on this book, the murder of nine church worshipers in Charleston took place. After those killings, media attention was also drawn towards a series of black church burnings.[5] The image of religious institutions as a safe area is challenged when such tragedies occur, and this discontinuity about how we think about religion may account for the attention such stories gain. Violence in a religious community should create a higher level of media interest than our scenario about university student groups.

Do stories of violence at religious institutions gain more traction when they occur with a non–Christian religious group, or is there an incentive to protect members of the majority religion? If there is more relative attention paid to Islamophobia than Christianophobia, then one would expect that the shooting at a Muslim mosque would attract more attention than a shooting at a Christian church. However, if media personnel tend to prioritize the concerns of Christians over Muslims, then a shooting at a Christian church should gain more attention. Islamophobia is described as antipathy towards Islam and an irrational fear of all or most Muslims (Ali 2012; Imhoff and Recker 2012). Islamophobia is an ideology that conflates the histories, politics, and cultures of the Middle East into an indistinguishable monolith (Semati 2010). This pan-ethnic group is held in comparison to Euro-American cultures and is found not only deficient, but also pathological. In particular, Islamophobia is intertwined with a fear of terrorism (Imhoff and Recker 2012; Semati 2010). Imhoff and Recker (2012) argue that Islamophobia and the increased fear of terror came after the attack on the World Trade Center on September 11, 2001. They also contend that Islamophobia has been evident in American culture since the Islamic Revolution in Iran in 1979, the Salman Rushdie affair in 1988, and the first Gulf War in 1991. Thus, Islamophobia is not only a fear of an enemy culture but a group of people. Perhaps, it should be called anti–Arab racism since it is not a religion that is a target of discrimination; individuals suffer discrimination. Institutional racism towards Islam is evident by Oklahoma's "Save Our State Amendment," which was put into place to ban Sharia law. This law is irrational and unwarranted because only one percent of Oklahomans are Muslim, and Sharia has never been used in a judicial decision within the state (Ali 2012).

However, we find weak evidence that media personnel have an interest in protecting the majority group religion. Newspaper reporters were more likely to place the mosque shooting in the front page or front section of the paper, but the difference was not significant (66.1% v. 55.4%: ns). They also were more likely to place the mosque shooting in the newspaper at all (81.8% v. 78.8%: ns), but the difference was even narrower than decisions about the front page/section. Furthermore, there was no greater desire to include the story online (64.3% v. 65.6%: ns). There was little religious difference in the inclusion of the story in television (39.0% v. 44.4%: ns) and social (35.4% v. 27.4%: ns) media. Therefore, it is not surprising that there was a non-significant higher likelihood of the mosque shooting being used when all media is taken into consideration (70.0% v 64.4%: ns). There is a slight possibility the story will be used more when a mosque is attacked, but it does not warrant further attention.

However, the real value of our data can be seen in the way the reporters and editors describe their interest in the story. Here, we find evidence that the respondents treat the story differently if a shooting occurs at a mosque instead at a church. When the religious institution is a mosque, the respondents were more willing to see this event as an example of discrimination (13.2% v. 2.5%: $p < .001$) and likely to see it as an example of a hate crime (15.9% v. 4.4%: $p < .001$).[6] Muslims could be seen as victims of an intentional bias crime of hate, while almost none of the respondents are willing to acknowledge when Christians are victimized by hateful discrimination. These respondents illustrate some of the spirit of the perspective of Muslims as victims of religious hate:

> Islamophobia is growing and must be covered more. Send a reporter there ASAP. (Newspaper Reporter, News Current Event beat, circulation 50,000–100,000)

> This is another potential hate crime that needs to be reported. (Television Reporter, multiple beats, circulation under 10,000)

> Also how the shooter had access to weapons and if it was motivated out of religious intolerance. (Newspaper Reporter and Editor, multiple beats, circulation under 10,000)

> This appears to be another example of a hate crime, which as stated earlier is big news. The most important information is that people were killed in an Islamic Center. (Newspaper Reporter, Crime beat, circulation 50,000–100,000)

There is a clear narrative in the story with the shooting of the mosque. It is to be featured as an example of religiously based hate crime, and one would expect a story that emphasizes the potential religious bigotry of this event. Just as the feminist group in the student organization example was more likely to be tied to larger issues of sexism, this situation is tied to larger issues of Islamophobia. This propensity to see Muslims as the victims of violence is not present in all, or even most, of the answers of our respondents, but the almost total lack of perception of religious violence when a church is shot up suggests that our respondents perceive that religious prejudice against Christians is non-existent. The scenarios did not differ in number of individuals killed or any comment from the shooter about how much he hates individuals in that religious group. Yet, there is almost no chance of the church story being cast as anti-religious hatred as a driving force behind the shooting.

Hence, if few media personnel entertain the possibility that those who may attack a Christian church may also be driven by anti-religious hatred, then we are left with the question of what they may see as responsible for a shooter when a Christian church is the target. The very act of shooting is one that is steeped in hatred of one's target. However, it is possible that a shooter is less driven by hatred than by dysfunctional psychological forces. Shooters of Christian churches may be seen as mentally unbalanced by psychological pressures that are not tied to larger sociological institutions. If churches are attacked by unbalanced individuals, instead of individuals influenced by social forces that contribute to religious bigotry, then one may divorce concerns of discrimination and hatred from attacks on Christian churches.

If this type of speculation is true then what should we expect from respondents who can only look at a potential scenario and do not have the ability to interview the shooter or talk with individuals who knew the shooter? One would expect that the respondents would put more of a focus on understanding Ferguson, the gunman, when they decide that the story of the church shooting is worth their attention. Indeed, this is what we have found (8.4% v. 1.1%: p < .01). An example of this focus can be seen in the comment of this respondent about what was important in the story (Newspaper Reporter, Government and Politics beat, circulation under 10,000): "The background and history of Jessie Ferguson. What motivated him to do this crime?" Other respondents were inquisitive about Ferguson and why he engaged in such violence when the church was the location of the shooting, but there was relatively little interest in Ferguson when the crime took place in the mosque.

Occasionally, the way Ferguson was analyzed did point to potential societal problems, but not the issue of hatred or discrimination. For example, this respondent (Newspaper Editor, News Current Events beat, circulation over 500,000) married the idea of learning about Ferguson with this gun violence emphasis:

> Where/how did Ferguson get the gun? Who is Ferguson and what possible motive did he have? What gun did he use? Did he leave a note? Humanize the victims. Flood the zone. Make Ferguson's gun an issue. How many does he have at home?

> How does he get them? What are the cops saying? What do state leaders say about the apparent proliferation of firearms in the hands of killers?

Thus, media personnel show relatively little interest in whether there are social propensities that may produce conditions that endanger the lives of Christian church members.[7] Instead, the church's shooting is an opportunity for some respondents to explore issues such as mental illness and gun violence. While some media personnel may use the story to examine a larger issue, the story is not about religious violence but violence in general and how society creates people who engage in murder. This is the reverse of what can potentially occur with the shooting at the mosque, as very few respondents mentioned the need to explore Ferguson. The story of anti-religion hatred and discrimination took precedent in that circumstance.

There is limited evidence that media personnel will pay more attention to a religious institution shooting when it is at a mosque than when it is at a church. This may be due to the spectacular nature of the scenario. Like the scenario of the kidnapping of a girl from her home we discussed in the last chapter, this may be a story that is too sensational to pass up. It is plausible that the insignificant difference can become significant in a religious discrimination scenario with more variability in our respondents' answers. This is speculation, but given the higher willingness of our respondents to focus on the religious discrimination aspect of Muslims as opposed to Christians, it is not a wild speculation.

When the Umpqua shooting occurred, we predicted that the media coverage would focus on the gun control debate and the mental fitness of the shooter. A Google search soon after the shooting indicated little conversation about the event being a hate crime, except at conservative or Christian websites. Our data strongly suggests that if the shooter had been reported as singling out Muslims for execution that Islamophobia and hate crimes would have been part of the discourse in the media. One benefit of this research is the manner in which it helps us to anticipate how media personnel report the social events.

We can see how the stories written in each version will be constructed with a focus on different elements. The story about the shooting at the mosque is more likely to focus on the possibility of a hate crime and is more likely to look at Islamophobia. It is an opportunity to focus on the problems Muslims face due to religious discrimination. There is almost no chance that our respondents would write a story about the church that included these elements. The story about the shooting at the church is more likely to focus on why Ferguson is violent and the problems associated with gun violence in our society. It is an opportunity to explore the problems of guns and violence in general society. Muslims are seen as victims more easily than Baptists in this particular scenario. We have speculated that journalists may be less willing to document problems imposed upon Christian groups relative to other religious groups, and our findings reinforce this speculation. With this scenario, we have some evidence for a lack of sympathy some media personnel have for Christians. However, Muslims are not traditionally known for being progressives in the culture war. Therefore, it is not yet possible to completely tie this lack of sympathy to culture war motivations. In our next scenario, we gain a chance to further investigate this possibility.

Hate Speech Scenario

In theory, hate crimes can apply to any religious group. But as the previous scenario suggests, violence perpetrated against Christians is relatively unlikely to be seen as a hate crime by media personnel. Does the designation of hate also have a contextualized meaning when looking at situations that fall short of actual criminal behavior? There has been talk of hate speech and the problems such speech creates in our society (Cortese 2006; Nielsen 2002; Tsesis 2002; Waldron 2012). Given that hate speech is likely recognized as a problem by journalists, we ask whether the media covers hateful speech against Christians in the same way they would cover it against another group. In this case, we will not look at another religious group, but instead explore a comparison of the treatment of Christians with treatment of the LGBT community. This allows us to compare Christians, often seen as a culturally conservative group, to a group often perceived as a key component of the culturally progressive movement. Differing treatments of Christians relative to the LGBT community will be especially useful for informing us of the possibility that journalists operate as agents for one side of the culture war.

As we found in our previous scenario, there was limited evidence that hate expressed against Christians gains less "ink" than hate against another group, but it was not a significant difference. These are similar to findings from our Hate Speech scenario. Newspaper personnel were insignificantly less likely to put the story of hate speech against Christian students, relative to gay students, on the front page or front section (27.6% v. 20.9%: ns), or to include it as an online article (56.3% v. 47.8%: ns). However, it was significantly more likely to be included in the newspaper at all when the hate speech was directed towards gay students (65.6% v. 51.7%: p < .05). When we looked at all of the media, we once again observed that hate speech against gay students was more likely to be included in a story, but the difference is not significant (50.3% v. 43.2%: ns).[8] We cannot make a strong argument that inclusion of the hate speech story depends on the group of students experiencing the hate. Now with all three Christian related scenarios analyzed, we are comfortable asserting that placement of a story is not likely to depend on whether the story includes Christians or not. Perhaps future research with other scenarios will generate a different conclusion.

However, as was true in the previous scenario, the focus of the story does appear to be tied to the group victimized. When the story was about hate speech against the LGBT community our respondents were about three times more concerned about how the university is going to treat, or punish, the professor (21.1% v. 7.5%: p < .001). Some respondents expressed interest in whether the university would retain Henderson. For example one respondent (Newspaper Editor, Lifestyle beat, circulation under 10,000) stated: "Sarah Henderson, tenured or not should be relieved from her job. She has no place in an educational facility." Others were concerned about whether the university can adequately deal with this situation, as expressed in this comment (Television Editor, Local beat, circulation 10,000–50,000): "What action will the university take? Is Henderson protected by tenure or is she fireable? How has the university handled other complaints about controversial/offensive comments by tenured faculty? Have they been consistent?" Thus, stories with hate towards gay students are more likely to center on how best to discipline the professor or even whether the professor can be disciplined. The professor may be the focus of the story, as someone to be cast as the "villain."

Perhaps, we are making too strong a statement by arguing that the professor would be cast as a villain. However, media personnel are more concerned about the homophobic professor, because they are about three times more likely to paint that professor, rather than the anti–Christian professor, as a bigot or homophobic/Christianophobic (18.6% v. 6.1%; p < .01).[9] Examples of how this manifested itself when provided the homophobic hate speech are:

Most important: that a state school is employing bigots. The story would have a short run without a statement from Ms. Henderson—who undoubtedly would be made to make herself available. (Newspaper Reporter, local beat, circulation 50,000–100,000)

It would be interesting to see the university's reaction to this—both the students' reaction and the administration's. A big question is who she made these comments to. The scenario is unclear whether this was a public speech or a private conversation. In other words: Is the professor a homophobe—or a really stupid homophobe? (Newspaper Reporter and Editor, multiple beats, circulation 50,000–100,000)

This reinforces the finding in the Religious Institution Shooting scenario that respondents are relatively unlikely to perceive Christians as victims of hatred or bigotry. Of course some of the respondents merely mentioned hate in passing, but it is clear that the notion of hate speech or bigotry is much more on the mind of newspaper personnel when thinking of a professor making anti-gay instead of anti–Christian remarks. The story to be written when dealing with hate speech with an anti-gay professor centers on the hateful nature of the speech and whether the professor can be punished.

Elements about punishing the professor or recognition of bigotry are comparatively absent when Christians are the targeted group. Thus, a different story is to be written if the professor is anti–Christian. The first clue is that our respondents were more likely to comment that this is not a big deal if it is hateful speech against Christians than when they answered the scenario of hate speech against the LGBT community, although the difference is not significant (13.3% v. 7.1%: $p < .1$).[10] Media personnel appear to be less able to recognize the possibility that Christians can experience the effects of hate. However, it is important to examine the focus of the story when media personnel still want to write the story. A few respondents focused on the right of the professor to offend her students (5.6% v. 1.0%: $p < .05$), such as this respondent (Newspaper Reporter and Editor, multiple beats, 10,000–50,000) who stated: "That someone was offended by another's personal beliefs ... happens all the time." The respondents were very unlikely to enunciate such a right when the professor made homophobic comments. A second important emphasis was the idea that the professor is exercising her free-speech rights, which was a more common theme when discussing the anti–Christian professor (8.9% v. 2.9%: $p < .05$). As noted below, such comments tended to defend the rights of the professor:

> Free speech policies are alive and well (Newspaper Editor, multiple beats, 50,000–100,000)

> If no sanctions are planed against the professor, I'd leave this one alone. The prof. has free-speech rights, and I won't let my stories be used as a sounding board for a one-sided debate. (Newspaper Reporter, all beats, circulation under 10,000)

The last comment is quite telling as several respondents were concerned about bringing the hate crime to the attention of the administrators when the hate speech is anti-gay, whereas this respondent took a much more passive attitude to the potential of discipline. For this respondent, disciplining the professor is up to the university administrators and they do not need any prodding by a newspaper story. The number of respondents who supported these ideas of free speech and the right to offend others is not large. However, combined with the propensity to not see the hate speech as a big deal, it tells of an attitude where the focus is not upon the offended student, but the rights of the professor. Respondents may be almost as likely to cover this story regardless of the group offended, but they also will write a different story when Christian students are the ones who complain.

We have contrasting stories based upon which group of students is offended. If LGBT students are offended, then a story about bigotry and potential punishment is more likely to be written. Such a story is less likely to occur if the professor is anti–Christian. However, there is a distinct possibility that we will have a story about the right to offend students and free-speech freedoms of college professors. Given that so few of the respondents enunciated a right to offend LGBT students, there is little reason to believe that any of them would write a story that concentrates on freedom to offend and free speech when the professor is deemed homophobic. The LGBT students are much more likely than the Christian students to gain a story addressing their grievances. These students are in a position to discuss generalized problems that plague their community, an opportunity that is not likely to be given to any Christian student who complains. As it concerns our television media personnel, we gain little insight, as we could not document strong differences in how the scenarios were treated. Lack of interest in this story seems to drive this inability to find sizeable differences among the television media personnel.

As we complete our assessment of the scenarios of Christians, we find consistency in the relatively low interest in the media personnel's concern about the issues facing the larger Christian community. There is some concern about a specific Christian student group, and we do not think that media personnel would be emotionally cold to a specific congregation that suffered from a horrific shooting. We are certain that some members of that congregation would be sympathetically interviewed. However, concerns that Christians may suffer these maladies because of a generalized anti–Christian hatred are largely dismissed by our respondents. This is not true for Muslims as it concerns Islamophobia, LGBT individuals as it concerns homophobia or the feminist group as it concerns sexism. Yet, for most of our respondents the possibility that Christians may suffer from the expressions of hatred is not seriously entertained. The difference in tone between Christians and other groups is more pronounced than the effects documented in the past two chapters. We have previously discussed how an accumulation of even small differences may lead to an overall change in cultural attitudes. If our previous discussion is accurate, then these even more distinctive differences between Christians and other social groups are highly likely to be tied to an alteration of cultural attitudes, or at least a reinforcement of previous cultural attitudes towards Christians.

Perhaps journalists are correct to dismiss those concerns since Christians can be seen as the majority religion in the United States, and we will discuss more of that possibility in the final chapter. However, there is little doubt that Christians are correct in arguing that they are treated differently than other social groups. Those who justify that difference would do well to admit to this differential treatment rather than argue that contrasting media approaches are nonexistent.

Culture War?

If a culture war in the United States is one between Christians and progressives, then indeed this chapter provides evidence of a Culture War News Ideology in which at least newspaper media personnel act as if they are on the side of the progressives. This may not be a surprise since there is some research indicating that journalists are more likely to be politically progressive than the general public (Lichter, Rothman and Lichter 1986; Patterson and Donsbach 1996). It is a mistake to think of Christians as a homogenous group and talk of a culture war generally pertaining to conservative Christians. The Christians in the hate speech scenario do not have to be conservative. Yet, we used "Baptist" to denote the type of Christian in the other two scenarios—a group that most individuals likely assume to be theologically conservative.[11] Thus, it is fair to assert that we have constructed an image of religious and cultural conservatism. This provides us with more confidence that our scenarios do provide our respondents with an opportunity to exhibit support for or opposition against cultural conservatives.

We mentioned earlier that any religious group could be the victim in a hate crime. Yet, it was fairly clear that many of our respondents have a difficult time envisioning Christians as potential victims of hate. Previous work has indicated that individuals with relative animosity towards conservative Christians tend to be well educated (Bolce and De Maio 2008; Yancey and Williamson 2014). Given that individuals in the media have a higher than average level of education, they may possess such animosity and have a relative inability to perceive hatred directed toward conservative Christians. If this is true then it will be difficult to conceive of news stories in which a conservative Christian can be portrayed as a victim of hate. This is not to say that such stories cannot occur, but clearly a higher degree of hatred, and more powerful evidence of that hatred, would have to be present for a comparable story of conservative Christian victimization to be written.

Claims of victimization can be a way social groups gain relative social power (Best 1997; Durfee 2011). If a group can be seen as a victim, then it has the right to make demands for redress. If the results of this chapter are accurate, then this way to gain power is not open to Christians if they want to utilize the media to obtain it. In our scenario in which a Baptist church is attacked, the media personnel tend to envision this as an opportunity to discuss issues of guns and violence. The scenario with the school groups provides our respondents with an opportunity to discuss relations between the school and the Baptist organization. The hate speech scenario provides many respondents with a format to discuss the perils and benefits of free speech. What is missing in these approaches to the stories is an attempt to gain attention for issues that generally concern Christians. The events surrounding the Christians in these scenarios allow the reporters and editors to address the issues of interest to them instead of to the Christians in the scenario. This was quite different than how the respondents dealt with scenarios that did not specifically involve Christians. There was concern for the plight of same-sex couples and the bigotry they personally face, for the Muslims who may be victims of hate crimes and for the feminist organizations with the possibility that sexism is at play. Our respondents appeared to be very hesitant to shift the focus away from the particular concerns of these groups.

Media critics who argue that the media possess a non–Christian bias would be unable to sufficiently document this bias if all we presented was the quantitative results. Those results suggest very weak evidence that stories that contain Christians are less likely to be run than stories not overtly about Christians. How the story is covered is likely to be quite different when Christians are involved. If objectivity is a goal that journalists seek, then it is important to not only look at the level of inclusion of stories that contain Christians, but also to explore how particular stories are covered by the media.

Why are stories covered differently depending on whether Christians are the focus of the story? Previous research has indicated that individuals with anti–Christian animosity are more likely to be highly educated (Bolce and De Maio 2008; Yancey and Williamson 2014). On the other hand, education is inversely related to overt racist and sexist expressions (Coenders and Scheepers 2003; Kane and Kyyrö 2001). Higher levels of education may feed into the propensity of journalists to be sensitive to issues dealing with race and gender but not those dealing with anti–Christian animosity. Furthermore, the progressive political and relatively irreligious nature of the typical journalist may also be connected to higher levels of anti–Christian sentiment (Yancey and Williamson 2014) and lower levels of animosity towards racial minorities and women. The type of highly educated, progressive and irreligious professionals that tend to be in journalism may be less likely to accept overt racism and sexism but be more open to having an anti–Christian bias due to the type of educational subculture where journalists are socialized. These contrasting social pressures may help to account for why we documented bias against Christians but did not document racial and gender bias.

There are limited implications for the possibility of a Majority Group Power News Ideology. Christians can be seen as a majority group; however, their shrinking numbers and power provide evidence that this majority group status is not stable. To the degree that Christians can be seen as a majority group, the evidence from these scenarios also buttress the notion that majority group support is not the primary motivational force driving journalists. Instead our findings point to a Culture War News Ideology in which journalists are relatively unsympathetic to the concerns of cultural and religious conservatives. Stories where such conservatives can be seen as victimized tend to be refocused to address alternate issues (i.e., gun control, free speech) rather than bring out the issues of concern to those conservatives.

One may speculate whether ignoring the concerns of Christians is tied to larger concerns about political conservatism. We did not have many scenarios that tested whether our respondents treated political conservatives differently than political progressives. However, we did have one scenario (Congressman and Prostitute) that tested whether our respondents would treat a scandal differently depending on whether it occurs to a Republican or a Democrat. We found little difference in whether the scandal was covered due to political affiliation. Newspaper respondents were not significantly more likely to publish the story on the front page or front section if it was a Democrat rather than a Republican (60.3% v. 57.5%: ns), put it in the paper at all (86.9% v. 89.5%; ns) and online (84.5% v. 77.5%: ns), and there was no real difference in the coverage for all media outlets (75.4% v. 76.8%: ns).[12] None of these differences are large enough to warrant a suspicion of bias. Analysis of the qualitative data indicated that there was not much difference in the answers to the open-ended questions except for the fact that newspaper media respondents were twice as likely to state that this is not an important story (16.1% v. 7.2%: $p < .05$) when the scenario was about a Democrat. This does indicate some potential of bias, perhaps a desire to see whether the Republican is a hypocrite that campaigned on "family value" issues. It is quite plausible that if we had a scenario with a scandal that exposed hypocrisy among progressives, for example extravagant use of electricity in one's home after pushing for a green agenda, then we would have found a similar tendency to see stories of Republicans as less likely to be seen as important.

Otherwise, we found little evidence of a political bias against conservatives in our data. Future research with different scenarios may dispute this claim, but until that occurs, we assume no overarching political bias is driving the results of this chapter. Since there is no strong evidence of such a political bias we assert that ignoring the concerns of Christians is not likely because they are seen as an arm of political conservatism. Rather, the unique characteristics perceived in Christians can play a role in some of our respondents' answers. If that is accurate, then it is plausible that one of those unique characteristics can be the perception of Christians as conservative enemies in the culture war.[13] Not all political conservatives are envisioned to be members of a right-wing conservative cultural movement, but Christians, who are often seen as conservatives, are generally seen as the force behind that movement.

This image of the media's lack of support of Christians as leaders of a cultural movement helps explain why interest groups serving racial minorities can influence media personnel in ways that escape interest groups serving Christians. If media personnel envision themselves as members of a new information professional class, then they likely lack the same degree of respect for Christian activists that they have for activists for racial minorities. It is not merely the economic or political power of activists that determine the type of influence they have, but whether the perspectives those activists promote resonates with the philosophical and epistemological presuppositions of the journalists.

However, it is not sufficient to merely document the unwillingness of journalists to take seriously the concerns of conservatives of the culture war. It is also vital to assess how willing those journalists are to address the concerns of cultural progressives. We have seen a bit of this with the Hate Speech scenario where we observed that there is evidence that our respondents are open to highlighting the concerns of LGBT communities. Clearly, recent events have shown that the desires of LGBT are seen as progressive expressions in the culture war. However, our survey allows us to examine other possible stories that allow the respondents to offer support for or to ignore the concerns of that community. Only by exploring the willingness of reporters and editors to take the desires of those in the LGBT community into consideration can we gain a holistic perspective of whether the Culture War News Ideology is accurate.

5

Homophobia

In some ways, sexuality issues cut across both Majority Group Power and Culture War news ideologies. Since heterosexuals can be seen as a majority sexuality group, scenarios that explore attitudes toward the LGBT community may be shaped by a desire to support the majority sexuality group. On the other hand, issues of sexuality have played a central role in the culture war. Indeed, the *Obergefell v. Hodges* case may have marked the beginning of the end of that war in the favor of cultural progressives. More than our examination of potential racial, gender, and religious bias, an examination of sexuality bias acts as a comparison of the power of majority group power and culture war explanations.

Do media personnel seek to defend a dominant group's traditional understanding of sexuality? Or are they progressive culture proponents who seek to replace that traditional understanding with modernist notions of sexuality? The findings from our previous three chapters suggest the latter to be true. If those chapters are an accurate way of understanding the perspectives of media, then we should expect media personnel to be supportive of issues important to LGBT activists. However, if that assertion is not accurate, then media personnel should be neutral, or even hostile, to those activists.

It is not hard to find representations of the LGBT in mass media. For example, one well-known television show that features gay men is Bravo's "Queer Eye for the Straight Guy." In this show, five gay men makeover a heterosexual man. Ramsey and Santiago (2004) argue that homosexuality is present in opposition to masculinity in "Queer Eye for the Straight Guy." The focus is not on the lives of the five gay men but rather on grooming and style appropriate for straight men. Homosexuality is counter to our heteronormative culture. As for television news, one prominent issue was the "Don't Ask, Don't Tell" policy of the U.S. military. Steel (1997) contends that journalists choose unofficial sources that abide by heterosexual norms. Instead of finding social scientists or other neutral experts, journalists picked retired officers or former public officials to speak about issues concerning sexuality in the military. Merely because sexual minorities are represented in the media does not mean that they are shown in a way that reflects support for their subcultural norms. However, in place of using a content analysis of television or news programs, we asked journalists themselves about how they place stories concerning sexuality to gain more insight into the efforts put forth to represent the LGBT community.

At times, we refer to the LGBT community or activists, which implies a larger group than simply gay men and lesbians. However, our scenarios do not deal with bisexuals or transgendered individuals. Such individuals can be seen as challenges to notions of traditional sexuality and thus attitudes of media personnel towards homosexuality likely impact bisexual or the transgender individuals. However, there are also possible distinct concerns of bisexuals and the transgender individuals in comparison to gay men and lesbians. The use of our results to argue about issues beyond gay men and lesbians should be done carefully, and future research utilizing scenarios of bisexual and transgender individuals may produce nuanced understandings of the similar and distinct challenges of contrasting sexual minority groups.

Review of Findings
from Hate Speech Scenario

Before we explore the results of our scenarios concerning sexuality, we should review the results of the hate speech scenario in the previous chapter. In that scenario we found that when the professor made anti–Christian statements there is a greater concern for the free speech rights of the professor; however, when anti-gay remarks were made, then there is a greater concern over how the university can control, or even fire, the professor. This suggests a greater concern for the plight of sexual minorities than for Christians, who are more likely to endorse some level of traditional sexual morality (Burdette, Ellison and Hill 2005; Rowatt et al. 2006; Schulte and Battle 2004). It is not clear whether media personnel automatically connect Christians in this scenario to an endorsement of traditional sexual morality, but given the job of media personnel to gather information about the larger society, it is likely that some acknowledgment of this correlation is known by many of our respondents. It is reasonable to argue that our respondents systematically choose to support a modern notion of sexuality over a traditional understanding.

In the last chapter, we focused upon the results of the scenario as it concerns Christians and how the focus on the rights of the instructor minimizes the concerns of Christians. However, there is also information to be gained by looking at this scenario from the perspective of sexual minorities. If media personnel want to support the concerns of sexual minorities, then emphasizing the hate speech implications of the professor is a powerful way to do so. Unlike Christians, when it comes to an anti-gay comment, there was a focus on hate and how manifestation of this hate may hurt the feelings of sexual minorities. We also noted that newspaper media personnel were more willing to discuss what the university should do in light of this hypothetical controversy. Such personnel were comparatively eager to see Henderson dismissed from her position. Such a priority can emerge due to a desire to protect sexual minorities from unfair treatment.

It can be argued that the LGBT community in our society is subject to a degree of hatred not experienced by other social groups. It is undoubtedly true that in the past sexual minorities were among the groups with the lowest levels of societal acceptance. However, it is not clear that this is still the case. Recent research indicates soaring levels of acceptance of those groups (Andersen and Fetner 2008; Avery et al. 2007). Furthermore, recent research has indicated a growing level of hatred against Christians (Bolce and De Maio 2008; Yancey and Williamson 2014). A recent survey indicates similar levels of willingness of Americans to support either a homosexual or evangelical presidential candidate (McCarthy 2015). The greater focus on the possible effects of hate speech on its intended target when it concerns the LGBT community instead of Christians likely reflects the philosophical priorities of the respondents at least as much as the existence of relative levels of hatred in the United States. The results of this scenario support the notion of media personnel as progressive culture advocates. However, it remains to be seen if this notion is a feature of a particularly unique scenario or if our other scenarios substantiate this claim.

Sexuality Scenarios

The rest of our analysis concerning issues of sexuality focuses upon two remaining scenarios. In the first scenario, we compare a rally between a group supportive of the LGBT community and one not supportive, since they define themselves as ex-gay. We constructed the scenario so that both groups are rallying over the same proposed law that would allow for reparative therapy. This is a controversial therapy, which is intended to alter sexual preference. In both scenarios, we postulate that the groups are concerned about the therapy since it threatens their community if it is supported (for PFLAG) or rejected (for PFOX). In this way, we hope to conceptualize similar concerns for each group to see if media personnel resonate more or less with the interests of the LGBT community. In the second scenario, we looked at a shooting of a couple. In one scenario, the couple is same-sex and in the other scenario the couple is interracial. This scenario does not allow for a direct comparison of sexual minorities to a group associated with traditional cultural morality. However, we still gain the opportunity to explore whether media personnel approach crimes based on sexuality in a different manner than crimes based on race.

Political Rally Scenario

In large metropolitan areas and college campuses, political rallies have become a way of life. They are almost expected to take place on a daily basis. Our media has to decide which rallies will be covered and which will be ignored. The expectations within media personnel on which issues are important undoubtedly play a role in which rallies gain space in newspapers and time in news shows. Furthermore, even if there is relatively equal willingness of media personnel to cover a rally, what they emphasize in that coverage will tell us quite a bit about the sort of story that will wind up in the media. Is it a story that is positive towards the protesting group or one that criticizes it? Will there be an effort to locate voices that disagree with the group or will the group's message go unchallenged? The qualitative answers to this scenario can provide clues to the sort of coverage we would see if these rallies took place. In our scenario we look at rallies of equal size and arguments that are identical—although the implications of the arguments may vary depending on the group running the rally. Our comparison of rallies by PFLAG or PFOX will be informative of the willingness of media personnel to consider the interest of sexual minorities.

The organization Parents, Families and Friends of Lesbians and Gays (PFLAG) was founded in 1972 and supports families with gay and/or lesbian members. PFLAG provides support, education, and advocacy for the LGBT community. The goals of PFLAG include bringing awareness of LGBT issues to the larger society, programming, and legislation to defend the human rights of the LGBT community (www.pflag.org). Parents and Friends of Ex-Gays & Gays (PFOX) was founded in 1998. It is a non-profit organization that supports ex-gays, parents, and friends of gays. The goals of PFOX are to educate, support, and advocate for individuals and parents on the issue of same-sex attraction and to increase understanding and awareness of the ex-gay community. PFOX advocates for the ex-gay movement, which is posited to be a civil rights movement that strives to ensure the safety and inclusion of former gay men and lesbians in society. PFOX contends that people can change their sexual preferences; therefore, ex-gays should be included in conversations about sexual orientation, diversity, and civil rights (www.pfox.org).

Journalists may be more likely to cover the PFLAG rally because of the larger societal belief that homosexuality is more acceptable than in times past (Newson and Richerson 2016). Another factor that may contribute to the journalists in this study being more open to covering PFLAG rallies is that those with higher education are more likely to be supportive of marriage equality (Becker 2014). Those who are more religious and conservative are less likely to support marriage equality. Thus, the relative irreligiosity and political progressiveness of journalists may be correlated to higher levels of support for sexual minorities.

Reparative therapy is a psychiatric attempt to convert gay and lesbian individuals to a heterosexual lifestyle (Moss 2014). Reparative therapy and other sexual orientation change efforts have undergone much criticism (Calvert et al. 2013) since the target audiences for this treatment are often minors with the consent of their parents (Moss 2014). It is reported that reparative therapy is not effective in changing sexual desire. In addition, some claim that it causes more harm than good. Consequently, conversion or reparative therapy has been banned in California (Calvert et al. 2013). PFOX and other ex-gay organizations have opposed this decision by claiming the ban is a violation of the First and Fourteenth Amendments (Fore 2014). PFLAG and other LGBT-friendly groups support the ban on reparative therapy because being gay is not a mental disorder that needs to be treated; instead, these organizations want LGBT identities not to be pathologized (Fore 2014; Moss 2014).

As it concerns the coverage of the story, there is strong evidence that media personnel are more open to such coverage when PFLAG, the group supportive of gay men and lesbians, hold their rally. Newspaper media personal were overwhelmingly more open to putting the story on the front page or front section (61.2% v. 37.4%: p < .001), but not whether to use the story at all (92.6% v. 90.0%; ns). Furthermore, there is no statistical difference when it came to placing the story online (89.8% v. 84.3%: ns). The respondents appear to agree that the story has at least some merit regardless of which group organizes the rally, as seen in their willingness to put the story online. They simply did not want to use it on the front page or section of the paper. We assert that the story with PFLAG will get much more prominent coverage than the one with PFOX. However, clearly the respondents prioritized the PFLAG story as more important than the PFOX story. We found that television (52.3% v. 44.4%; ns) and social (58.6% v. 53.5%; ns) media personnel were about equally likely to promote either story. So it is not surprising that there is a similar level of willingness of all the media to cover the story at all (79.3% v. 78.6 %: ns). The way the question was posed to the television and social media does not allow them to prioritize which stories will be put in more prominent positions. We have to allow the unique wording in the questions to the newspaper media personnel to inform us of the relative importance attached to each scenario. With that data, we can see the overall propensity of the PFLAG story to have more prominence than the PFOX story. However, both stories are likely to be mentioned by different segments of the media.

However, assessment of differences between how the rally stories are covered does not stop at where the story will be placed. A key difference in how the stories may be treated depends on whether the media seeks dissenting perspectives to the rally. Such efforts indicate whether a reporter or editor is careful to construct a one-sided perspective and make sure that the statements of the group do not go unchallenged. Our results indicate that the willingness to do this is greater in the PFOX scenario (20.1% v. 7.3%: p < .001).[1] The answers of the respondents indicate why such balance tends to be sought.

Ick. But in my small community, 150 people doing anything political is news. The critical thing is to get someone from the group supporting the law to get both sides. The important thing to be learned is sort of the tenor of the community. 150 PFOX people rallying would indicate a profoundly conservative community. (Newspaper Reporter and Editor, all beats, circulation under 10,000)

I'd use it, as I'd use a story about any gathering. But I would be sure [to talk to] a person/or persons who don't agree with this group for his/her/their opinion(s) and include this in the story. (Social Media Other Role, Local beat, circulation 50,000–100,000)

It's an interesting news story about a rather unusual political faction. Assuming the reporter covered the other side, the public could learn about both sides of a controversial issue (Newspaper Reporter, all beats, circulation under 10,000)

When the story is about the ex-gay group there was a strong urge to make sure that all sides of the story are told. If PFOX gets to tell their story, the newspaper personnel want to make sure that their opponents also are allowed to share their perspectives. This urge was not as strong when exploring the story for the gay and lesbian group—indicating more willingness to allow the arguments of the PFLAG group to go unchallenged.

As the story of the PFLAG group is nearly twice as likely to get front page or front section coverage as the PFOX group, it is reasonable that there are a lot of other factors shaping the desire of the respondents to use the PFLAG story. Indeed, we found that those given the PFLAG scenario were more concerned about getting a comment from the protesting group (33.1% v. 23.3%: $p < .1$),[2] and they wanted to know about the events that lead to the proposed legislation (27.0% v. 7.5%: $p < .001$). They were also concerned that the legislation allowing the therapy was proposed in the first place (29.6% v. 16.0%: $p < .01$).[3] These differences need to be considered together to gain a comprehensive understanding of how media personnel approach these stories differently. By itself, each finding may not be very important. But certain themes emerge from the patterns of these multiple findings.

One of the themes is the attention paid to the law. There was a focus on the proposed law that is not as prevalent in the PFOX scenarios.

Details of the law and local reaction to it by members of the PFLAG group. I would want a reporter to find a member of the gay and lesbian community to potentially profile on this issue to show the impact on families. (Newspaper Reporter, Crime beat, circulation 50,000–100,000)

Explore the topic of reparations therapy and whether it's sound lawmaking. Also, 150 people is a fairly large demonstration, which would encourage coverage. (Newspaper Editor, News Current Events beat, circulation 50,000–100,000)

How other communities have dealt with similar laws in the past and across the country. What scientific foundation is there for/against this kind of therapy. (Television Reporter and Editor, Multiple beats, circulation 100,000–500,000)

The respondents talked about a focus on the law as it may impact gays and lesbians or whether this is a sound law. The reporters and editors invest energy to investigate the law more deeply when the story is couched as a way that threatens the PFLAG community. One anticipates a more investigatory nature of the newspaper stories when talking about how the law impacts the members of PFLAG. This desire to seek out the implications of the law as it concerns sexual minorities may account for the greater attention paid to the law in the PFLAG scenario. The concerns of PFLAG are seen as legitimate and will be respected in the type of stories emerging from this scenario.

This assertion is strengthened when we consider a second theme that comes from these findings, which is the focus on the concerns brought up by the protesting group when the scenario includes PFLAG. Indeed, one respondent (Newspaper Editor, Local beat, circulation 10,000–50,000) stated a concern about how "…a law intrudes on personal life." However, there is also greater attention to the concerns of the group protesting when the group is PFLAG instead of PFOX. This typical tendency is expressed by this respondent (Newspaper Reporter and Editor, multiple beats, circulation 10,000–50,000) who stated that there is a focus on "reaction from the PFLAG participants." These are also patterns that reinforce a notion that the media personnel are concerned about the civil rights implications of the law and how it may impact LGBT individuals. We conceptualize these approaches as different ways by which the respondents want attention paid to the concerns of gays and lesbians. Some were concerned with the personal impact on the LGBT community (Newspaper Editor, News Current Events, circulation over 500,000): "Humanize the story by talking to PFLAG members about their children's experiences with coming out as gay and/or people who tried to 'repair' them." Others fear that this legislation may lead to more homophobic discrimination (Newspaper Reporter, multiple beats, circulation under 10,000): "I would think the concern would be the discrimination against members of the gay and lesbian community and not the loss of members of PFLAG." Finally, another respondent (Social Media Reporter and Editor, Current Event beat, Circulation over 500,000) notes that the story would be told in a way to bring "greater awareness of the issues facing gays, lesbians and their families." In a variety of different ways, the concerns of sexual minorities are addressed by the respondents in the PFLAG scenario,

It is not only the case that the story gains more prominence when the rally is of those favoring sexual minorities instead of ex-gay men and lesbians. The story of the PFLAG rally focuses on supporting sexual minorities. The manner of this support emerged in different ways; however, support for the rallying group was much stronger in the PFLAG story than the PFOX story. Indeed, even in the PFOX story there are concerns for the issues of PFLAG, since the major different focus in that scenario is whether there is a balance in the issues covered. In stories about PFLAG, the focus will nearly always be solely on the issues brought up by PFLAG; but stories with PFOX were more likely to contain attempts to balance their assertions with those who disagree with them. Consequently, the issues of PFLAG tend to be covered regardless of which group initiated the rally.

However, there were a few respondents who, when asked about PFOX, showed more interest in the numbers of attendees at the rallies, usually disparaging them for being too small (2.7% v. .03%: p < .1). For example, one respondent (Newspaper Editor, multiple beats, Circulation under 10,000) stated, "This is a small rally for just another political group." Indeed, many of the respondents did not only question the wisdom of the law but also the very existence of former gays and lesbians.

> That PFOX exists at all (Social Media Reporter, Lifestyle and Current Events beats, Circulation 50,000–100,000)
>
> Whether or not ex-gays have rights and if "ex-gay" is even possible (Newspaper Editor, Multiple beats, Lifestyle beat, circulation under 10,000)
>
> If you are gay or lesbian you cannot just "become "straight!! (Newspaper Reporter and Editor, Circulation 10,000–50,000)

Of course the nature of sexual preference is a hotly debated topic. Some researchers have made assertions of the genetic nature of homosexuality (Bailey and Pillard 1991; Hamer et al. 1993). However, other scholars (Edogbanya 2016; Mayer and McHugh 2016) have called such assertions into question.[4] It is beyond the scope of this work to speculate about the reality of sexual fluidity and what it means for claims of the innate nature of sexuality, but research has not appeared to produce a clear answer on the origins of homosexuality. It is not realistic to think that most media personnel will be on top of the latest research on sexuality. However, the assumption by many media personnel that individuals cannot be "ex-gays" is a clear indicator of their perception of a movement such as PFOX. The lack of legitimacy they attached to that movement likely influences the lesser importance they attach to a PFOX rally as opposed to a PFLAG gathering.

We should expect a quite different story for PFOX than what would be written or produced for PFLAG. We would expect a story built upon doubts about the legitimacy of the PFOX organization. It will be a story where the assertions of the PFOX representatives are more likely to be countered by claims of an opponent of the group. The care that many of our respondents mention in making certain that the media they constructed did not harm sexual minorities is more likely to be missing when the story is about those who claim to be ex-gay.

In Chapter 4, we talked about the ability of special interest groups to motivate the manner in which a story is covered. In that chapter, we argued that racial minority groups might influence the willingness of editors and reporters to cover stories and how those stories might be covered. But not all interest groups have this type of power in the media. It is clear from the results in the previous chapter that Christian interest groups do not command the attention given to racial minority groups. In this scenario we see more evidence that not all interest groups have the power to motivate the media. The media is relatively willing to get the story of PFLAG out to the general public in a fairly undiluted manner. On the other hand, the PFOX story was more likely to be told with qualifiers. This difference has important meaning as it concerns the groups' incentives to interact with the media. Groups supportive of sexual minorities may have some degree of confidence that the message they seek to enunciate will be transmitted to the larger audience. Groups that oppose the agenda of sexual minority interest groups would do well not to trust the media to present their message and may be incentivized to seek out sympathetic alternative media that allows them to promote their message.

The results of this scenario indicate that issues that trouble sexual minorities are not ignored by media personnel. Individuals in the group of ex-gays may not automatically be cultural conservatives, but they have a message supportive of the interest of cultural conservatives. However, their perspectives are seen as something that needs to be balanced. This scenario, combined with the scenario of the previous chapter, can be seen as viable comparisons of the Majority Group Power and Culture War News Ideologies. If they are, then evidence is that the Majority Group Power News Ideology does not have nearly the explanatory power on the decisions of media personnel as the Culture War News Ideology. However, part of these results may be due to the unique perspective that respondents have toward issues of sexuality. Those issues may possess a qualitatively higher priority than that provided to other interest groups. To assess this possibility, it is useful to compare the reaction of the respondents to sexual minorities and to a group not associated with cultural progressives—interracial couples.

COUPLE SHOOTING SCENARIO

We have already introduced scenarios of hate crimes and hate speech. Intolerance and the hatred that comes from it are topics that naturally draw the attention of media personnel. For this reason, it is not surprising that our scenarios overrepresented situations seemingly motivated by hate or bigotry. This is also the case with our scenario of the shooting of a couple. Drive-by shootings are not uncommon in some of the more dangerous areas of our country. They tend to be motivated more by gang violence than by prejudice and bigotry. However, there are exceptions to this pattern such as the drive-by shooting of the Rev. Dr. Augustus Sealy in Hartford, Connecticut, which is suspected as a racial hate crime. We conceptualize that a drive-by shooting believed to be a hate crime would draw a lot of attention from our respondents. Indeed, 77.9% of them wanted to put the story on the front page, not just the front section of the paper, regardless of whether it was an interracial couple or a same-sex couple that was shot.

This scenario cannot be used to assess the Majority Group Power News Ideology, since both interracial and same-sex couples can be considered alternatives to the general understanding of a racially homogenous, heterosexual couple. However, it may provide some insight into the Culture War News Ideology, as interracial coupling is generally not seen as a culture war issue anymore. As such, we are in a position to see whether the attitudes towards a potential hate crime vary depending on whether elements of the culture war are included in the mix. We are a little surprised that the shooting of the interracial couple was slightly more likely to be included in the front page or front section of the newspaper than the same-sex shooting (89.4% v. 80.7%: p < .1), and nearly all of the newspaper respondents wanted the story somewhere in the paper (99.0% v. 98.7%; ns). However, there is no difference in the online coverage of newspapers, a high percentage of respondents felt the story had a place there as well (95.6% v. 96.0%: ns). There was also no real difference when it comes to coverage in all three media areas, although the total coverage was a bit lower in television and social media than in newspapers (85.4% v. 85.0%: ns).[5]

Although both events are highly likely to get coverage, the nature of the stories ultimately written appears to differ. When it is an interracial couple that is shot, there is a higher likelihood that this will be treated as a crime story. There was also a higher concern about the evidence and the police report (31.4% v. 20.8%: p < .05).[6] Comments from the respondents demonstrate the stronger inclination to investigate the event when it concerned the attack on the interracial couple.

> If there were witnesses who heard racial epithets and there is a police report, this is front-page news. (Newspaper Reporter and Editor, multiple beats, circulation under 10,000)
>
> Many interesting aspects to this story. I would want to see what the witnesses had to say. (How many witnesses were there, and how credible are they?) I'd also be interested in the information from the police report regarding the racial motivation for the crime. (Social Media Editor, News Current Events beat, circulation 50,000–100,000)
>
> Are police identifying the shootings as a hate crime? Have there been any other, similar offenses in the community recently? If so, how many? Is there any evidence the shooters were part of an organized group? (Newspaper Reporter, Multiple beats, circulation 10,000–50,000)

This desire to gather the evidence should not be interpreted as an attempt to delay or ignore this story. We have already seen that the shooting of the interracial couple may be more likely to be prominently placed than the story about the same-sex couple. What this desire shows is that the details of the shooting and the evidence surrounding the event weigh more heavily in the minds of the respondents when told that the crime may be racist rather than homophobic. This may indicate a desire to gain an accurate story so that larger racial issues can be explored.

Perhaps, the desire to make sure to get the details right is tied to the concern the respondents have for the potential reaction from minority interest groups. We did find that when the scenario concerned the shooting of the interracial couple there was a stronger focus on the larger community conflict and/or a desire to talk to a racial/sexuality special interest organization (14.2% v. 6.2%: p < .05).[7] This respondent (Newspaper Editor, Education and Government beat, circulation under 10,000) sums up such sentiment well: "Any shooting story is worthy of the front page. The racial element adds to the intrigue and also serves as a way to determine community feelings on such matters." The racial issue clearly caught the attention of the respondents even more than the sexuality issue in the same-sex couple shooting. As such, the respondents showed concern for the attitudes of the communities of color more than for LGBT communities. When we match this finding with the focus in the interracial couple shooting on the criminal story and local police, it appears that the interracial shooting results in a focus on the local community and how the circumstances will impact nearby people of color.

The story to be written about the interracial couple shooting is at least partially shaped by the concerns of local minority racial groups. This concern may influence reporters and editors to get the details correct. Some of the recent racialized police shooting incidents may have incentivized the respondents to make sure they are accurate in the event's description. This emphasis may explain why the respondents pay more attention to the racial element of the interracial couple shooting than the homosexuality element in the same-sex couple shooting. The racial element may trigger the concern that the media presentation will be criticized by the larger racialized community. As we argued in Chapter 4, there are reasons to believe that pressure from racial minority civil rights organizations may impact the way media present stories with a racialized element. This is different than our comparison between LGBT issues and ex-gays in the political rally scenario, where there was an attempt to investigate the details of the law so that the concerns of the larger LGBT, instead of the ex-gay, community could be addressed. Therefore, it truly does matter to whom the LGBT community is compared when considering whether their larger concerns will be addressed. When the culture war element is removed from the potential story, then concerns of the local LGBT community are not as relatively important to the coverage.

If the focus on the racialized element and details of the shooting is the focus of the interracial couple shooting, then why is interest in the same-sex couple shooting about as strong as the interracial couple shooting? What aspect of this event draws the attention of the reporters and editors? That becomes evident when looking at the comments of those given the same-sex couple–shooting version of the scenario. The most prominent difference is that the respondents are more likely to bring up the feature of hate crimes in their comments (47.2% v. 31.0%: p < .01)[8] when told that the shooting is of a same-sex couple. We see the tenor of these comments that drives this emphasis on hate crimes.

> As long as police agreed this was potentially a hate crime, it would most likely lead our news. Since the shooters are still out there, they could attack another gay couple if they are not caught. (Television Reporter, multiple beats, circulation under 10,000)

> The most important information is that anti-gay sentiments are still very strong everywhere and that more needs to be done to educate the public, or perhaps the law should provide stiffer penalties for hate crimes. (Newspaper Reporter, multiple beats, circulation 10,000–50,000)
>
> A broad-daylight public shooting is news in any case, and especially when it appears to be a hate-crime. (Newspaper Reporter, Government beat, circulation 10,000–50,000)
>
> Was this a hate crime and what can be done to prevent such crimes? (Social Media Editor, News Current Events beat, circulation under 10,000)

There was some focus on the sexuality elements of the crime when it came to the same-sex shooting just as there is some focus on hate crimes when it is the interracial couple shooting. However, there was a focus on the hate crime elements in the same-sex couple shooting that is not as strong with the interracial couple–shooting version. As these comments indicate, this focus was seen as motivation to inform the community and to warn against and fight hate crimes. The difference between this and the community concerns about the interracial couple is that the notion of hate crimes are often, although not always, tied to concerns for sexual minorities in general and not merely those in the local community. Given the recent controversies about same-sex marriage and religious liberties, it is reasonable to consider whether the respondents are reacting to larger society issues not available for the story about interracial couples. In other words, there are not contemporary, although there clearly have been historical, debates in the larger society about interracial couples, yet there has been a good deal of recent debate about same-sex couplings. This larger debate can provoke respondents to tie local events, such as this shooting, to larger societal concerns about hatred and violence. The attention paid to each event is the same and this is not a case, as it was with the hate speech scenario, where the respondents act in concern of the protesting group in one case but disregard their concern with a different protesting group. However, there is concern for both groups with a different emphasis depending on the type of national coverage or community interest connected to the group.

In this scenario, we have two groups that are generally recognized as minority groups in our society. This eliminates the possibility of examining whether majority group status matters in how this crime is reported. However, there does appear to be more local community focus when an interracial couple is shot and more national focus on hate crimes when it is a same-sex couple. The unique challenges each type of minority group faces may account for the distinct ways the shooting of each particular type of couple is handled by media personnel. These distinct challenges also remind us that it is a mistake to argue that the experiences of racial minorities and sexual minorities are identical.

Consistently, when we construct scenarios including LGBT individuals, our respondents are more willing to discuss hate crimes in comparison to any other group. This is true even with a group that has been historically defined as victims of hate crimes—interracial couples. This is not a coincidence. Whatever we learn about media coverage of sexuality issues, linking hate crime victimization to LGBT communities is quite powerful among media personnel. We have noted that one of the ways that groups gain power is with an image of victimization that allows them to make claims on others in society. If claims of victimization do lead to social power, then one of the reasons why we have seen a spike in support for LGBT individuals may be a willingness of media personnel to support the image of victimization based on minority sexuality status even more than racial identity.

Sexuality and the Media

The findings from this research indicate the type of attitudes media personnel likely have towards sexual minorities. The clear finding is that there is a certain level of sympathy towards those individuals. This was especially true when they are compared to Christians or ex-gays, but it was also evident when they are compared to an interracial couple. When respondents were asked about the shooting of the interracial couple, there was more of a focus on the community response and the event rather than a cry for addressing the potential hate crime. Hate crimes designation seems strongly tied to those with a sexual minority identity.

The concept of the victimization of sexual minorities is of particular interest in all three relevant scenarios. Hate was a major concept in the Hate Speech and Couple Shooting scenarios, and the civil rights implications of the law were a strong factor in the Political Rally scenario. The theme of racial minorities as victims did not strongly resonate in the Kidnapping scenario. Furthermore, some respondents pushed colorblind perspectives in the Airport Robbery and Research Study scenarios, although at times people of color were seen as victims. Women also were not as likely to be seen as victims in the scenarios where we tested for gender. While there was some reinforcement of the traditional gender norms, the idea of women as victims or being mistreated did not often come up. It is likely that the nature of the type of scenarios we constructed helped to create this higher tendency to see sexual minorities as victims. We can imagine other scenarios in which the respondents may be more likely to portray either racial minorities or women as victims in comparison to whites or men. However, we sought selected scenarios that fit with the sort of stories that reporters and editors might encounter. For example, although it is unlikely for a professor to use the term "fags" in class, it seems even less likely for them to use the word "bitches" to describe women. We suspect that such a scenario would not be believed by our respondents; and in attempting to create realistic scenarios, we may have created those that invited the respondents to see the LGBT community as victims. Thus, while our construction of these scenarios may have enhanced the propensity of the respondents to describe sexual minorities as victims, we do not believe that the entire effect is due to the nature of these scenarios.

If media personnel are qualitatively more likely to envision sexual minorities as victims than even other minority groups that have traditionally been seen as victims of hate, then what does this say about the type of news ideologies that dominate the media? We suspect that it indicates that while there are powerful social pressures to avoid mistreatment of other minority groups, there is a unique pressure tied to the outcomes faced by those in the LGBT community. One potential explanation for this exceptional situation can be the culture war implications of supporting them. There is little to be gained in the culture war in the defense of racial minorities or women. Cultural conservatism is generally silent on issues of race, and conservatives likely promote a colorblind policy more than an overt racist effort. Some cultural conservatives endorse a traditional gender framework that can work to the disadvantage of women, but the answers of some of our respondents also reinforced that framework. The real culture war implications are found in the reaction towards the LGBT community. Our final analysis indicates clear support for the Culture War News Ideology and very tepid, or even no, support for the Majority Group Power News Ideology.

Summary of Analysis of Scenarios

Now that we have completed our analysis of the data collected, it is advantageous for us to summarize these findings and consider some of their initial implications. It is clear that at this point we favor the Culture

War News Ideology, instead of the Majority Group Power News Ideology, as the best explanation for the motivations of media personnel. The only evidence supporting the Majority Group Power News Ideology is found in the slight willingness of our respondents to reinforce some of the traditional gender stereotypes that some feminists have found to be problematic (Basow 1992; Bolzendahl and Myers 2004; Enns 1997). On the other hand, we found consistent evidence of the Culture War News Ideology in the strong support of sexual minorities and the relative dismissal of the concerns of Christians. In the last chapter, we will explore more implications of the Culture War News Ideology as we seek to understand the way media presents important issues in our society.

Beyond the Culture War News Ideology, there are other important issues addressed by our findings. One of those issues is the importance of interest groups. We perceived this importance most directly through our analysis of racial groups, but also in the sexuality scenarios. Despite the values of neutrality often discussed by those in the media, our work provides evidence that activism indeed does have an impact in how media personnel write their stories and whether they are going to include those stories. The media are supposed to be fair referees when reporting on controversial issues, and referees are not supposed to change their call because of the complaints from one of the teams. Yet, we have evidence that this does occur at times when it comes to the media's presentation of certain issues. Of course, the Christian scenarios did not reveal the power of Christian interest groups to shape the news ideology of the media personnel, so pressure from external groups is not always going to bring about the result desired by group members. We speculate that if the media personnel do not respect the members of an interest group, then they do not allow them to influence the way an issue is covered. The referee analogy can be supplemented with the image of a referee who listens only to certain teams and ignores the concerns of other teams.

Another lesson can be seen in the conceptualization of hate by the media. We have already pointed out that the concept of being hated is highly likely to be tied to sexual minorities, even relative to racial minorities.[9] It is also noteworthy that in the exact same situation as was described about a gay student, that Christians were not seen as the victims of hate. Hate was also more likely to be tied to a shooting of a mosque than a church. The implication of this observation is that hate is not merely defined by media personnel according to the actions of a person whose acts can be called hateful; it is also dependent upon the group targeted by that action. The exact same action done to a sexual or religious minority group and seen as hateful by the respondents often will not be seen as hateful if conducted against other social groups. If media personnel represent other well-educated professionals in industries that help to create our culture, then we may have insight into how notions of hate are socially constructed and promoted by cultural leaders in our society.

Beyond the propensities discussed with the Culture War News Ideology, it is useful to speculate why certain groups can be "hated" in our society while others cannot. Our country's history is one in which members of different types of majority groups (i.e., white, male, heterosexual) have enjoyed tremendous advantages in our society. They have enjoyed these advantages at the expense of those in the minority groups. Our respondents are educated individuals who likely learned about this history while obtaining that education. Such information should make the respondents more sensitive to charges of mistreatment from a group that has historically faced societal disadvantages compared to other groups that may or may not currently face disadvantages but do not have the marginalized history of minority groups. This explanation does not indicate why a same-sex shooting is more likely to engender issues of hate crime than an interracial couple, but that distinction may be tied to culture war considerations. (It must be remembered that some respondents did talk about hate crime with the interracial couple. It is not that hate crime implications were totally ignored. However, this topic came up less often than when a same-sex couple was described in the scenario.) However, media personnel may have a limited ability to conceptualize victimization when the group is not recognized as historically having experienced social discrimination and prejudice. We have strong evidence that bias against members in those groups is real, and it may be problematic if those individuals are ever indeed victimized.

However, we did discover that in certain ways media personnel are able to be relatively neutral in how they cover a story. This is most clearly seen in the Kidnapping scenario whereby the race of the child did not matter significantly in whether the story was included and how the story would be covered. The horror of a child being kidnapped may have motivated the respondents so much that any implicit bias they may have possessed disappeared. Furthermore, while there is some potential reinforcement of traditional notions of aggressive masculinity in our Daughter into Slavery scenario, there is the same level of concern about helping to find the daughter regardless of the sex of the parent. To some degree, there is also a great deal of desire to celebrate Pat's success in Homeless to Millionaire scenario regardless of the sex of Pat. Finally, in a Congressman and Prostitute scenario that we did not spend a lot of time discussing, there is not much difference in the coverage of the politician's scandal regardless of whether the politician is a Republican or Democrat. Issues of religion and sexuality tend to produce distinct ways in which a story may be covered. However, issues of individual peril or victory seem to negate many of those distinctions. Stories that are sensational or horrific will be covered no matter which groups are involved in a story.

It is likely that this would not have been the case a few decades ago. The notions of traditional gender stereotypes may have been too powerful to allow the respondents to celebrate the business success of Pat the woman as much as Pat the man, and concern for a kidnapped child may have been influenced by the race of that child. Clearly our society has changed so that overt expressions of racism and sexism are taboo within highly educated professional groups. However, it is also likely that the occupational training that many of the media personnel have received has helped them to avoid making distinctions when they are not warranted. This training is obviously incomplete, as we have demonstrated with the scenarios concerning religion and sexuality. However, we should credit the occupational training in creating neutrality in some of the situations where it has experienced success.

WHAT DOES IT ALL MEAN?

This research is not an attack on media in the United States, but rather it is an aid for individuals in the media so that they can improve their craft. Our research indicates that media personnel possess certain biases, and those biases help to shape how our news is covered. Their possession of biases does not make them evil, or bad, reporters or editors. All that it means is that they are human. Understanding those biases can help media personnel to be careful about how the news is reported. For that reason we will spend our last chapter looking more intently into the implications of our findings and offer some suggestions for improving how the media presents the news.

6

Where to Go from Here?

We have pointed out that individuals are likely to perceive media bias, at least in part, based on how this perception feeds their particular social interest. Our research does not touch on the potential for confirmation bias to shape media personnel's ability to accurately perceive media bias. We developed a methodology that allowed us to assess which perceptions of media bias are more likely to be true. According to this data, bias toward racial minorities is more likely to be positive than negative, and bias against women is very slight. Our more powerful findings indicate negative bias against Christians and positive bias toward sexual minorities. These findings are much more supportive of the notion that the Culture War, rather than the Majority Group Power or No Bias, News Ideology drives the perceptions of media personnel.

In our concluding chapter, we want to explore the implications of this finding. There are ethical values one must consider in order to decide how to address the pervading Culture War Ideology. The ramifications of the decision to address this bias need to be considered as well. We also recognize the limitations of our current study and want to consider how future research can explore media bias.

PARTICULAR VERSUS GENERALIZED CONCERNS

Some who complain about media bias seem to imply that media personnel ignore groups for which they lack sympathy. We cannot completely rule out this possibility. Such an argument appears to have support in our Political Rally scenario where clearly the group supportive of the LGBT community gained more attention than the group supportive of ex-gays.

However, generally there was not a great deal of difference in the level of attention given to the various religious and sexuality groups in our scenarios, although the way these groups were treated differed significantly. The argument that the media hides stories about groups it does not like is not supported by our work. The way the Culture War News Ideology operated was not to ignore culturally conservative groups but to treat those groups in a distinctive manner.

When media personnel addressed the concerns of culturally progressive groups, they did so in ways that tied these concerns to the larger generalized issues that would be advocated by special interest elements tied to that group. For example, the hate speech is about hate and homophobia, which brings up the need to punish the professor. In the other version, the professor may be a jerk, but there is not a great deal of concern about hate when the professor is anti–Christian. The larger concerns of Christians are ignored, and there is more focus on the particular incident. Although not a culturally progressive group, we saw the same pattern when comparing Muslims to Christians in the shooting at their religious institution. The shooting at the mosque ties to larger issues of Islamophobia, while the shooting at the church brings up concerns of that particular shooter. This may be a generalized progressive effect and not merely one linked to cultural progressives, as we observed this difference in the attention paid to sexism when a feminist student group faced possible discrimination compared to the specific religious/campus conflict when it was the Baptist student group.

If this general pattern holds for similar stories, then we can start to predict how differences may emerge depending on the attributes of the individuals in the story. For example, a story of a man accusing his employer of firing him because of his Christian faith will be covered differently than a man accusing his employer of firing him because he is bisexual. We do not predict that the former story will not be covered. However, it is likely to be covered as a local conflict between that man and his employer. There indeed may be evidence that the employer is an anti–Christian bigot. But that information will only be brought to bear to impeach his claims of neutrality and not to consider larger issues of religious hostility. On the other hand, the story of the bisexual man will not merely focus upon the details of that particular incident. We suspect that even if the evidence comes out to show that the firing was legitimate, that media personnel would still take advantage of this opportunity to discuss problems that bisexual individuals face. For culturally conservative groups, generally only the local story matters. For cultural progressive, and perhaps other progressive groups, larger generalizable issues can also be addressed.

This difference is powerful as it concerns the ability of special interest groups to call attention to issues they want to promote. For some groups, perhaps the best they can hope for is to point out specific unjust situations. However, attempts to tie these issues to how social structures or cultural patterns contribute to the possible injustice are not likely to be accepted by most media personnel. On the other hand, those in groups towards which media personnel have sympathy may have the ability to discuss the larger social and cultural concerns that influence their complaints. This may be a critical way in which the media influences our society, as only certain groups are allowed to make arguments of structural inequality and cultural oppression that are substantiated by the larger media.

MAJORITY GROUP POWER?

We entered this research with two major possible pathways in which bias can challenge the efforts of media personnel to practice a norm of objectivity, we also tested the possibility that objectivity is the key component to media coverage. We basically argued that media personnel may either support, intentionally or not, a social structure that enhances the power and prestige of the majority group, or they may support the arguments of cultural progressives. We have found the latter rather than the former to be accurate. In the latter half of this chapter, we will look at the implications of this finding and suggest some ways media personnel may consider dealing with this bias. However, at this time, it is wise for us to consider our lack of finding of the Majority Group Power News Ideology.

Few individuals believe that the media is filled with overt racist, sexist and homophobic individuals who seek to re-victimize social minority groups. However, it is quite reasonable to consider whether members of the media, who are more likely to enjoy various types of majority group status, are relatively uninformed about how social structures in the United States reinforce the challenges of social minority groups. If that is the case, then the media may reinforce a status quo that locks in position the type of social structures working against these social minority groups. It is also possible that there are corporate organizational interests that influence members of the media to protect the status quo as well. However, the opposite seems to be the case. Minority social groups may have the ability to take a news story and have media personnel use that story as a vehicle for addressing some of the larger social concerns (racism, sexism, homophobia) that motivate activists within these groups. Rather than ignoring these social structures, media personnel are in a position to help bring light to the ways these social structures may harm social minority groups, and the results of our work suggest that this is precisely what tends to happen.

A good example of how this may happen can be seen in the recent rise of the Black Lives Matter movement. The movement arguably began with the acquittal of George Zimmerman in the 2013 death of Trayvon Martin. The members of the movement were also able to organize after the police-shooting deaths of Michael Brown and Tamir Rice, as well as the non-shooting deaths of Eric Garner and Freddy Gray among others. What the movement was able to do was to go beyond the actual details of these individual events to facilitate a discussion about the role of the criminal justice system in the lives of African-Americans. If the media was willing to report on these particular encounters, our research suggests that they often also go on to discuss the criminal justice system. This gave these activists the ability to highlight the work of scholars who have documented some of the abuses of that system (Alexander 2012; Cole 2000; Snyder 2015). Regardless of the level of success this movement ultimately has in addressing these issues, it is clear that the media personnel in our sample would be quite open to allowing these activists to discuss larger issues, even if the details of some of the police encounters do not precisely fit the narrative of their movement.[1] If the Majority Group Power News Ideology was the best explanation of potential media bias then it is unlikely that such activists would have relatively easy access to a media that allowed them to air their grievances. Instead, groups such as Black Lives Matter would struggle to get significant airtime. Thus, our findings help to at least partially explain the visibility of groups such as Black Lives Matter.[2]

While we are not in a position to completely explain the failure of the Majority Group Power News Ideology, we can speculate about why it is not a good explanation of the potential bias in the media. Previous research has indicated that understanding the way social structures impact social minority groups is positively correlated to educational attainment (Glick, Lameiras and Castro 2002; Kane and Kyyrö 2001; Schaefer 1996). Media personnel are more highly educated than the average individual and likely were exposed to different educational efforts to expose them to the problems of institutional racism, sexism, and homophobia. This level of awareness on the behalf of media personnel likely enables them to be sensitive to the power of social structures to shape the lives of social minority groups and helps them to be open to allowing activists from those groups to use particular news events to discuss larger structural and social issues.

Is it possible that despite our findings, there are indeed ways in which the media supports the majority groups? We cannot discount this possibility, since many of the ways inequality works today are not overt but rather through subtle mechanisms. It is possible that future research using a different set of scenarios may discover some of the hidden ways the media may reify social inequalities. However, until there is more solid evidence of such a process, we will assert that the ideology driving the media's attempt to understand social inequalities does not aid majority group, but rather it provides minority interest groups ways to articulate their issues.

Do Christians Have a Right to Complain?

In contrast to the visibility given to racial minority groups, we find that media personnel are less willing to consider the larger generalized complaints Christians may make about disparate treatment. This finding has to be contextualized with information gathered from other research. For example, Kerr (2003) finds evidence that fundamentalist Christians were reported on in a consistently mildly negative manner between 1980 and 2000. Contrary to our findings that political affinity does not shape media reporting, some of this negativity is tied to the political threat this group represents (Kerr 2003; Kerr and Moy 2002). Pieper (2011) suggests that some of this hostility may be linked to images created in 1992 by Patrick Buchannan declaring a culture war on leftists at the Republican National Convention. This event appears to have created a fear among many on the left of the power of Christian conservatives to take the country backwards, and this fear may have motivated some in the media to take a more critical stance toward Christians and other cultural conservatives. Our finding that political affiliation is relatively unimportant when shaping media coverage may not account for a unique political fear that is aimed at those cultural conservatives. This fear, and a heightened desire to use a critical framework when dealing with Christians, may account for part of the reluctance of media personnel to take seriously the larger societal concerns of Christians.

However, it is also possible that this reluctance has emerged simply because there is insufficient evidence of legitimacy in the complaints of Christians. Few would doubt that there are isolated cases whereby individual Christians, or small Christian groups, face prejudice or discrimination. However, one can ask whether the case has been made that these incidents are due to the unique circumstances of a given situation or that there are larger anti–Christian social forces that need to be unpacked.[3] Media personnel, especially those more inclined to take a critical stance towards Christians, would want to be extra careful not to unduly allow members of the majority religion to claim a victim status.

A few years ago it was much easier to maintain such an argument. However, there is mounting evidence that at least in higher education, there is an anti–Christian bias not merely due to a few religious bigots (Hyers 2008; Tobin and Weinberg 2007; Yancey 2011). Findings from Rothman and Lichter (2008) indicate that cultural, but not necessarily political, conservatives find themselves in lower status positions even after controlling for their academic achievements. It has become harder to maintain a fiction that there is not a systematic bias against Christians in academia. If this bias exists, then it is not surprising that we have a dearth of research documenting anti–Christian perspectives in our larger society. Given our findings of the unwillingness of journalists to appreciate the possibility of systematic anti–Christian social effects, we may have another institution that generally investigates social dysfunctions but ignores those dysfunctions when it comes to social forces that disadvantage Christians.

Beyond possible anti–Christian academic bias, recent work has documented what has been termed Christianophobia (Yancey and Williamson 2014). Christianophobia is defined as "an irrational animosity towards or hatred of Christians, or Christianity in general." The level of animosity aimed at Christians rivals that directed at Muslims. However, generally those with Christianophobia are more likely to be white, male, wealthy, and highly educated. Thus, they have more per-capita social power than the average person. It is reasonable to suspect that individuals in such positions of power would buttress social mechanisms that work to the disadvantage of Christians. The potential failure of academics and journalists to take this possibility seriously likely allows these mechanisms to exist without large scale critical challenge from those in non-sectarian academic or media institutions. It is not feasible to argue that Christians generally are overstating their potential victimization until there has been a more honest vetting of their complaints from academics and journalists determined to find the truth behind those complaints. In this sense, the contention that journalists do not respect the generalized concerns of conservative Christians because those concerns are not well founded is premature.

Overarching News Ideologies?

One of the questions we wanted to address in our work is whether there are overarching news ideologies relevant to different types of news media. Our ability to make definitive assertions about these three media dimensions is somewhat limited given the low numbers of television and social media personnel in our sample. However, we assert that our work provides us an ability to speculate about what distinctions and commonalities we may see between the different types of media. This speculation can provide direction for future work with higher numbers of non-newspaper media personnel.

We only used one scenario to assess potential political bias, so we are limited in our assessment of it. However, it was noteworthy that while newspaper and television media personnel did not differ in preference for either scenario that social media personnel displayed a strong preference for the story where the Democrat was arrested.[4] Indeed, we found that about a quarter (23.4%) of those given the scenario with the Democrat were likely to mention the arrest as a way of justifying putting the story online. It is easy to see why the fact of the arrest would make this a more newsworthy story. Without the arrest, this story may just be a rumor. Why is the arrest more relevant with a Democrat than with a Republican? Since we have eliminated the possibility that it is the conservatives driving this result, we have to look at other factors for this political bias.

It is possible that this result is driven by the context in which we conducted this study. We collected the data during a Democratic presidential administration. That may color social media personnel's priorities. We speculate that the nature of social media may attract those with a rebellious perspective, regardless of their own political orientation. Thus, under a Democratic administration there may be more desire to point out the flaws of the members of that party than of the opposing party. This is an explanation that may also explain other divergent social media results. This can especially be the case if social media personnel believe that there is a "politically correct" nature in those inhabiting other media. There may be a rebel orientation that produces more of a willingness to run a story about research that white workers work harder. Furthermore, personal interest stories may not draw interest from social media personnel simply because they do not present controversies that allow a more rebellious nature among social media personnel to be expressed. After all, what is the controversy in opposing sexual slavery or a kidnapping of a child? While we only have this single scenario to look at potential political bias, this scenario may provide an important clue into why social media personnel differ from their peers.

It is in the context of this speculation about the rebellious nature of social media that we have a theory about the differences between them and other media personnel. It is a theory connected to social media as a way to challenge the norms and values of the larger society. If social media attracts those who are innovators in their use of technology, then it may also encourage them to "think outside the box" as it concerns social and political issues as well. Some have observed how those engaging in social media often engaging in rude and anti-social behavior in their comments and blogs (Dutton 1996; Hill and Hughes 1998; Papacharissi 2002; Shandwick 2011). This rebellious attitude may not be limited to overthrowing traditional mores, a distaste for the notion of politeness and political correctness may also motivate those who work in more traditional media occupations.

With such small numbers and given our methodology, we are limited in how much we could speculate about the differences between social media personnel and our other respondents. However, the notion that social media personnel have more rebellious attitudes than other media offers valuable explanatory power for these differences. Previous literature has suggested that social media is quite different from other types of media based on who consumes it (Correa, Hinsley and De Zuniga 2010; Duggan and Brenner 2013; Lenhart et al. 2010). These individuals may be more conditioned to receive information in distinct ways than those who receive information from traditional media outlets. Indeed, research has demonstrated that consumers of social media may have different social interactions than other individuals due to their participation in this medium (Fischer and Reuber 2011; Hogan 2010). These are key differences that may alter the approach of those in social media.

For example, Teresa Correa et al. (2010) found that social media use is positively related to extraversion and openness to experiences while negatively related to emotional stability. Such individuals may place a high priority in external excitement and opposition to a status quo that seeks conformity. This may contribute to the rebellious attitude in the social media we postulate to have captured. Social media personnel may realize the need to reflect this type of non-conformity to the established media norms in order to attract and maintain a large audience. This need would be more easily met with social media personnel focused upon projecting a rebellious image. For this reason, we argue that there are certain overarching news ideologies, but social media is an alteration of those news ideologies that at times reinforces them and at other times challenges them. If there is an argument for the presence of a Majority Group Power News Ideology, then it would be found among social media personnel. However, we speculate that there is less of a desire to push for majority group power and more of a desire to rebel against the perception of political correctness that social media personnel may envision as part of traditional media structures.

While we found that there are certain propensities common among newspaper, television and social media personnel, there were also important distinctions that help us to understand how news ideologies may be contextualized for certain groups. Understanding these similarities and differences can better help us comprehend how news ideologies can impact media bias. For example, in none of these groups was there a strong desire to postulate a majority group ideology concerning race. While the social media personnel were more willing to publish the story of the white robber, there was still more concern about a possible racial motivation for the robbery when they were told that the robber is white. Social media personnel had roughly an equal propensity to state that race was unimportant, while other media personnel were more likely to state this propensity when asked about African-Americans.[5] It is possible that the unwillingness of social media personnel and other media to pursue an agenda whereby majority group interests are furthered may develop from contrasting motivations. For newspaper and television media personnel there can be motivation to meet the interest of people of color. This may produce a more proactive media that seeks positive stories for people of color, as we can see in the research scenario. For social media there appears to be a desire to hold to a colorblind perspective that makes them hesitant to openly promote a majority group agenda. However, that comes with its own set of problems. Other scholars (Armstrong and Wildman 2008; Bonilla-Silva 2003; Carr 1997) have argued that colorblindness can lead to the promotion of a racial status quo that supports whites. Indeed, we speculate that our findings of the social media promoting research favoring whites more than Hispanics may attempt to reject "political correctness" so that they do not have to ignore a positive story for whites. Thus, members in all the media groups talk about downplaying race, but it is the social media personnel who also are less open to exploring issues of modern, non-overt forms of racism.

As it concerns gender, there are once again similarities and differences between the groups. All of them tended to envision the father as dangerous. The social media personnel were not as interested in the story as the other media personnel, but the tenor of the story they would pursue did not greatly differ. However, there was a difference in whether media personnel envision Pat the businessman as more inspirational. Social media personnel did not accept the narrative of an inspiring businessman as easily as other media personnel. Perhaps, social media personnel are not as interested in the human-interest angle of these scenarios as other media personnel. This would account for why they were less interested in the welfare of a kidnapped child and why they were not looking for inspiration from Pat. It is plausible that social media personnel are more interested in larger social and political issues than the happenings of individuals or single families. As we already suggested, such human-interest stories do not have the potential for displaying the type of rebellious attitudes that may be part of the social media atmosphere. Nevertheless, for all three groups there was some portrayal of traditional gender roles, but not necessarily in ways that would substantiate a Majority Group Power News Ideology. After all, there was more anger put forth at the dangerous father than the mother. However, that the media may play on traditional gender roles in subtle ways is evident in all three media sources.

The rejection of attitudes from the general media culture also came out in some of the findings connected to attitudes towards Christians. We found that social media personnel were not significantly more likely to include the story of the church shooting than the mosque shooting (35.4% v. 27.4%), in contrast to the other media personnel. (Although they reflected the same attitudes as other media personnel when it came to hate speech). This finding has to be taken with a huge grain of salt, since it is insignificant and based on such a small number or respondents. But if this finding held up with larger numbers of social media respondents then it is plausible that social media personnel are rejecting a narrative of Muslims as victims. As the election of President Donald Trump has shown there is a market for an ethnic and religious nativism that may be tied to an unwillingness to recognize the potential victimization of Muslims. It is possible that the differential ways the other media outlets treat the shooting of the mosque and the church (emphasizing hatred as it concerns the mosque and the traits of the shooter as it concerns the church) minimizes the potential victimization of the Baptists. If social media personnel sense a propensity of other media personnel to favor Muslims over Baptists then they may be inclined to buck against this trend by being more willing to run the story with the Baptist church.

However, it should be noted that many of the other factors covered in our analysis of the potential bias against Christians showed social media personnel to be similar to other media personnel. Thus, they may share a similar level of antipathy towards Christians with other media personnel. If it is only in comparison to Muslims that social media personnel potentially diverge from other media personnel then it is plausible that these media personnel have more of an anti-religious attitude than an anti–Christian perspective. Such an attitude would indicate not only rebellion against the attitude driving other media but against the otherworldly norms of our society.

It is in that context that we can look at the perspectives of social media personnel as they concern issues of sexuality. Social media personnel were more open to using the shooting of an interracial couple than a same-sex couple, which was divergent from the rest of the media. Here too we have a difference that is not significant, but given our low numbers of respondents is worth noting (p = .096). However, outside of this difference social media personnel do not seem to diverge that greatly from the general narrative that media personnel are quite sensitive to the interests of sexual minorities. Thus, the potential "rebellion" of the social media personnel appears to have certain limitations. Concerning issues connected to sexuality, they do not differ much from the rest of the media. If social media personnel possess a general anti-religious attitude then such conformity to the rest of the media in this aspect of the Culture War News Ideology is not surprising.

We emphasize once again that this speculation is preliminary and there is a need for future work to verify our general premise about the differences between social media and other media outlets. However, even given the low numbers of social media respondents, it seems unlikely that we would document many differences between social media and other media respondents if there were not a qualitative difference between the two groups. For this reason, we assert with some confidence that social media personnel are distinct from other media personnel. Future research with higher numbers of social media respondents is needed to confirm or refute this assertion.

JOURNALISM AND OBJECTIVITY

Current journalistic culture in the United States promotes the ideas of neutrality and fairness. It may be impossible for journalists to maintain that standard due to the social and psychological factors that inhibit their ability to be objective. However, because objectivity is impossible does not mean that it is not a value to be sought. Attempts to present non-biased media may fall short, but they produce a superior product than what we would have obtained if we had not made the attempt to be objective. If that is the perspective of journalists, then our work can be valuable in helping journalists recognize the mechanism in which they fail to be relatively fair in their presentation of news stories. Understanding those mechanisms will help us to fashion potential solutions.

The good news is that we did find some evidence of relative objectivity among media personnel, especially as it pertains to issues of gender and race. As it concerned issues of gender, the differences in how men and women are portrayed are not overwhelming. However, as we have noted, it is quite possible that even small differences can have strong influence if multiplied across several stories. There were stronger differences when looking at racial issues, but not in a direction that substantiates majority group dominance. Our one scenario that tested for political effects indicates that there is not a preference for either political party. Furthermore, it is also clear that if a story is sensational enough, issues of gender and race become nearly irrelevant. Our scenarios of kidnapping and slavery created minor or no differences in the attention given to the story or the way it was covered. We argue that this is likely because the news value of such controversial events is so great that the vast majority of media personnel are unlikely to take note of the gender or racial components of these stories. One reassurance our findings bring is that if a story is traumatic enough, then media bias is not a substantive issue.

However, the good news ends when we consider the evaluation of stories that include participants in the culture war. The concerns of groups connected to a conservative cultural perspective tend to be ignored while the concerns of groups connected to a progressive cultural perspective are taken seriously. To the degree that lack of objectivity is a problem in the media, it is a problem linked to a Culture War News Ideology that shapes how stories are covered rather than whether a story is to be covered.

One barrier to objective reporting is the presence of special interest groups motivated to shape the news in ways that are advantageous for their group. Clearly, the ability of groups to shape the media is not equal. Those that fit the goals and interests of cultural progressives are in a better position to influence media personnel. However, racial minority groups are generally not seen as having a position in the culture war, but they appear to have higher than normal influence over the tone given to news stories. Our research cannot answer why such groups have this influence; however, we speculate that this effect may be due to a strong desire on the part of journalists to avoid information that stigmatizes people of color. Perhaps, the media personnel are very familiar with our history of racial abuse, and this sensitizes them to the plight of people of color. However, they do not seem quite as sensitive to the plight of women despite our patriarchal history. This difference may be due to a belief in an innate difference based on sex, but not race. Ideally, future research can investigate this possibility.

However, differences between how media personnel treat race and gender is not the place where media personal have the greatest difficulty in losing objectivity. The real issue of objectivity concerns the promotion of the Culture War News Ideology. If objectivity is important, then there should be minimal effort towards protecting the image of women and racial minorities and a great deal of effort towards addressing the biases connected to cultural progressivism. However, it may be the case that news media personnel do not want to challenge this news ideology. A belief that it is important to side with cultural progressives may be so strong that it is more powerful than a desire for objectivity. Indeed, it is not hard to imagine that newspaper and television journalists may celebrate court victories concerning same-sex marriage and take some pride in playing a role in those victories. If that is the case, then discussions about how to deal with this bias are a waste of time. For the sake of honesty, media personnel should simply acknowledge this bias and then allow the consumers of that media to assess their work in light of it.

It is our hope that most media personnel are uncomfortable with evidence that indicates a need for a more balanced media. Even if they do support culturally progressive ideologies, the value of having a media that can be trusted is simply too important. However, there may still be others who are not concerned about the type of biases outlined in our research. For this reason, it is valuable to consider the implications of the Culture War News Ideology as they impact our media.

IMPLICATIONS OF CULTURE WAR NEWS IDEOLOGY

The sensitivity that media personnel have towards issues of race appears to be magnified when issues of sexuality are in play. In particular, it is clear that media personnel are quick to explore conflicts that include members of the LGBT community with an understanding that members of that community are often victims of hate crimes. We are less interested in the accuracy of such assertions than we are of the impact this perception has in the shaping of media coverage. If media members approach stories with a preconceived notion that members of any community are the ones likely to have been victimized by hate, then it is hard to write a story that does not contain this notion, regardless of what the facts on the ground may be. With regard to objectivity, media personnel's strong belief about the victimization of the LGBT community does not serve them well in a quest to make objective reports about the news.

This portrayal of victimization is relevant given our changing culture. Some have noted what can be called "competitive victimization" (Noor et al. 2012; Sullivan et al. 2012) whereby social groups argue over who has faced the greatest hardship. Campbell and Manning (2014) argue that there is a distinction between being a victim and being an offender, whereas the "victim" experiences a gain in moral status. If this analysis is accurate, then we can appreciate the advantage of a media that is willing to portray one particular group (the LGBT community) as victims of something as heinous as hate crimes, while those in another group (Christians) are rarely seen as victimized due to their social status. This elevates those who can obtain a portrayal of victimization, which raises their status and allows them to make demands upon the society in ways not feasible for groups that are rarely seen as victims.

Looking at one of our scenarios can indicate how such a bias can create an advantage for certain groups relative to others. In the Religious Institution Shooting scenario we observed how media personnel framed the shooting as a hate crime or Islamophobic situation when a mosque was attacked, but they took the opportunity to discuss why people become violent and the need for gun control when the church was attacked. In the former case, there is a recognition that attention needs to be paid to the possible victimization of Muslims, because they are Muslims. We noted the 2015 shooting in Roseburg where there was some evidence that the shooter singled out some of his victims for their Christian faith. Given the results of our work, we suspect that this possibility would be played up much more if there was evidence that potential Muslim victims are being singled out. This incident would be less likely to be treated as an isolated instance of hatred, but rather it would have been an opportunity to explore the poisonous Islamophobia in the United States. Such an examination could have kept the story in the headlines longer, regardless of the level of evidence that the shooting was at least partially based on anti-religious hatred.

This type of more in-depth examination of Islamophobia opens up the possibility of legal protections that are specifically geared toward protecting Muslims from violence. In the church version of the scenario, the story framed was about how we can make societal wide changes to combat violence. There is little opportunity for Christians to discuss whether they may be uniquely vulnerable to violence. Christian groups are not able to address their concerns as Christians but are relegated to discussing their concerns as part of the larger society. Even though both versions of the scenarios offered the same level of evidence of religious specific "hate," the victimization framework provided to the mosque shooting allows Muslims to make societal claims in ways that escape Christians.

It can be argued that it is appropriate for Muslims to have an ability to make claims on our society that escapes conservative Christians. This "right" may emerge due to the higher levels of hatred and bigotry that Muslims face. Yet, it is not clear that there is a greater level of hatred towards Muslims than towards Christians, particularity if they are the type of Christians that are culturally conservative. Recent research (Yancey and Williamson 2014) indicates that the level of disaffinity towards conservative Christians at least rivals the disaffinity towards American Muslims. This work indicates that some of those with this level of hostility exhibit characteristics of dehumanization, bigotry and prejudice against Christians. Furthermore, those who tend to engage in such beliefs have higher levels of social status than other individuals.[6] This is not to state that the plight of conservative Christians is the same as that of Muslims. Clearly, that is not the case.

Indeed, one can reasonably argue that the higher educated, relatively wealthy individuals with disdain for conservative Christians are less likely to engage in violence than individuals who tend to have Islamophobia. However, there is at least some evidence that Christians experience social rejection due to their social identity as Christians (Yancey and Williamson 2014). Media moving towards objective coverage of the culture war would exhibit some degree of curiosity about what that rejection looks like. However, one with the type of social presuppositions demonstrated by our respondents is unlikely to show such curiosity and thus will fail to provide a complete picture of the culturally based social conflicts of our day. To the extent that this complete picture is not fleshed out by the general media, there is a distorted image that prevents media consumers from gaining near-complete information of the stories of the day and that allows the media to shape the social issues of the day based on the spread of selective information.

We believe that there are costs of such a failure to consider the position of culturally conservative groups, such as Christians, to the larger media enterprise. We have seen the rise of decentralized media institutions that serve different subcultures in our society. These institutions are often popular within their social niches and can sustain themselves with smaller audiences than general media institutions. Such fragmentation of the media threatens the larger media institutions, which continue to suffer losses of their share of the consumers of media. At least one of the reasons for the emergence of these niche media institutions is the lack of confidence individuals in certain subgroups have towards the media.[7] The biases illustrated in our research provide some reasons why there is a lack of trust. Those in culturally conservative subcultures may identify these biases rather easily since they are looking for them and thus be more willing to seek out alternate sources of information. Thus, the biases documented in our work may encourage the development of the type of niche media institutions threatening the dominant media organizations of today. Media personnel should consider dealing with this news ideology to lessen, or even eliminate the need for some of the niche media institutions that have developed in recent years.

Whether there should be an effort to challenge the Culture War News Ideology is a question connected to one's system of priorities. If victory in the culture war is a higher priority than providing an accurate portrayal of society or eliminating the need for the niche media that is least trusting of the general media, then an argument can be made that media personnel should engage in partisan media. Despite our explorations of the implications of this news ideology, there undoubtedly will be some who believe that the value of promoting issues of sexual identity, reproductive control and same-sex sexuality is such a high priority that they are willing to engage in the partisan journalism supporting such goals. However, we suspect that most journalists do not share such a ranking of their priorities and are open to looking at ways to deal with the subtle ways that bias may slip into their work. We do not believe that most media personnel want to do partisan work. They want to present the world in as accurate a manner as possible. However they, like most other individuals, are vulnerable to the type of confirmation bias that undoubtedly explains part of our findings. For those journalists, we offer the following advice in light of our findings.

DEALING WITH CULTURE WAR NEWS IDEOLOGY

A problem of dealing with the processes connected to news ideologies is that it is difficult for individuals to see how those biases play themselves out in their cognitive framework. It is easier for individuals to locate information that supports their presuppositions and ignore information that challenges them. Anyone wanting to deal with their presuppositions has to consider that those assumptions are not objective reality. They also have to accept that others have different ideas about our society, and those ideas may have developed in as careful and intellectual a manner as theirs have. The obvious first step media personnel have to take if they want to minimize the power of a Culture War News Ideology to influence their reporting is to carefully consider the presuppositions they have developed about society. Once they recognize those assumptions, they will be in a position to consider how they influence their work.

It is not enough to merely understand one's assumptions about social reality. It is also vital to develop a proper level of respect for ideas that differ from one's own. It is quite tempting to dismiss alternative perspectives as unworthy of consideration. Indeed, if we had sufficient reasons for why we should not believe a certain assumption about reality, then we would change our assumptions. Changing one's beliefs is not necessarily needed in order to respect the beliefs of others. However, it will take some degree of effort to respect, although not agree with, alternate beliefs. To this end, there is value in attempting to understand the disagreeing perspectives. For media personnel who recognize that they operate in a Culture War News Ideology, this means making efforts to read primary literature by cultural conservatives. We assume that some degree of research is conducted before stories concerning culturally conservative groups are written. However, there are many stories media personnel conduct research for and there can be only so much depth to the research conducted for a particular story. However, given the overall propensity in media to be influenced by the Culture War News Ideology, extra attention to literature by cultural conservatives is warranted in an effort to make certain that common presuppositions among media personnel have been countered by other perspectives.

There would also be value in developing friendships and relationships with individuals from those subcultures. Contact hypothesis (Pettigrew 1998; Sigelman and Welch 1993; Yancey 2007) indicates that intergroup contact often allows individuals to develop a higher level of respect for those in social out-groups. It is quite viable that many media personnel dwell in subcultures that do not have many individuals with culturally conservative beliefs. If media personnel have the characteristics linked to individuals with anti–Christian animosity (highly educated, progressive, irreligious), then the social networks of media personnel may actually exacerbate their propensity to dismiss and marginalize the perspectives of cultural conservatives. Contact theory has indicated that close relationships are not needed to produce respect for out-group members; however, there has to be a sufficient saturation of those members in a social network to enjoy the positive benefits of intergroup contact (Jackman and Crane 1986; Wilder 1984). Thus, attempts to introduce cultural conservatives into a media personnel's social network do not demand bringing individuals into one's intimate circle of friends. This is an effort that would not be easily achieved given the difficulty of having close friends with divergent social values. However, it is important that media personnel expose themselves to those with different values in multiple ways.

When individuals consider whether they have contact with individuals from social groups they are not a part of, they may overstate their acceptance of such groups since they likely know some individuals from that group. Even if media personnel live in relatively secular areas of the country, it is likely that they can name at least a few acquaintances whom they know to be a cultural conservative. However, merely having some cultural conservatives in one's social network does not necessarily provide many of the positive benefits connected to intergroup contact. Contact hypothesis theories have identified the value of having contact with out-group members who enjoy some degree of equality with them. If those in the out-group are in subordinate positions, then it becomes relatively easy to dismiss the ideas of such individuals as irrelevant. Since culturally conservative groups, such as conservative Christians, are relatively unlikely to be proportionately represented in non-sectarian media organizations, it is quite likely that the contacts media personnel have with members of that group will lie outside of their work environment, and it is quite possible that this contact will be with individuals who may be in subordinate social positions, such as office workers or landscapers. If media personnel want to neutralize the bias that comes from lack of intergroup contact, then there has to be an intentional effort to create consistent contact with individuals who are members of that group and have some degree of social prestige. It is a tall order, but overcoming the type of confirmation bias that develops from lack of exposure to those from other social groups will be difficult.

There is an operational value in the extension of media personnel's social networks. In the Political Rally scenario, we observed that our respondents were relatively eager to find alternative perspectives to the comments by PFOX. Yet, there was little to no effort to find alternate perspectives to PFLAG. While this finding was mostly limited to this particular scenario, we cannot discount the possibility that there are other situations in which media personnel are relatively unlikely to seek out alternate perspectives. It may be that having a lack of individuals who have culturally conservative perspectives in one's social network makes it harder for media personnel to introduce that balance into their work. If media personnel want to combat the tendency to rely on a Culture War News Ideology to shape their work, then there must be an effort to find balance, especially for the issues that one is particularly emotionally invested in supporting. To this end, even if media personnel do not, or cannot, sufficiently create an ideologically diverse social network, there should be an intentional effort to provide alternate perspectives on issues related to the culture war. Such issues cannot be dismissed as unworthy of discussion with cultural conservatives, since they are often driven by different cultural values rather than objective assertions about reality.

A key difference between how Christians were addressed by media personnel compared to other groups was whether they had the ability to go beyond a particular event to discuss larger issues that may be connected to those issues. We have already discussed how the Black Lives Matter activists have been able to use certain social events to create a social movement that addresses some of the structural problems embedded within the criminal justice system. This is a pathway by which social groups can use the media to highlight their concerns through social events that are media events. It is an important pathway that is more difficult for a cultural conservative to take. At the time of this writing, cultural conservatives have been attempting to make the release of videos from the Center for Medical Progress an important media event that can be used to energize their pro-life movement. We predict that this is likely to fail since media personnel are unlikely to provide the same degree of attention to such individuals as they did for the Black Lives Matter movement.

This difference has important ramifications for media personnel. If media personnel are to be referees between the conflicts of American social groups, then the same rules have to be available to all groups. This means that if progressive activist groups are allowed to use media news to discuss larger issues of concern to them, then the same opportunity should be provided to conservative activists groups. The natural biases within media personnel will limit this propensity unless there is a concerted, intentional effort to treat groups relatively equal. Such an effort does not require media personnel to accept the arguments supporting the larger concerns of the culturally conservative group any more than a referee has to root for one team or another to win. However, if a journalist is not going to be partisan, then one of the costs of that goal is to be fair to perspectives with which one disagrees. We suggest that media personnel make an intentional decision to either focus only on a specific event to avoid discussions of larger issues, or to allow activist groups of all sorts to make larger social assertions about specific media issues and to have this policy for all activist groups.

We do not minimize the challenge to overcome one's own presuppositions. Perhaps one of the most difficult tasks we can achieve as humans is to put our biases and expectations aside to gain a clean look at a given social situation or event. We hope that our work may aid media personnel by identifying a major area in which many, but not all or perhaps even most, personnel have a blind spot. If our work only allows them to consider the reality of this bias in their potential work, then we are confident that they will be in a better position to reach goals of objectivives that many of them have set.

6. *Where to Go from Here?*

EXTENSIONS TO THIS RESEARCH

We have utilized a unique experimental audit technique to go beyond observations of news media to assess in their own words how journalists consider the placement of stories. It is a technique that is limited because our respondents answer relatively few "scenario" questions. The questions require more reading than a normal attitudinal question and asking many more than a dozen is certain to tax the patience of a busy journalist.[8] Perhaps, if we had the resources to pay the respondents a substantial amount for their participation, then we could ask more questions.[9] However, most scholars will not have the level of funding to pay a large number of professionals the money it takes to have them fill out a survey that takes 40 minute to an hour to complete. We realize that our few statements are not definitive in any of the dimensions tested, as we are relegated to a few scenarios to test for potential racism, sexism, homophobia and anti–Christian sentiment. Our hope is that in producing these preliminary results, we have introduced a way in which future researchers can further explore the contours of media news ideologies with additional testing of other scenarios.

For example, two of our examples concerning race dealt with crime. Perhaps, the propensity of journalists to engage in protection of the majority group is neutralized in stories that involve crime. More variety of scenarios may elicit responses that fit with a Majority Group Power News Ideology. Until we see more evidence for this news ideology, we will stay with our current conclusion while remaining open to the possibility that testing of future scenarios may indicate that our finding is contextualized to only certain types of stories. In a different dimension, we touched upon the possibility of political differences with only one scenario. With so many dimensions (race, politics, gender, sexuality, religion) and being able to use only a few scenarios, it was inevitable that one of those dimensions would be short-shifted. In our current research project, that dimension is possible political bias. We are somewhat comfortable with this focus since we assert that generalized political bias is not likely to be a powerful explanation of media bias. Despite this assertion, and even though our one scenario suggests that media political bias is a myth, we are interested in seeing further tests of the possibility of political bias. Just as race and political identity are dimensions that would benefit from future research that assesses more scenarios of those potential aspects of bias, we argue that all of the dimensions would also benefit from further scrutiny. Even if our original assertions hold up to this testing, we suspect that this testing would allow us to understand more of the nuanced differences that account for the news ideologies dominating our media.

While we were able to use our television and social media data to look at the entire media culture, not just newspaper media culture, we are not under the illusion that we have done a masterful job of assessing how news ideologies play themselves out across different media outlets. We were unable to gather enough respondents to make the type of strong conclusions that are more clearly in our newspaper media personnel data. Clearly, another extension to this work would be a more concerted effort to gather enough responses by those in the television and social media institutions to assess whether the findings of this project are strongly replicated in a different medium. To that end, much of the new media is online, and the emergence of social media cannot be ignored. Given our previous theoretical construction of the rebellious nature of social media, there is great potential value in concentrating on gathering a list of social media personnel for study. Research with sufficient numbers of social media personnel, especially if they can be gathered in a manner that creates at least a somewhat representative sample that provides adequate statistical power, can help to either further document or refute our "social media as rebellion" theory.

In addition to adding other scenarios and attempts to collect the responses necessary to more fully evaluate other forms of media, we are mindful of the problem of obtaining respondents who work for media outlets that have a high circulation. It is quite likely that such individuals are more dismissive of such research attempts and perhaps even more financial compensation will not allow us to include them in our sample. We support attempts to reach them, as many of the other respondents were not reached in this study; however, future researchers must also be open to the possibility that reporters and editors at large newspapers or television media outlets simply do not see it worth their time to fill out an online or mailed questionnaire. While our comparisons of the different versions of the scenarios were weighted for the circulation of the newspapers the respondents worked at, it is quite possible that had we been able to obtain more respondents from larger papers that we would have seen important distinctions that we have missed with this current sample.

Given that the voices of media personnel at larger outlets may have more impact on how the media shapes our culture, they are voices that we do not want to miss. To this end, we suggest that future researchers have more flexibility in gathering information from media personnel at larger outlets. For example, it may be that these individuals are less willing to dismiss an invitation to an interview rather than an impersonal questionnaire. Even though an interview may take more time, it can be harder to say no to a personal invitation than an email. Of course the disadvantage of using interviews is that one is limited in the number of interviews that can be feasibly performed. The upside of interviews is that it becomes possible to use follow-up questions and probes to elicit the type of information that will not come out in an internet survey. Given the importance of the opinions of those at larger media outlets who often set the trend for other media personnel, we consider it advisable to conduct a qualitative project to assess how such media personnel make decisions about what news stories they would use and what approach they would take in writing them. Perhaps, such a project could precede or coincide with a similar project that assesses media personnel from smaller outlets to determine if there is really a difference in the outlook of media personnel from institutions of different sizes.

Finally, there has been a good deal of de-centralization of media into distinct institutions that cater to a certain subculture. This makes the task of assessing media bias more difficult, since the way bias plays out with media of certain perspectives is likely quite different than the way it plays out with those motivated by different ideologies. There is little doubt that social media outlets such as Salon, Think Progress and Occupy Democrats have different biases than National Review, TownHall and World Net Daily. However, it is not enough to merely assess one group as having progressive political biases while the other group has conservative political biases. Future research with some variation of the experimental audit design we showcased here may also be able to determine the degree to which certain types of media outlets are open to contrasting opinions and whether issues on certain themes are more likely to activate these biases than others. It may be possible to flesh out the different news ideologies not only for media centered on political ideologies but also for social lifestyles or religious theologies. Such efforts would allow researchers to gain a more holistic understanding of the competing news ideologies that dominate our current media culture.

Conclusion

Even though there has been a great deal of research on media bias in the past, we have pioneered a technique that allows us to assess how media personnel weigh the issues that enable them to make decisions about which media stories to use and how to use them. As such, we hope that our techniques launch the beginning of a new phase of media research. Ideally, future researchers will improve on this technique and find other creative ways to implement it. If such efforts allow researchers to gain more understanding about the media and help the professionals in the media to better combat the problems associated with news ideologies that distort media coverage, then we are gratified to have started this methodological trend.

We engaged in this project because we believe that potential media bias is an important topic. That bias can inhibit the ability of media personnel to be believed and create social myths that are difficult to dispel. Our conclusion is that media bias is a problem contextualized into certain aspects of media coverage. We do not know whether complete objectivity is possible, and indeed there is a good deal of previous psychological and sociological work that indicates that it is not. However, this does not mean that our media should not strive towards that impossible goal. Even if the goal is unobtainable, striving towards that goal will produce a higher level of the type of balanced reporting that has the chance of winning over skeptical media consumers.

Appendix:
Methodology and the
Study of Media Bias

As mentioned in the main body of this text, there are quite a few challenges in the assessment of media bias. For example, it is difficult to assess potential media given our difficulty in controlling all relevant factors. If the media pays more attention to stories with black robbers than with white robbers, it may be that the manner in which blacks rob others is systematically different in ways that demand more media attention. Thus, if blacks are more likely to use a gun, then this potential difference may demand more attention. It is the gun, rather than the race of robber influencing the degree of media attention. But how is a researcher going to anticipate all of the potential differences that may arise when we look at stories across a variety of categories? It is difficult, if not impossible, to control for all potential differences that might arise. So comparisons between actual news stories will never capture all possible effects that can account for differential treatment of media stories.

We must assess whether media personnel make distinctive decisions based on the social and demographic characteristics of the individuals in the story and do so in a way that holds other factors in control. However, research has generally failed to look into why media personnel make the choices they do about what is published. Usually research is utilized to demonstrate a difference in how a story featuring those with different characteristics is covered, and it is implied that these characteristics motivate this distinction. Beyond the problem of possible mediating variables that explain the relationships between those characteristics and whether, or how, a story is covered, we are making assertions about motivations without asking the media personnel about their motivations. To this end, we decided on a mixed-methods approach that allows us to determine with experimental quantitative data that assesses the level of importance media personnel attach to certain demographic and social characteristics, but also with qualitative data to help us understand why they made those decisions.

Researching Media Bias

The vast majority of research on media bias is tied to observations of how media responds to outside stimuli. In other words, researchers observe current stories in a newspaper or media broadcast and then assess whether the characteristics of the principles in the story matter in how the story is treated. In a hypothetical example, if a Republican presidential candidate was caught having an affair and a Democrat presidential candidate was caught having an affair, then a researcher can assess the placement of each story and the tone used to report that story. If political bias is nonexistent, and the information in the stories is basically the same, then we should have stories of similar importance and tone reported by the media. With some exceptions, a variation of this strategy is how academics have attempted to determine whether we have media bias.

A key issue with such a strategy is that it is rare that one can find events that are exactly alike except for a key demographic or social characteristic. For example, if in the example above the Republican candidate had children and the Democrat candidate did not, then a media organization may pay more attention to the affair of the Republican because of the presence of children rather than political bias of media personnel. In almost any two stories, there are many, perhaps dozens, of differences that may play a role in how the story is treated by media personnel. Some studies attempt to look at multiple occurrences to see if there is a pattern that transcends idiosyncratic issues; however, given the phenomenological aspect of news stories, it is hard to get a large enough sample to overcome problems of statistical power. Furthermore, there may be conditions related to demographic differences that also have an impact in how a story is covered. For example, differential treatment of African-American criminal suspects may be due to impressions driven by socio-economic status rather than racial stereotypes. This makes it quite likely for a researcher to mistakenly link differential treatment to an incorrect independent effect.

Furthermore, we gain limited information from just the placement of a story. For example, without gauging tone or how a story is covered, it is quite possible that a story will be placed in the same position but written in a completely different manner. In our aforementioned example of affairs and presidential candidates, if a newspaper places both stories on page 2, yet emphasizes hypocrisy for the Republican but the likeability of the Democrat, then we still have a case for media bias. Developing ways to assess the type of tone taken in a story is important to gain a comprehensive understanding of potential media bias.[1] However, given the potential problems of confirmation bias within the researcher, there is the danger that interpretations of tone will conform to the expected theory proposed in a particular study.

To accomplish our goals, we develop an experimental design. Our design is not perfect as it is not done in a natural setting, and it is not clear whether the actions of a respondent in an experiment will be the same in real life. However, our design does allow us to control for all factors except for the experimental variable. We rely on an experimental audit design to disentangle possible media bias from other possible independent effects. Butler and Schofield (2010) used an experimental design whereby they sent letters to editors, half supporting McCain and half supporting Obama. They found more support for the McCain letters and more support for the candidate the newspaper does not endorse. However, this experiment does not inform us about the type of news coverage a paper offers and is of limited use for this particular research question. The closest experimental study that addressed potential newspaper coverage may be Patterson and Donsbach's (1996) work. They used a survey to assess the political attitudes of journalists in five Western democracies (the United States, the United Kingdom, Germany, Italy, and Sweden) using an experimental question that asked them to assess whether a story is newsworthy and whether to use photos that enhance either conservative or progressive perspectives on a story. Findings indicated that a journalist's political beliefs are correlated with his/her news coverage. However, because this research is international in nature, it is unable to focus on the unique manner racial, gender, political and religious issues are represented by U.S. media. Furthermore, respondents were all given the same scenarios which allowed the researchers to make comparisons across the countries, but it does not allow the researchers to assess whether the media personnel would have provided different answers if the scenarios focused on alternative groups.

Our strategy utilizes an experimental audit design to examine media personnel in the United States. An audit study is typically used to measure discrimination directly with experimental fieldwork. For example, with certain audit studies, researchers carefully select, match, and train testers to play the role of a job seeker. The testers have matched equal characteristics aside from the experimental variable—often race. From this procedure, researchers can assess the effect that variable has in regards to access to opportunities and exposure to discrimination (Pager and Shepard 2008). In addition to providing a more realistic social context, audit studies produce similar results to experimental studies (Correll 2007) and thus provide additional support for the conclusions of both studies. Unlike laboratory experiments, audit studies allow for more realism when conducting research. In addition, audit studies avoid the external validity problem of laboratory experiments, which are conducted in artificial settings (Pager 2007; Pager and Shepard 2008; Samson 2013). Audit studies take into account social contexts when assessing the causes of various forms of discrimination and other social disparities (Pager and Shepard 2008). Although many audit studies focus on racial effects, the same principles can also be used to assess potential gender, sexuality, political and religious effects.

However, we cannot completely replicate the type of audit studies done by trained testers in a real world setting. It is simply not viable to send real news stories with contrasting demographic/social characteristics in our assessment of news media personnel. Thus, we are forced to use a somewhat artificial laboratory design with this current research project. Instead of a traditional audit study, we have an experimental audit design that will allow us to isolate each particular social/demographic characteristic to account for their possible effect in media coverage. Pager (2003) used a similar design to isolate the effect of a previous criminal record for whites and blacks and their opportunity to obtain a job. With this methodology, Pager found that having a previous criminal record had an especially detrimental effect on blacks. We do not exactly replicate Pager's techniques, as she used individuals of different races trained to act similarly, but we still will have the ability to isolate potential effects of certain social/demographic characteristics in the decisions of media personnel.[2]

The quantitative elements of our design can at their very best only tell us whether media personnel place stories differently due to the characteristics of the principles in the story. However, the design is powerless to inform us about why there may be such differences. Perhaps those differences are connected to very real circumstances that should dictate differential treatment of the story. On the other hand, certain stereotypes and prejudices may also influence how individuals with certain social and demographic characteristics are treated in the media. After we have determined where a respondent will place a given story, it is important to ask them for their reasons for this placement. This provides us the sort of qualitative data that will reveal the intended tone that the respondent plans on providing the article. We can assess how the changed characteristic alters the ways reporters and editors frame a given story. Looking at the intended tone of hypothetical stories, rather than assessing differential treatment of actual contrasting stories, is a superior way to assess whether media personnel are treating a story differently based on demographic or social differences of the individuals in the story, since we are getting our information directly from the "horse's mouth" instead of implying our own interpretation of potential differences.

Methodology

In the initial stage of this research, we sent out a survey to 2400 newspaper editors and reporters collected by a listing purchased from Meltwater—a media intelligence company. We used Meltwater to gain access to a nationwide list of newspaper journalists and editors. We then selected potential respondents from specific beats. After collecting data from these newspaper personnel, we followed up with a survey to 2400 television media personnel and 2400 social media personnel. All respondents who had access to the online survey were randomly selected.

For our newspaper study, we limited our sample to only individuals in the following roles: assignment desk, assistant editor, associate editor, bureau chief, columnist, contributor, correspondent, department head, deputy editor, editor, editor-at-large, editor-in-chief, editorial assistant, editorial editor, executive editor, freelance journalist, news editor, online editor, op-ed editor, reporter, senior editor, staff writer or sub editor.[3] Additionally, we limited our study to respondents who were assigned to crime, culture, education, government, legal, lifestyle, local, news and current affairs, news and media, politics, religion, or science beats. Once we accumulated a list of all personnel who fit our parameters (a total population of 29,682 potential respondents), we assigned a number to all of the individuals and then selected 2400 numbers using a random number generator. Half of the respondents were sent one version of the survey, while the other half received the alternate version. The respondents were sent two reminders after the initial email with a link to the survey.[4] To encourage completion of the survey, the respondents who completed the survey were allowed to enter a drawing for one of three $200 Amazon gift cards. To be entered in the drawing, the respondent had to answer all of the survey's questions, since the survey was set up to not allow them to complete it if they skipped any questions.

The response rate of the survey was 12.17 percent. Since it is low, our sample may systematically differ from the entire population. Non-response is a common problem when using online surveys to gather data (Dillman et al. 2009; Shih and Fan 2008), especially from busy professionals. Couper and Miller (2008) argue that research using online surveys may be at a disadvantage compared to other modes of data collection. Yet, low response rates do not necessarily mean response bias (Groves 2006; Keeter et al. 2000). Singer and Ye (2014) suggest a focus on non-response error rather than non-response rates. Indeed, Groves (2006) argues that non-response rates alone are not a good predictor of the extent of response bias. This is especially the case if the characteristics, where the sample and population differ, show no impact on the dependent variable. He recommends, among other remedies, comparison of response rates across subgroups and comparing the sample to estimates from other sources. We ran a series of regression models[5] using social and demographic information as the independent variables and where a respondent placed a story as the dependent variable. These models indicated that the most consistent and powerful predictor of where a respondent placed a story was the circulation level at their newspaper.

The Meltwater listing allowed us to obtain the circulation levels for the vast majority of members on the list. When we compared our respondents to the entire population in the listing with regards to the circulation of the newspapers where they worked, we found that our respondents tended to work at papers with lower levels of circulation. It is not surprising that our response rate would be lower among individuals working at larger newspapers, as they are more likely to not have the time for our survey or, assuming that they are better paid than those in smaller newspapers, to be less motivated by our incentive of a gift card. Pike (2008) contends that weighting adjustments can be used to compensate for non-response error due to non-response rates, and so we use weights in this study to compensate for circulation size using the circulation levels of the population in the Meltwater listing. Thus, weighing for circulation is the most efficient way to account for possible non-response bias due to possible differences between the sample and the general population.[6]

Since this is an audit design, we sent out two different surveys to our complete sample. We compared the responses from the two different surveys utilized in this research. We found that after application of circulation weights, the sample did not significantly differ on paper circulation, size of city or region where the paper is located. The respondents for each survey type also did not differ on race or sex. Finally, the percentage of individuals in each beat did not significantly vary between those who answered either survey. Differences in the answers between the contrasting surveys are not due to any demographic differences between the respondents.

We used similar techniques to collect data from television and social media personnel. We examined the same beats as we did with the newspaper media respondents, but the roles examined differed somewhat. The roles for the television media personnel were analyst, assignment desk, blogger, bureau chief, columnist, contributor, correspondent, critic, department head, deputy editor, editor, editor-at-large, editor-in-chief, editorial assistant, executive editor, foreign correspondent, freelance journalist, host, manager, managing editor, news editor, online editor, photo editor, producer, reporter, senior editor, or staff writer. The roles for the social media personnel were assignment desk, assistant editor, associate editor, blogger, bureau chief, columnist, contributor, correspondent, critic, department head, deputy editor, editor, editor-at-large, editor-in-chief, editorial assistant, editorial editor, executive producer, foreign correspondent, freelance journalist, host, manager, managing editor, news editor, online editor, photo editor, producer, reporter, senior editor, or staff writer. Our final sample was 105 television media personnel and 72 social media personnel. However, the response rate was disappointedly low for our television media (4.83%) and social media (3%) personnel. Given our discussions in the previous paragraphs, we are not as concerned with non-response bias as we are with potential statistical power in making audit comparisons.

The survey is an audit examination containing 11 scenarios that varied by a single critical characteristic. These scenarios are seen in Table 1-1 with the character alteration in *italicized* wording. Half of the respondents received the scenarios without italics. Those surveys were labeled Survey A. The other half of the respondents received surveys with the scenarios with the italicized term included in the scenarios. Those surveys were labeled Survey B. This introduced the experimental aspect of the research, since the only difference between the scenarios was tied to a gender, political, racial, religious, or sexuality dimension studied with that particular scenario. After each scenario, we asked the respondent: Do you think that this story should be used: (1) On the front page (2) In the front section but not front page (3) In the local section (4) A small news brief, but not a full story (5) Not used at all.[7] We followed this question with a second one: Do you think that it should be used as an online story? This created the dependent variables of our quantitative research. We also asked the respondents about their own sex, race, city size of where their paper is located, circulation of paper and region of the country where the paper is located.

As it concerned our television media respondents, we asked them whether they would use the story. They could either reply (1) Yes, we would use this story, (2) Maybe, if we had a slow news day, we would use the story or (3) No, we would not use the story. In the main part of the book, we used only answer number 1 to indicate a complete willingness to use a potential story. For our social media personnel, we asked if they would use the story as the basis for a blog, Twitter feed, an online story on the organization's website, or not use the story at all. We found that in all 11 scenarios, inclusion on the organization's website as a story was more common than blog or Twitter use. In the main part of our book, we noted whether the social media respondent agrees to use a story on the organization website. This will simplify our presentation and allow us to be as inclusive as possible with the social media personnel.

In the first scenario, we describe an airport robbery. We interchange the race of the robber and victim so that in one version the robber is black and the victim is white, while the races are switched in the second version. In the second scenario, we describe a small political rally where in the first version the group is PFLAG, a group that supports the LGBT community, and in the second version the group is PFOX, a group of ex-gays. In the third scenario, we have a rags-to-riches story where in the first version the individual is male and in the second version the individual is female. In the fourth scenario, we describe a conflict between a university and a student organization whereas in the first version the group is Baptist, and the second version the group is feminist. The fifth scenario concerns a peer-review study where one racial group is shown to work harder than another group. The first version highlights whites as the hard working group, and the second version highlights Hispanics. In the sixth scenario, we talk about the drive-by shooting of a romantic couple apparently motivated by hate, with the first version the couple being interracial and the second version the couple being same-sex. We describe a congressman caught in solicitation in the seventh scenario using a Republican in the first version and a Democrat in the second. The eighth scenario describes a kidnapping of a girl who in the first version is white and is black in the second version. The ninth scenario documents a shooting at a religious institution—a Baptist church in the first version and a mosque in the second version. In the tenth scenario, we used a story of a professor using hate speech against LGBT individuals in the first version and conservative Christians in the second version. Finally, in the eleventh scenario, a parent is accused of selling a daughter into slavery. The parent is the mother in the first version and the father in the second.

With this variety of scenarios, we are able to assess dimensions of politics, race, religion, gender, and sexuality. It is not possible to look at all possible aspects of these dimensions with so few scenarios, but we are able to assess some of the major accusations of media bias commonly heard. For example, some conservatives argue that the media pays more attention to scandals of conservatives than of progressives (Huston 2011; Olasky and Smith 2013). With our fourth scenario, we test this possibility. Along the lines of the media being more sensitive to progressive groups, we test their willingness to see LGBT individuals as victims in the second, sixth and tenth scenario. On the other hand, conservative Christians may represent a test of the willingness to see a conservative interest group as victims in the fourth, ninth and tenth scenarios. These scenarios obviously also have implications about whether there is media bias concerning sexuality and religion.

Scholars of race and gender have argued that the concerns of racial minorities and women have been overlooked in our society (Feagin and O'Brien 2004; Omi and Winant 2014; Pratto and Stewart 2012; Wildman and David 1994). Furthermore, some have argued that the media perpetuates stereotypes that marginalize minority ethnic groups and women (Amaya 2013; Giroux 1998; Smith, Choueiti and Gall 2011). We test the willingness of media personnel to perpetuate stereotypes of criminality and work ethic of people of color in the first and fifth scenarios, while the sixth and eighth scenarios help us to see if media personnel are sensitive to the victimization of people of color. Concerning women, the third scenario helps us test whether the media personnel can comparatively envision a successful businesswoman in a similar manner as a successful businessman, while the eleventh scenario helps us test the possibility that the traditional gender role of mother may create more judgment from media personnel when a parent sells his/her child into slavery.

The focus in the quantitative portion of our findings centers on whether a respondent places a story differently based on the potential scenario due to our changing a single component in that scenario and whether the story will be used in an online story. Since this is an experiential setting, there is no assurance that their stated treatment of a given scenario will match what will occur if they encounter such a story in reality. However, if the respondents react differently, even in this experiment, when told scenarios that differ in race, gender, religion, political affiliation or sexual preference, then there is little reason to doubt that they would provide a distinct treatment of a story in reality based on the particular demographic or social difference examined in a given scenario.

At the conclusion of all of these scenarios, we ask the respondents about why they place that story where they choose to place it or why they choose not to use the story at all. We coded these open-ended answers, and then we calculated how often a type of answer was used in each version of our survey. We engaged in an open-coding technique whereby one of us engaged in open coding for the first 100 respondents.[8] The codes naturally emerged from the data. Once we had the codes from those first 100 respondents, we used them on the rest of the sample. If a new code emerged, we talked about including it. Very few codes that did not emerge from the first 100 respondents occur often enough to be a factor in our analysis. We both coded the first 100 respondents and compared our answers to assess inter-rater reliability.[9] Where there was conflict between us, we went with the results of the first coder, since that researcher would code the rest of the sample.

The experimental nature of our design allows us to assess whether the respondents provide different answers based on the contrasting characteristics in these scenarios. It also allows us to see why they may be more likely to provide a favorable placement for one scenario than another scenario. Even if the placement of the two scenarios are nearly identical, these answers provide important insight about the possible different tones that articles may have depending on the demographic or social characteristics of the principles in the article. A discussion of our qualitative findings and their implications for understanding possible media bias are provided in the previous chapters.

Many themes we hope to evaluate will be evident in our qualitative data. For example, it is possible that media personnel will pay more attention when a mother offers her child up for sex slavery than if a father does so. Our quantitative data informs us whether stories with the version including a mother are placed in more prominent positions than stories featuring a father. However, even if we have such a finding, it is quite possible that this placement is due to factors not tied to our original theorizing. With the qualitative data, we are in a position to assess whether the notion of a violation of the traditional notion of a nurturing mother is driving the decision about where such a story is placed. In this way, we are able to assess the tone that each scenario likely generates and capture possible patterns of bias that are not evidently clear by merely examining whether a story is included and where that story is placed.

We have a methodology that allows us to quantitatively assess whether there is a different propensity to place a story based on certain social and demographic characteristics of the principles in the story, as well as an assessment from our respondents about why they made their decisions. This mixed-methods approach provides a more complete assessment of the possibility of media bias than previous research. It suffers from a lack of scenarios when sending a survey to a group as busy as media personnel, but we see this as a template for future possible work that uses scenarios to test dimensions we cannot address in this particular study.

Issues of Interpretation

There are important issues of our interpretation when using this methodology. One problem with interpreting short answer open-ended questions is that respondents generally provide short answers, and there is not an opportunity to probe those underdeveloped answers. There is a tendency to gain too little information. This is especially problematic with our current research design, since the respondents have motivation to answer the open-ended questions as quickly as possible. This issue is further complicated by the relatively low number of respondents in this project. This makes it harder to find trends within the answers of the respondents that correspond to the different scenarios.

Given these concerns, we discussed specific differences in the responses to the contrasting scenarios, but with a perspective of how the differences make sense in tandem with each other. For example, if we developed codes indicating that respondents are worried about the outrage a study will generate when whites are shown to be hard workers and codes showing a concern about whether the study should be done at all, then it is important to consider whether these respondents are exhibiting a similar motivation with only slightly distinct ideas. While those items would be coded separately, we would argue these themes likely work together, and a fair interpretation would be that hostility to the study motivates a fear of social backlash and a desire to question whether such a study should be done. This interpretative technique better allowed us to gauge general themes in the epistemological culture in media communities and how that culture can shape the presentation of information.

Due to the relatively small number of respondents and our desire to find themes from multiple differences, we did some findings at the .1 level and even mention some non-significant findings. However, we only did this if such findings supported a larger theme documented elsewhere. This fits with our intention to look for groups of codings, rather than (with some exceptions) a single overarching explanatory code to gain a nuanced understanding of the epistemological culture within the media. This is less than desirable, but we are not attempting to conduct a strict statistical analysis with our qualitative data. This technique fits with our attempt to locate epistemological patterns in our respondents' approach to news stories.

Chapter Notes

Introduction

1. A more in-depth discussion of the methods in this book can be found in the appendix, where we discussed how our sample was collected and the rationale behind our audit experimental methodology.

2. Perhaps this attitude is best typified by the arguably best known radio media personality—Rush Limbaugh. He often says that his conservative show does not need equal time, but that it is equal time.

Chapter 1

1. It is important to note that the majority group should be seen in terms of power and not numbers. Having disproportionate power is a common metric by which we have defined majority groups (Brinkerhoff, David B., Suzanne T. Ortega, and Rose Weitz. 2012. *Essentials of Sociology*. Belmont, CA: Wadsworth/Thompson Learning; Parillo, Vincent N. 1997. "Strangers to these shores." Boston: Allyn and Bacon). Thus even though white heterosexual males are a declining percentage of the population, they are still generally seen as the "majority" group in terms of societal power.

2. Recent work (Yancey, George, Sam Reimer, and Jake O'Connell. 2015. "How academics view conservative Protestants." *Sociology of Religion* 76(3):315–36) suggests that at least some academics define fundamentalists as those accepting the Bible as the Word of God. According to the 2012 American National Election Studies, this would include about a third of all Americans.

3. In the appendix we discussed why we weighted the data by circulation.

4. Power analysis calculations indicted a power score of .4866 for the Research Study scenario and .488 for the Couples Shooting scenario at $p < .05$ level. Since we would expect to see medium size effects at .5 we may not pick up differences if there are medium effects, and it is clearly the case that this sample will not detect small effects on these variables. Thus, attention to possible effects at $p < .1$ is warranted.

5. Once again, power analysis indicates a power score of .4925, indicating an inability to determine small differences with this data on this particular scenario.

6. The mean for the percentages of scenarios used for online stories is 82.71 with a standard deviation of 15.46.

7. The respondents had the option of stating that they would definitely run a story, maybe run a story or would not run a story at all.

8. Elimination of the social media respondents did not have a similar effect for any of the other scenarios.

Chapter 2

1. There is a fourth scenario where we switched an interracial couple with a same-sex couple, but in these three scenarios we directly switched one racial group for another racial group enabling us to make direct assertions about potential racial effects.

2. OLS Regression analysis with city size, circulation, whether the respondent is a reporter, sex and region of the United States as well as which scenario used indicated that survey and newspaper circulation were significant in predicting the level of placement of the story in the newspaper. Thus, the tendency of respondents to place the story in a more prominent position if the robber is white is not due to different characteristics of the respondents given that scenario.

3. We suspected that much of this effect is tied to the presence of social media personnel with a politically conservative focus. In our sample five of the six social media personnel who identified with a politically conservative perspective received the scenario with the black robber. Out of these five respondents, five of them stated that they would put the story online. However, eliminating social media personnel did not make a dramatic alteration in the percentage favoring the story of the black robber (63.2% v. 53.6%; ns). Thus, we may be looking at a subcultural effect tied to social media personnel rather than a result tied to the inclusion of political conservatives.

4. All three types of media groups were more likely to be interested if the robbery was racially motivated when the robber was white, although for television and social media respondents the difference was not significant due to lack of statistical power.

5. It is reasonable to consider the $p < .1$ level with the social media respondent since the number who provided answers that could be coded ($n = 40$) is small.

6. Once again of the 6 social media respondents who identified themselves as conservative, 5 of them received the version of the survey with White workers as the hard working workers. Four of the five stated that they would run the story online. However, removal of the six conservative social media personnel did not dramatically alter our statistical results (47.8% v. 22.3%: ns). One must consider the possibility that there is some unique dynamic in social media that is creating this divergent result.

7. In our weighted sample, 88.1% of our respondents are white. It is possible that whites are not overrepresented in the general media, in comparison to the general population, and that we oversampled racial majority group members. However, given the high percentage of whites in this current sample, it is not feasible to argue that our results are due to our sampling a high percentage of racial minorities.

Chapter 3

1. There is an argument about gender identity that minimizes the importance of male/female physical differences. However, most Americans still cling to the notion that men are physically different than woman and this distinguishes gender-issue concerns from racial-issue concerns.

2. An interesting way of conceptualizing the notion among Christians that sex differences are innate while racial differences are not can be found in research concerning gender attitudes in multiracial congregations (Yancey and Kim 2008). This research found that in theologically

conservative congregations, racial diversity was positively related to more traditional gender attitudes. The authors speculate that conservative Christian congregations with more progressive racial attitudes may feel more freedom to articulate less progressive gender attitudes. Yet, one still may ask why those who are proactive in addressing a racialized society lag behind as it concerns confronting patriarchy. A reasonable answer is that these Christians are motivated to deal with racial problems since they perceive individuals of different races as the same before God, but still hold on to notions of innate male/female differences that justify divinely inspired contrasting gender roles.

3. In both scenarios we were very conscious about making sure that we used androgynous names so that the same name would be used in both versions of the scenario. This made the scenarios exactly alike except for the sex of the principle and greatly reduced the possibility of any other factor within the scenarios contributing to differential treatment of the potential story.

4. This also may be the result tied to the fact that five of the six social media personnel who identify as conservative also received the scenario where Pat was male. Of those five respondents, four would include the story online. This is a small effect but with our sample size of social media personnel, it may be enough of an effect to create the distinction between the social media sample and the other samples. However, when we removed the conservative social media personnel the difference was not greatly abated (66.9% v. 40,8%; ns).

5. We found the same propensity to look at the male Pat as an encouragement among television media personnel but not among social media personnel. In neither case is the difference significant.

6. For example, today females receive more undergraduate degrees than males.

7. In this case we found the same higher propensity to see the story as a feel good story for the male Pat among both the television and newspaper personnel. In fact, this propensity was significantly higher among the social media personnel, despite the low numbers in the sample (24% v. 0%: $p < .05$).

8. For example whether they mention that Pat was a man or woman in the statement or through pronouns.

9. However, it should be noted that social media personnel were much less likely to include this story than newspaper or television media personnel. A little less than half of all social media personnel (49.5%) were interested in putting the story online. Even though this is a sensationalist story, social media personnel may have a distinctive criteria for what will draw attention to websites.

10. Indeed, we found that our respondents were slightly more likely to mention being shocked when the story concerned the father than the mother, although this difference was not significant (18.7% v. 13.9%; ns).

11. Our weighted sample is 44.3% female. Indicating women are underrepresented in this sample. The underrepresentation in the sample is relative to the general population. However, this does not suggest there would be an effect on the social atmosphere of the newsroom, but rather buttressing of a potential egalitarian attitude.

12. Of course there is a whole range of other possible male/female differences than these obvious physical distinctions. Exploring these possible sex differences is an enterprise unto itself and one that we are not willing to explore in the context of this particular research effort. Thus, we only point out the obvious physical differences to make our point in a noncontroversial manner that men and women do possess noticeable distinctions.

13. We distinguish between issues of sex and gender as we take a traditional approach to these two concepts. Thus, sex is biologically driven while gender, and by extension some issues of sexuality, are determined by society expectations. In our treatment of these principles, we ignore the debate over the transgendered to maintain simplicity in our examination. Issues of sexuality can also be tied to arguments within gender studies, but we treat them distinctly given the culture war implications of those issues.

Chapter 4

1. There is a plethora of research indicating that intergroup contact has a powerful effect on moderating hostile attitudes (Yancey 2007; Pettigrew 1998; Pettigrew and Tropp 2000; Powers and Ellison 1995; Herek and Capitanio 1996; Heinze and Horn 2009; Lee, Farrell, and Link 2004). This research has generally focused on racial, sexuality and socioeconomic status groups. Contact effects with minority religious groups has also been analyzed (Jung 2012; Gervais 2011), but little research has been done about contact effects with Christians.

2. This concern is not without merit. Kelley (Kelley, Dean M. 1977. *Why conservative churches are growing: A study in sociology of religion*: Mercer University Press) argues that Christian institutions that do not maintain their epistemological boundaries are more likely to lose members than more "strict" churches.

3. The differences in the use of the story in television and social media did not significantly differ from each other, although the social media personnel did show more willingness to use the story of the Baptist rather than feminist organization (61.8% v. 46.5: ns) at a high enough level to believe that with a larger sample that a significant difference may emerge in this media dimension.

4. However, it should be noted that such majority group status may no longer be the case or that Christians may lose that status. Yancey and Williamson's (Yancey, George A., and David A. Williamson. 2014. *So Many Christians, So Few Lions: Is There Christianophobia in the United States?*: Rowman & Littlefield) work indicates that those who tend to have animosity towards conservative Christians also tend to have higher levels of education and socioeconomic status. It is plausible that they currently have the social power to significantly marginalize this religious out-group or that they soon will have such power. Given this changing social reality, it may be useful to rethink the assumption that simply because Christianity has been the majority religious group in the United States that this will be the state of that faith for the conceivable future.

5. However it is not clear how many of these burnings are the result of arson (Ellis, Ralph, and Mariano Castillo. 2015. "No Hate Crimes Found in 6 Black Church Fires, Authorities Say." St. Louis, MO: Fox2 Now). Yet the possibility that religious organizations had been attacked so soon after the Charleston tragedy certainly found its place in the news cycle.

6. These differences hold up, although they are not significant, when looking at television and social media personnel as it concerns measures of discrimination. However, in measurement of concern about hate crimes the distinctions between the scenarios with mosque and church are not notable.

7. While it may be tempting to dismiss the possibility that there are societal values and conflicts that can lead to violence against Christians, one only need to look at the actions of Floyd Corkins, who attempted to kill members of the Family Research Council, a Christian activist group. Reportedly, Corkins was influenced by culture war arguments offered by progressive groups before attempting murder. While he failed to actually take a life, his attempt was deemed serious enough for him to be sentence to 25 years in prison.

8. We found that among television news media that there was a slight (non-significant) tendency to favor the story of hate speech against Christians.

9. However, this tendency was not true for television media personnel, as none of them saw the homophobic professor as bigoted.

10. The actual probability score is .056.

11. Although it should be recognized that American Baptist is a denomination known for being relatively theologically progressive.

12. However, there was a strong propensity for the story among social media personnel (61.7% v. 29.1%; p < .1) when the congressman was a Democrat. This may be simply due to the fact that five of the six conservative social media personnel happen to disproportionately

receive that option from our survey. Four of those respondents stated that the story should go online. However, this propensity was not greatly reduced when we removed those six respondents from the sample (61.7% v. 32.2%: ns). Political allegiance of the conservative respondents is not driving this result.

13. This tendency may not be limited to journalists. Previous work (Bolce, Louis, and Gerald De Maio. 2008. "A prejudice for the thinking classes." *American Politics Research* 36(2):155–85; Yancey, George A., and David A Williamson. 2014. *So Many Christians, So Few Lions: Is There Christianophobia in the United States?*: Rowman & Littlefield) has found that academics are more hostile to conservative Protestants than political conservatives. It is possible that both academics and journalists are the type of professionals that serve as advocates for a culturally progressive agenda. Such professionals would have the ability to dictate the type of issues that gain attention in the larger culture.

Chapter 5

1. This same difference was found in all separate samples of newspaper, television and social media personnel, although the latter two samples did not produce significant findings due to low numbers of respondents.

2. Although this difference does not reach the standard level of significance it is so close (p = .053) that we feel it is worth mentioning. The main reason why this difference does not reach a level of significance is because television media personnel were more open to getting a comment from PFOX than PFLAG, although this difference was not significant (22.8% v. 18.4%: ns). When we eliminated the television media personnel from the sample then the difference between the two scenarios was significant (37.2% v. 23.4%: p < .05). It is not clear whether there are dynamics of television news that produce a higher desire to gain the perspective of a group like PFOX than PFLAG, and our sample size does not make an examination of this possibility feasible.

3. However most of this effect was due to the overwhelming tendency of newspaper media personnel to favor the PFLAG scenario.

4. It can also be argued that homosexuality may not be genetic but that the way a child is socialized creates a situation whereby his or her sexuality is beyond volitional choice (Bradley, Susan J., and Kenneth J. Zucker. 1997. "Gender Identity Disorder: A Review of the Past 10 Years." *Journal of the American Academy of Child & Adolescent Psychiatry* 36(7):872–80; Burton, Simon. 2006. "The Causes of Homosexuality: What Science Tells Us." *The Jubilee Centre, Cambridge*). Those are the types of issues that we are not ready to assess at this present time but only wish to point out that this is a research question that is currently in flux.

5. There is a higher tendency to cover the interracial couple shooting than the same-sex couple shooting among social media personnel (65% v. 36.9%: p < .1). It is also worth noting that only 56.3% of the television media personnel and 55.1% of the social media personnel will use the story in their reports. It is not clear why newspaper media personnel are more committed to reporting on this story than other media personnel, but there is little doubt that this is the case in our sample.

6. This same tendency was found in each separate sample, although the difference was not significant for the television and social media sample.

7. However, television media personnel actually were less inclined to be concerned about the larger community for the interracial couple than the same-sex couple, although the difference was slight and not significant.

8. This same relations was found in all three samples although it was not significant in the Social Media sample, it was significant at p < .1 among television media personnel and p < .05 among newspaper media personnel.

9. Even though our scenario deals with an interracial couple, it is likely that the respon-

dents envision at least one of the members of the couple as a racial minority. Indeed, if both members of the couple are white, then by definition they cannot be an interracial couple.

Chapter 6

1. For example, the finding of the Holder justice department does not indicate strong evidence that Michael Brown was surrendering when he was shot and thus, the common chant "hands up, don't shoot" is not substantiated. Nevertheless, the shooting in Ferguson was still an important catalyst for the Black Lives Matter movement as they had the attention of media personnel to open up a larger conversation on the criminal justice system.

2. However, there clearly are other factors that are relevant in the visibility of Black Lives Matters. For example, their savvy use of social media should not be discounted (Grossmann, Matt. 2017. "Media Bias (Real and Preceived) and the Rise of Partisan Media." Washington, DC: Niskanen Center; Shapiro, Ben. 2011. *Primetime Propaganda: The True Hollywood Story of How the Left Took Over Your TV*. Northampton, MA: Broadside Books).

3. This is not unlike the argument made by race scholars that whites can experience individual prejudice and discrimination in a certain situation, but racism is about prejudice plus power. As such, whites are not in a position to experience true racism (Asante, Molefi Kete. 2003. *Afrocentricity, the theory of social change*. Chicago, IL: African American Images; Omi, Michael, and Howard Winant. 2014. *Racial formation in the United States*: Routledge).

4. While all of our social media results are tentative due to the low number of respondents, we have more confidence in this one due to the strength of our findings. The difference between the two scenarios resulted in a p score that barely missed significance (p = .052). While not technically significant it is a very impressive p score given our low number of social media personnel respondents.

5. For newspaper media personnel there was a very low percentage (5.7%) that stated that race was unimportant, while the percent of social media personnel that stated that race was unimportant when asked about blacks was not much higher than it was for social media personnel (19.9% v. 17.7%). Thus, the difference for social media personnel was their willingness to state that race was unimportant when discussing a white robber as well as a black one.

6. According to Yancey and Williamson, those with anti–Christian hostility are more educated, more likely to be white, wealthier and more likely to be male than other individuals.

7. Of course this is not the only reason for the development of such media organizations. Indeed, one can think of several such organizations that support culturally progressive ideals (i.e., Mother Jones, Huffington Post). However, those who tend to support these media outlets may not necessarily be as hostile towards traditional media institutions as those who support culturally conservative perspectives. Even as there are niche media outlets that are not threatened by the biases documented in our work, the individuals served by these outlets are more trusting of the general media and more willing to look to that media for some of their information.

8. We originally used 12 questions; however, one of the questions was flawed and did not generate answers that fit into how we operationalized our variables.

9. Indeed, one potential respondent emailed us and offered to fill out the survey if he was guaranteed to win the prize. Of course, we are not able to make such a guarantee or pay all of our respondents the amount we offered as a prize.

Appendix

1. Of course when asking media personnel after a story is published, a researcher is certain to run into problems of social desirability bias. Media personnel have a powerful incentive to

project an image of objectivity and thus are highly motivated to justify contrasting treatment of similar stories. Thus, confronting media personnel with accusations of favoritism, which is a common tactic of different activists, is much more likely to generate attempts at defensive evasions rather than honest assessments of potential bias.

2. Pager is able to conduct her research in a more natural setting than we are. Yet our work has the advantage that we are not dependent on the actions of trained testers, who may not always be able to act in an identical manner, and thus we can better isolate the potential effect of the characteristic we wish to test.

3. Clearly some of these roles (i.e., editor-in-chief) are more central to determining what stories are published and how they are framed than others. However, we decided to cast a wide net since we contend that the media operates in a general social atmosphere that influences those who write and edit the content. As such, there is value in understanding the perspectives of those individuals that some might consider as having a periphery position (i.e., correspondents) in the social system. Including such individuals not only increased the statistical power of our analysis, but it also provided us with a broader understanding of the general social culture in the media.

4. After the initial contact, we replaced any emails that bounced back to us, but we did not do this after sending out the reminder emails. This allowed us to be certain that we made 2400 initial good contacts.

5. The use of unweighted data in regression models has been shown by Winship and Radbill (Winship, Christopher, and Larry Radbill. 1994. "Sampling Weights and Regression Analysis." *Sociological Method and Research* 23(2):230–57) to create larger than warranted standard errors. Thus, the use of weighted data is unwarranted in our exploratory regression models to identify possible mediating variables between the scenarios and hypothetical placement in a newspaper.

6. This is not to say that there are no other potentially important factors such as race, sex, region, etc.; however, we have no way of measuring those qualities within the larger Meltwater listing.

7. In some ways, we are fortunate that a majority of our respondents are in newspaper media. This question not only assesses whether a story will be included in media but the importance attached to that story. It is the sort of question we are not able to ask television and social media personnel. Within those institutions we can only assess if a story is to be used or not. While ideally, we would have a better response rate in all three areas of media, if we are to have only one media group with a high response rate, it is best for it to be the newspaper media personnel.

8. For the information in the television media sample, both authors coded all of the responses. We did not do an inter-rater reliability check with the social media sample, as we felt that the information from the two larger samples was sufficient. Furthermore, the small sample of the social media personnel did not allow us to have enough of a sample to feel confident in any inter-rater reliability scores.

9. The average inter-rater reliability score is 92.195 with a median of 94 and standard deviation of 8.105. There were variables with lower than desired ratings. The major difference in the two ratings was the higher tendency of one author to assign codes than the other researcher. We disregarded scores below a .8 threshold with one exception. We had several scores between .7 and .8 in the Homeless to Millionaire scenario. We considered dropping this scenario, but we only had one other gender-based scenario. So we changed one of the variables to objectively measure gender and kept another variable, dealing with encouragement of businesspersons, for our analysis. While the findings fit the general conclusions of other findings concerning gender and to a lesser extent race, we acknowledge the need to confirm these results in future research.

References

Abrajano, M. (2010). Are blacks and Latinos responsible for the passage of Proposition 8? Analyzing voter attitudes on California's proposal to ban same-sex marriage in 2008. *Political Research Quarterly, 63*(4), 922–932.

Aday, S. (2010). Chasing the bad news: An analysis of 2005 Iraq and Afghanistan War coverage on NBC and Fox News channel. *Journal of Communication, 60,* 144–164.

Akbarzadeh, S., & Smith, B. (2005). The representation of Islam and Muslims in the media. *School of Political and Social Inquiry.*

Alexander, M. (2012). *The new Jim Crow: Mass incarceration in the age of colorblindness.* New York: The New Press.

Ali, Y. (2012). Shariah and citizenship—How Islamophobia is creating a second-class citizenry in America. *California Law Review, 100*(4) 1027–1068.

Alterman, E. (2008). *What liberal media? The truth about bias and the news.* New York: Basic Books.

Amaya, H. (2013). *Citizenship excess: Latino/as, media, and the nation.* New York: NYU Press.

An, J., Cha, M., Gummadi, K. P., Crowcroft, J., & Quercia, D. (2012). *Visualizing media bias through twitter.* Paper presented at the Sixth International AAAI Conference on Weblogs and Social Media.

Andersen, R., & Fetner, T. (2008). Cohort differences in tolerance of homosexuality attitudinal change in Canada and the United States, 1981–2000. *Public Opinion Quarterly, 72*(2), 311–330.

Anderson, B. C. (2013). *South Park conservatives: The revolt against liberal media bias.* Washington, D.C.: Regnery Publishing.

Appiah, O., Knobloch-Westerwick, S., & Alter, S. (2013). Ingroup favoritism and outgroup derogation: Effects of news valence, character race, and recipient race on selective news reading. *Journal of Communication, 63*(3), 517–534.

Armstrong, M. J., & Wildman, S. M. (2008). Teaching race/teaching whiteness: Transforming colorblindness to color insight. *Santa Clara Univ. Legal Studies Research Paper,* No. 08–51.

Asante, M. K. (2003). *Afrocentricity, the theory of social change.* Chicago, IL: African American Images.

Avery, A., Chase, J., Johansson, L., Litvak, S., Montero, D., & Wydra, M. (2007). America's changing attitudes toward homosexuality, civil unions, and same-gender marriage: 1977–2004. *Social Work, 52*(1), 71–79.

Awad, I. (2011). Latinas/os and the mainstream press: The exclusions of professional diversity. *Journalism, 12*(5), 515–532.

References

Bagdikian, B. H. (2014). *The new media monopoly: A completely revised and updated edition with seven new chapters*. Boston, MA: Beacon Press.

Bailey, J. M., & Pillard, R. C. (1991). A genetic study of male sexual orientation. *Archives of general psychiatry, 48*(12), 1089–1096.

Balkaran, S. (1999). Mass media and racism. *Yale Political Quarterly, 21*(1), 10–13.

Baron, D. P. (2005). Persistent media bias. *Journal of Public Economics, 90*, 1–36.

Basow, S. A. (1992). *Gender: Stereotypes and roles*. Belmont, CA: Thomson Brooks/Cole Publishing Co.

Baum, M. A., & Groeling, T. (2008). New media and the polarization of American political discourse. *Political Communication, 25*, 345–365.

Baunach, D. M. (2012). Changing same-sex marriage attitudes in America from 1988 through 2010. *Public Opinion Quarterly, 76*(2), 364–378.

Becker, A. B. (2014). Employment discrimination, local school boards, and LGBT civil rights: Reviewing 25 years of public opinion data. *International Journal of Public Opinion Research*, edu003.

Becker, J., Niehaves, B., & Klose, K. (2005). A framework for epistemological perspectives on simulation. *Journal of artificial societies and social simulation, 8*(4). Retrieved from http://jasss.soc.surrey.ac.uk/8/4/1.html

Behr, R. L., & Iyengar, S. (1985). Television news, real-world cues, and changes in the public agenda. *Public Opinion Quarterly, 49*(1), 38–57.

Berger, P. (1986). *The capitalist revolution*. New York: Basic Books.

Berkowitz, P. (2015). The left's crusade against free speech. Retrieved from http://www.realclearpolitics.com/articles/2015/05/10/the_lefts_crusade_against_free_speech_126535.html

Bernhardt, D., Krasa, S., & Polborn, M. (2008). Political polarization and the electoral effects of media bias. *Journal of Public Economics, 92*, 1092–1104.

Berry, P., & Franks, T. J. (2010). Women in the world of corporate business: Looking at the glass ceiling. *Contemporary Issues in Education Research, 3*(2), 1.

Best, J. (1997). Victimization and the victim industry. *Society, 34*(4), 9–17.

Black, J., Steele, B., & Barney, R. (1999). Doing ethics in journalism: A handbook with case studies. (3rd ed.). Boston: Allyn and Bacon.

Blumenfeld, W. J. (2006). Christian privilege and the promotion of "secular" and not-so "secular" mainline Christianity in public schooling and in the larger society. *Equity & Excellence in Education, 39*(3), 195–210.

Bohrmann, H., Klaus, E., & Machill, M. (2007). *Media industry, journalism culture and communication policies in Europe*. Cologne, Germany: Halem.

Bolce, L., & De Maio, G. (2008). A prejudice for the thinking classes. *American Politics Research, 36*(2), 155–185.

Bolzendahl, C. I., & Myers, D. J. (2004). Feminist attitudes and support for gender equality: Opinion change in women and men, 1974–1998. *Social Forces, 83*(2), 759–789.

Bonilla-Silva, E. (2003). *Racism without racists: Color-blind racism and the persistence of racial inequality in the United States*. New York: Rowman and Littlefield.

Bonilla-Silva, E., Lewis, A., & Embrick, D. G. (2004). "I did not get that job because of a black man...": The story lines and testimonies of color-blind racism. *Sociological Forum. 19*(4), 555–581.

Bradley, S. J., & Zucker, K. J. (1997). Gender identity disorder: A review of the past 10 years. *Journal of the American Academy of Child & Adolescent Psychiatry, 36*(7), 872–880.

Branton, R. P., & Dunaway, J. (2009). Slanted newspaper coverage of immigration: The importance of economics and geography. *Policy Studies Journal, 37*(2), 257–273.

Brinkerhoff, D. B., Ortega, S. T., & Weitz, R. (2012). *Essentials of sociology* (9th ed.). Belmont, CA: Wadsworth/Thompson Learning.

Bullock, K. H., & Jafri, G. J. (2000). Media (mis) representations: Muslim women in the Canadian nation. *Canadian Woman Studies, 20*(2), 35.

Burdette, A. M., Ellison, C. G., & Hill, T. D. (2005). Conservative Protestantism and tolerance toward homosexuals: An examination of potential mechanisms. *Sociological Inquiry, 75*(2), 177–196.

Burgoon, J. K., & Burgoon, M. (1980). Predictors of newspaper readership. *Journalism and Mass Communication Quarterly, 57*(4), 589.

Burton, S. (2006). The causes of homosexuality: What science tells us. *The Jubilee Centre, Cambridge.* Retrieved from http://www.jubilee-centre.org/causes-homosexuality-science-tells-us-simon-burton/

Butler, D. M., & Schofield, E. (2010). Were newspapers more interested in pro-Obama letters to the editor in 2008? Evidence from a field experiment. *American Politics Research, 38*(2), 356–371.

Cabrera, N. L. (2014). Exposing whiteness in higher education: White male college students minimizing racism, claiming victimization, and recreating white supremacy. *Race Ethnicity and Education, 17*(1), 30–55.

Callanan, V. J. (2012). Media consumption, perceptions of crime risk and fear of crime: Examining race/ethnic differences. *Sociological Perspectives, 55*(1), 93–115.

Calvert, C., Carnley, K., Link, B., & Riedemann, L. (2013). Conversion therapy and free speech: A doctrinal and theoretical first amendment analysis. *William & Mary Journal Women and Law, 20,* 525–571.

Campbell, B., & Manning, J. (2014). Microaggression and moral cultures. *Comparative Sociology, 13*(6), 692–726.

Campbell, R., & Wasco, S. M. (2000). Feminist approaches to social science: Epistemological and methodological tenets. *American Journal of Community Psychology, 28*(6), 773–791.

Carr, L. G. (1997). *Color-blind racism.* Thousand Oaks, CA: Sage Publications.

Caspari, G. G. (1982). *The impatient press: Placing black newspapers in the ideologies of black progress.* Paper presented at the Annual Meeting of the Association for Education in Journalism and Mass Communication, Corvallis, OR.

Chapman, M. W. (2015). The Reverend Graham defends FRC: 'We are targets of the liberal media's anti–Christian bias, but it doesn't mean that we stop.' Retrieved from https://www.cnsnews.com/blog/michael-w-chapman/rev-graham-defends-frc-we-are-targets-liberal-medias-anti-christian-bias-it

Coenders, M., & Scheepers, P. (2003). The effect of education on nationalism and ethnic exclusionism: An international comparison. *Political Psychology, 24*(2), 313–343.

Cohan, W. D. (2014). *The price of silence: The duke lacrosse scandal, the power of the elite, and the corruption of our great universities.* New York: Scribner.

Cole, D. (2000). *No equal justice: Race and class in the American criminal justice system.* New York: The New Press.

Collins, R. L. (2011). Content analysis of gender roles in media: Where are we now and where should we go? *Sex Roles, 64*(3–4), 290–298.

Cooper, A. (2006). Diagnosing "missing white woman syndrome." *Anderson Cooper 360 Blog.* Retrieved from http://www.cnn.com/CNN/Programs/anderson.cooper.360/blog/2006/03/diagnosing-missing-white-woman.html

Correa, T., Hinsley, A. W., & De Zuniga, H. G. (2010). Who interacts on the web? The intersection of users' personality and social media use. *Computers in Human Behavior, 26*(2), 247–253.

Correll, S. J. (2007). Getting a job: Is there a motherhood penalty? *American Journal of Sociology, 112,* 1297–1338.

Cortese, A. J. P. (2006). *Opposing hate speech.* Santa Barbara, CA: Greenwood Publishing Group.

Coulter, A. (2002). *Slander: Liberal lies about the American right.* New York: Three Rivers Press.

Couper, M. P., & Miller, P. B. (2008). Web survey methods: Introduction. *The Public Opinion Quarterly, 5*(72), 831–835.

Covert, T. J., & Wasburn, P. C. (2007). Measuring media bias: A content analysis of *Time* and

References

Newsweek coverage of domestic social issues, 1975–2000. *Social Science Quarterly, 88*(3), 690–706.

Cromwell, D., & Edwards, D. (2006). Guardians of power: The myth of the liberal media. *London: Pluto.*

D'Alessio, D., & Allen, M. (2000). Media bias in presidential elections: A meta-analysis. *Journal of Communication, 50*(4), 133–156.

Dalton, R. J., Beck, P. A., & Huckfeldt, R. (1998). Partisan cues and the media: Information flows in the 1992 presidential election. *American Political Science Review, 92*(1), 111–126.

Dautrich, K., & Hartley, T. H. (1999). *How the news media fail American voters: Causes, consequences, and remedies.* New York: Columbia University Press.

Dempsey, K. (2013). Christians continue to be undermined by mainstream media. Retrieved from https://www.christianpost.com/news/christians-continue-to-be-undermined-by-mainstream-media-103620/

Dennis, E. E. (1997). How "liberal" are the media anyway? The continuing conflict of professionalism and partisanship. *Journal of Press/Politics, 2*(4), 115–119.

Deuze, M. (2003). The web and its journalisms: Considering the consequences of different types of newsmedia online. *New Media & Society, 5*(2), 203–230.

De Waal, E., Schönbach, K., & Lauf, E. (2005). Online newspapers: A substitute or complement for print newspapers and other information channels? *Communications, 30*(1), 55–72.

Dillman, D. A., Phelps, G., Tortora, R., Swift, K., Kohrell, J., Berck, J., & Messer, B. L. (2009). Response rate and measurement differences in mixed-mode surveys using mail, telephone, interactive voice response (IVR) and the Internet. *Social Science Research, 38*(1), 1–18.

Dimmick, J., Chen, Y., & Li, Z. (2004). Competition between the Internet and traditional news media: The gratification-opportunities niche dimension. *The Journal of Media Economics, 17*(1), 19–33.

Dixon, T. L., & Linz, D. (2000). Overrepresentation and underrepresentation of African Americans and Latinos as lawbreakers on television news. *Journal of Communication, 50*(2), 131–154.

Doane, A. W., & Bonilla-Silva, E. (2003). *White out: The continuing significance of racism.* New York: Routledge.

Domke, D., Fan, D. P., Fibison, M., Shah, D. V., Smith, S. S., & Watts, M. D. (1997). News media, candidates and issues, and public opinion in the 1996 presidential campaign. *Journalism & Mass Communication Quarterly, 74*(4), 718–737.

Donsbach, W., & Klett, B. (1993). Subjective objectivity. How journalists in four countries define a key term of their profession. *Gazette (Leiden, Netherlands), 51*(1), 53–83.

Douglas, S. J. (1995). *Where the girls are: Growing up female with the mass media.* New York: Three Rivers Press.

Dowler, K. (2002). Media influence on attitudes toward guns and gun control. *American Journal of Criminal Justice, 26*(2), 235–247.

Dreher, R. (2014). A response from Vandy's misfit Christian. Retrieved from http://www.theamericanconservative.com/dreher/vanderbilt-misfit-christian-tish-harrison-warren/

Drew, E. M. (2011). "Coming to terms with our own racism": Journalists grapple with the racialization of their news. *Critical Studies in Media Communication, 28*(4), 353–373.

Duggan, M., & Brenner, J. (2013). *The demographics of social media users, 2012.* Washington, D.C: Pew Research Center's Internet & American Life Project. Retrieved from http://www.pewinternet.org/2013/02/14/the-demographics-of-social-media-users-2012/

Durfee, A. (2011). "I'm not a victim, she's an abuser": Masculinity, victimization, and protection orders. *Gender & Society, 25*(3), 316–334.

Dutton, W. H. (1996). Network rules of order: Regulating speech in public electronic fora. *Media, Culture & Society, 18*(2), 269–290.

Eagly, A. H. (2013). *Sex differences in social behavior: A social-role interpretation.* New York: Psychology Press.

References

Edogbanya, O. P. (2016). Homosexuality: Innate or acquired? *MAYFEB Journal of Biology, 1,* 7–21.

Ehrenreich, B., & Ehrenreich, J. (1977). The professional managerial class. *Radical America, 11,* 7–31.

Eisinger, R. M., Veenstra, L. R., & Koehn, J. P. (2007). What media bias? Conservative and liberal labeling in major U.S. newspapers. *The Harvard International Journal of Press/Politics, 12*(1), 17–36.

Ellis, R., & Castillo, M. (2015). No hate crimes found in 6 black church fires, authorities say. Retrieved from http://fox2now.com/2015/06/30/fires-at-black-churches-prompts-federal-investigation/

Ellison, C. G., Echevarria, S., & Smith, B. (2005). Religion and abortion attitudes among US Hispanics: Findings from the 1990 Latino national political survey. *Social Science Quarterly, 86*(1), 192–208.

Embrick, D. G., & Henricks, K. (2013). Discursive color lines at work: How epithets and stereotypes are racially unequal. *Symbolic Interaction, 36*(2), 197–215.

England, P. (2010). The gender revolution uneven and stalled. *Gender & Society, 24*(2), 149–166.

Enns, C. Z. (1997). *Feminist theories and feminist psychotherapies: Origins, themes, and variations.* Binghamton, NY: Harrington Park Press/The Haworth Press.

Entman, R. M., & Rojecki, A. (2001). The black image in the white mind: Media and race in America. *Journal of Communication, 51*(1), 196–227.

Eveland, W. P., & Shah, D. V. (2003). The impact of individual and interpersonal factors on perceived news media bias. *Political Psychology, 24*(1), 101–117.

Everbach, T. (2013). Women's (mis) representation in news media. In C. L. Armstrong (Ed.), *Media disparity: A gender battleground* (pp. 15–26). Lanham, MD: Rowman & Littlefield.

Feagin, J. R., & O'Brien, E. (2004). *White men on race: Power, privilege, and the shaping of cultural consciousness.* Boston: Beacon Press.

Fields, S. (2015). The slow death of free speech: How the illiberal left silences those who won't go along to get along. Retrieved from http://www.washingtontimes.com/news/2015/may/20/suzanne-fields-how-the-liberal-left-is-killing-fre/

Figdor, C. (2010). Objectivity in the news: Finding a way forward. *Journal of Mass Media Ethics, 25*(1), 19–33.

Fiorina, M. P., Abrams, S. J., & Pope, J. (2006). *Culture war? The myth of a polarized America.* Boston : Longman Publishing.

Fischer, E., & Reuber, A. R. (2011). Social interaction via new social media: (How) can interactions on twitter affect effectual thinking and behavior? *Journal of Business Venturing, 26*(1), 1–18.

Fishman, M. (1988). *Manufacturing the news.* Austin, TX : University of Texas Press.

Fore, W. (2014). Joyful heart is good medicine: Sexuality conversion bans in the courts. *Michigan Journal of Gender and Law, 21*(2), 311–340.

Frith, S., & Meech, P. (2007). Becoming a journalist: Journalism education and journalism culture. *Journalism, 8*(2), 137–164.

Funt, D. (2015). Gender doesn't tell the whole story for Clinton coverage. Retrieved from http://www.cjr.org/watchdog/press_gender_bias_of_clinton_a_new_york_state_of_mind.php

Gallagher, C. A. (2003). Color-blind privilege: The social and political functions of erasing the color line in post race America. *Race, Gender & Class,* 22–37.

Gentzkow, M., & Shapiro, J. M. (2006). Media bias and reputation. *Journal of Political Economy, 114*(2), 280–316.

Gershon, S. A. (2012). When race, gender, and the media intersect: Campaign news coverage of minority congresswomen. *Journal of Women, Politics & Policy, 33*(2), 105–125.

Gershon, S. A. (2013). Media coverage of minority congresswomen and voter evaluations: Evidence from an online experimental study. *Political Research Quarterly, 66*(3), 702–714.

References

Gilliam, F. D., Jr., & Iyengar, S. (2000). Prime suspects: The influence of local television news on the viewing public. *American Journal of Political Science, 44*(3), 560–573.

Giroux, H. A. (1998). *Channel surfing: Racism, the media, and the destruction of today's youth.* New York: Palgrave Macmillan.

Glick, P., Lameiras, M., & Castro, Y. R. (2002). Education and Catholic religiosity as predictors of hostile and benevolent sexism toward women and men. *Sex Roles, 47*(9), 433–441.

Glynn, C. J., & Huge, M. E. (2014). How pervasive are perceptions of bias? Exploring judgments of media bias in financial news. *International Journal of Public Opinion Research, 26*(4), 543–553.

Goldberg, B. (2014). *Bias: A CBS insider exposes how the media distorts the news.* Washington, DC: Regnery Publishing.

Gouldner, A. W. (1978). The new class project. *Theory and Society, 6,* 153–204.

Grabe, M. E., Kamhawi, R., & Yegiyan, N. (2009). Informing citizens: How people with different levels of education process television, newspaper, and web news. *Journal of Broadcasting & Electronic Media, 53*(1), 90–111.

Groeling, T. (2008). Who's the fairest of them all? An empirical test for partisan bias on ABC, CBS, NBC and Fox News. *Presidential Studies Quarterly, 38*(4), 631–656.

Groeling, T. (2013). Media bias by the numbers: Challenges and opportunities in the empirical study of partisan news. *Annual Review of Political Science, 16,* 129–151.

Groseclose, T. (2012). *Left turn: How liberal media bias distorts the American mind.* New York: St Martin's Griffin.

Groseclose, T., & Milyo, J. (2005). A measure of media bias. *The Quarterly Journal of Economics, 120*(4), 1191–1237.

Grossmann, M. (2017). Media bias (real and perceived) and the rise of partisan media. Retrieved from https://niskanencenter.org/blog/media-bias-real-perceived-rise-partisan-media/

Groves, R. (2006). Nonresponse rates and nonresponse bias in household surveys. *Public Opinion Quarterly, 70*(5), 646–675.

Gunther, A. C. (1992). Biased press or biased public? Attitudes toward media coverage of social groups. *Public Opinion Quarterly, 56*(2), 147–167.

Hagan, J. (2005, November 8). Circulation continues to decline at most major newspapers. *The Wall Street Journal,* p. B7.

Hamer, D. H., Hu, S., Magnuson, V. L., Hu, N., & Pattatucci, A. M. (1993). A linkage between DNA markers on the X chromosome and male sexual orientation. *Science, 261*(5119), 321–327.

Hanitzsch, T. (2007). Deconstructing journalism culture: Toward a universal theory. *Communication Theory, 17*(4), 367–385.

Hanson, R. E. (1997). Objectivity and narrative in contemporary reporting: A formal analysis. *Symbolic Interaction, 20*(4), 385–396.

Hellmueller, L., Vos, T. P., & Poepsel, M. A. (2013). Shifting journalistic capital? Transparency and objectivity in the twenty-first century. *Journalism Studies, 14*(3), 287–304.

Herek, G. M. (2002). Heterosexuals' attitudes toward bisexual men and women in the United States. *Journal of Sex Research, 39*(4), 264–274.

Hill, K. A., & Hughes, J. E. (1998). *Cyberpolitics: Citizen activism in the age of the Internet.* Lanham, MD: Rowman & Littlefield.

Ho, D. E., & Quinn, K. M. (2008). Measuring explicit political positions in media. *Quarterly Journal of Political Science, 3,* 353–377.

Hogan, B. (2010). The presentation of self in the age of social media: Distinguishing performances and exhibitions online. *Bulletin of Science, Technology & Society, 30*(6), 377–386.

Hughey, M. W. (2010). The (dis)similarities of white racial identities: The conceptual framework of 'hegemonic whiteness.' *Ethnic and Racial Studies, 33*(8), 1289–1309.

Hunter, J. D. (1991). *Culture war: The struggle to define America.* New York: Basic Books.

References

Huston, W. T. (2011). The top 50 liberal media bias examples. *Western Journalism*. Retrieved from http://www.westernjournalism.com/top-50-examples-liberal-media-bias/

Hyers, L. L. (2008). Everyday discrimination experienced by conservative Christians at the secular university. *Analyses of Social Issues and Public Policy, 8*(1), 113–137.

Imhoff, R., & Recker, J. (2012). Differentiating Islamophobia: Introducing a new scale to measure Islamo prejudice and secular Islam critique. *Political Psychology, 33*(6), 811–824.

Irvine, D. (2015). What media bias? CNN neglects to mention that op-ed writer raised more than $1 million for Hillary in 2008. Retrieved from http://www.aim.org/don-irvine-blog/what-media-bias-cnn-neglects-to-mention-that-op-ed-writer-raised-more-than-1-million-for-hillary-in-2008/

Iyengar, S., & Hahn, K. S. (2009). Red media, blue media: Evidence of ideological selectivity in media use. *Journal of Communication, 59*(1), 19–39.

Jackman, M. R., & Crane, M. (1986). "Some of my best friends are black...": Interracial friendship and whites' racial attitudes. *Public Opinion Quarterly, 50*(4), 459–486.

James, C. (2007). Reverse racism? Students' responses to equity programs. In T. Das Gupta, C. E. James, R. C. A. Maaka, G.-E. Galabuzi, & C. Andersen (Eds.) *Race and racialization essential readings* (pp. 356–362). Toronto: Canadian Scholars' Press.

Jayaratne, T. E., Ybarra, O., Sheldon, J. P., Brown, T. N., Feldbaum, M., Pfeffer, C. A., & Petty, E. M. (2006). White Americans' genetic lay theories of race differences and sexual orientation: Their relationship with prejudice toward blacks, and gay men and lesbians. *Group Processes & Intergroup Relations, 9*(1), 77–94.

Johnson, K. A. (1991). Objective news and other myths: The poisoning of young black minds. *The Journal of Negro Education, 60*(3), 328–341.

Johnson, M. A. (2004). Damsels in distress: If you're missing, it helps to be young, white and female. Retrieved from http://www.nbcnews.com/id/5325808/ns/us_news-crime_and_courts/t/damsels-distress/#.VZ_7Ok1FDIU

Johnson, T., & Kaye, B. (2010). Choosing is believing? How web gratifications and reliance affect Internet credibility among politically interested users. *Atlantic Journal of Communication, 18*(1), 1–21.

Judge, T. A., & Livingston, B. A. (2008). Is the gap more than gender? A longitudinal analysis of gender, gender role orientation, and earnings. *Journal of Applied Psychology, 93*(5), 994.

Kahn, K. F. (1994). Does gender make a difference? An experimental examination of sex stereotypes and press patterns in statewide campaigns. *American Journal of Political Science, 38*(1), 162–195.

Kane, E. W., & Kyyrö, E. K. (2001). For whom does education enlighten? Race, gender, education, and beliefs about social inequality. *Gender & Society, 15*(5), 710–733.

Katz, E., Haas, H., & Gurevitch, M. (1973). On the use of the mass media for important things. *American Sociological Review, 38*(2), 164–181.

Katz-Wise, S. L., Priess, H. A., & Hyde, J. S. (2010). Gender-role attitudes and behavior across the transition to parenthood. *Developmental psychology, 46*(1), 18.

Kaufmann, K. M. (1998). Racial conflict and political choice a study of mayoral voting behavior in Los Angeles and New York. *Urban Affairs Review, 33*(5), 655–685.

Keene, J. R., & Quadagno, J. (2004). Predictors of perceived work-family balance: Gender difference or gender similarity? *Sociological Perspectives, 47*(1), 1–23.

Keeter, S., Miller, C., Kohut, A., Groves, R., & Presser, S. (2000). Consequences of reducing nonresponse in a national telephone survey. *Public Opinion Quarterly, 64*(2), 125–148.

Kelley, Dean M. (1996). *Why Conservative Churches Are Growing: A Study in Sociology of Religion*. Macon, GA: Mercer University Press (originally published by Harper & Row in 1972).

Kelsey, G. D. (1965). *Racism and the Christian understanding of man*. New York: Scribner.

Kenney, K., & Simpson, C. (1993). Was coverage of the 1988 presidential race by Washington's two major dailies biased? *Journalism Quarterly, 70*(2), 345–355.

Kerr, P. A. (2003). The framing of fundamentalist Christians: Network television news, 1980–2000. *Journal of Media and Religion, 2*(4), 203–235.

Kerr, P. A., & Moy, P. (2002). Newspaper coverage of fundamentalist Christians, 1980–2000. *Journalism & Mass Communication Quarterly, 79*(1), 54–72.

Klayman, J. (1995). Varieties of confirmation bias. *Psychology of Learning and Motivation, 32,* 385–418.

Kperogi, F. A. (2013). Clash of civilization or clash of newspaper ideologies? An analysis of the ideological split in British newspaper commentaries on the 2002 Miss World riots in Nigeria. *Asia Pacific Media Educator, 23*(1), 121–143.

Kristol, I. (1979). The adversary culture of intellectuals. In S. M. Lipset (Ed.), *The third century* (pp. 327–343). Stanford, CA: Hoover Institution.

Kuhn, D., Cheney, R., & Weinstock, M. (2000). The development of epistemological understanding. *Cognitive development, 15*(3), 309–328.

Kuklinski, J. H., & Sigelman, L. (1992). When objectivity is not objective: Network television news coverage of U.S. Senators and the "paradox of objectivity." *The Journal of Politics, 54*(3), 810–833.

Kuypers, J. A. (2002). *Press bias and politics: How the media frame controversial issues.* Westport, CT: Praeger.

Lawrence, R. G., & Rose, M. (2010). *Hillary Clinton's race for the White House: Gender politics and the media on the campaign trail.* Boulder, CO: Lynne Rienner.

Lee, E. J. (2012). That's not the way it is: How user-generated comments on the news affect perceived media bias. *Journal of Computer-Mediated Communication, 18*(1), 32–45.

Lee, T.-T. (2010). The liberal media myth revisited: An examination of factors influencing perceptions of media bias. *Journal of Broadcasting and Electronic Media, 49*(1), 43–64.

Legge, J. S., Jr. (1983). The determinants of attitudes toward abortion in the American electorate. *Western Political Quarterly, 36,* 479–490.

Len-Rios, M. E., Rodgers, S., Thorson, E., & Yoon, D. (2005). Representation of women in news and photos: Comparing content to perceptions. *Journal of Communication, 55*(1), 152–168.

Lenhart, A., Purcell, K., Smith, A., & Zickuhr, K. (2010). Social media & mobile Internet use among teens and young adults. *Pew Internet & American Life Project.* Retrieved from http://www.pewinternet.org/2010/02/03/social-media-and-young-adults/

Lichter, S. R. (1990). *The media elite: America's new powerbrokers.* New York: Hastings House.

Lichter, S. R., Rothman, S., & Lichter, L. (1986). *The media elite.* Chevy Chase, MD: Adler & Adler.

Lin, M.-C., Haridakis, P. M., & Hanson, G. (2016). The role of political identity and media selection on perceptions of hostile media bias during the 2012 presidential campaign. *Journal of Broadcasting & Electronic Media, 60*(3), 425–447.

Lippa, R. A. (2005). *Gender, nature, and nurture.* New York: Routledge.

Loftus, J. (2001). America's liberalization in attitudes toward homosexuality, 1973 to 1998. *American Sociological Review, 66*(5), 762–782.

Long, H. (2016). Female CEOs are at record level in 2016, but its still only 5%. *CNN Money.* Retrieved from http://money.cnn.com/2016/09/29/investing/female-ceos-record-high/

Lorde, A. (2003). The master's tools will never dismantle the master's house. In R. Lewis & S. Mills (Eds.), *Feminist postcolonial theory: A reader* (pp. 25–27). New York: Routledge.

Losey, K. M., & Kurthen, H. (1995). The rhetoric of "political correctness" in the US media. *Amerikastudien, 40*(2), 227–245.

Lowry, D. T. (2008). Network TV news framing of good vs. bad economic news under democrat and republican presidents: A lexical analysis of political bias. *Journalism & Mass Communication Quarterly, 85*(3), 483–498.

Lowry, D. T., & Shidler, J. A. (1995). The sound bites, the biters, and the bitten: An analysis of network TV news bias in campaign '92. *Journalism & Mass Communication Quarterly, 72*(1), 33–44.

References

Lu, L., & Nicholson-Crotty, S. (2010). Reassessing the impact of Hispanic stereotypes on white Americans' immigration preferences. *Social Science Quarterly, 91*(5), 1312–1328.

Martin, P. Y., Osmond, M. W., Hesselbart, S., & Wood, M. (1980). The significance of gender as a social and demographic correlate of sex role attitudes. *Sociological Focus, 13*(4), 383–396.

Mastro, D., & Tukachinsky, R. (2011). The influence of exemplar versus prototype-based media primes on racial/ethnic evaluations. *Journal of Communication, 61*(5), 916–937.

Mayer, L. S., & McHugh, P. R. (2016). Special report—Sexuality and gender: Findings from the biological, psychological and social sciences. *The New Atlantis: A Journal of Technology & Society, 50*. Retrieved from https://www.thenewatlantis.com/docLib/20160819_TNA50 SexualityandGender.pdf

McCarthy, J. (2015). In U.S., socialist presidential candidates least appealing. Retrieved from http://www.gallup.com/poll/183713/socialist-presidential-candidates-least-appealing. aspx?utm_source=tagrss&utm_medium=rss&utm_campaign=syndication

McCombs, M. E., & Shaw, D. L. (1972). The agenda-setting function of mass media. *Public Opinion Quarterly, 36*(2), 176–187.

McConahay, J. B. (1986). Modern racism, ambivalence, and the Modern Racism Scale. In J. F. Dovidio & S. L. Gaertner (Eds.), *Prejudice, discrimination, and racism* (pp. 91–125). San Diego, CA, US: Academic Press.

McEwan, C. (2001). Postcolonialism, feminism and development: Intersections and dilemmas. *Progress in Development Studies, 1*(2), 93–111.

McNerney, S. (2011). Confirmation bias and art. Retrieved from http://blogs.scientificamerican. com/guest-blog/confirmation-bias-and-art/

Megill, A. (1994). *Rethinking objectivity*. Durham, NC: Duke University Press.

Mellado, C., Moreira, S. V., Lagos, C., & Hernández, M. E. (2012). Comparing journalism cultures in Latin America the case of Chile, Brazil and Mexico. *International Communication Gazette, 74*(1), 60–77.

Mendes, K. (2012). 'Feminism rules! Now, where's my swimsuit?' Re-evaluating feminist discourse in print media 1968–2008. *Media, Culture & Society, 34*(5), 554–570.

Meyers, M. (2004). African American women and violence: Gender, race, and class in the news. *Critical Studies in Media Communication, 21*(2), 95–118.

Miller, P. M. (1996). Teaching women in the news: Exposing the "invisible majority." *Political Science and Politics, 29*(3), 513–517.

Moore, K. S. (2008). Class formations: Competing forms of black middle-class identity. *Ethnicities, 8*(4), 492–517.

Morgan, M. Y. (1987). The impact of religion on gender-role attitudes. *Psychology of Women Quarterly, 11*(3), 301–310.

Morris, J. S., & Francia, P. L. (2010). Cable news, public opinion, and the 2004 party conventions. *Political Research Quarterly, 63*(4), 834–849.

Moss, I. (2014). Ending reparative therapy in minors: An appropriate legislative response. *Family Court Review, 52*(2), 316–329.

Nadal, K. L., Issa, A., Griffin, K. E., Hamit, S., & Lyons, O. B. (2010). Religious microaggressions in the United States: Mental health implications for religious minority groups. In D. W. Sue (Ed.), *Microaggressions and marginality: Manifestation, dynamics, and impact* (pp. 287–310.) Hoboken, NJ: John Wiley & Sons.

Newson, L., & Richerson, P. J. (2016). Moral beliefs about homosexuality: Testing a cultural evolutionary hypothesis. *ASEBL Journal, 12*(1), 2–21.

Nickerson, R. S. (1998). Confirmation bias: A ubiquitous phenomenon in many guises. *Review of general psychology, 2*(2), 175.

Nielsen, L. B. (2002). Subtle, pervasive, harmful: Racist and sexist remarks in public as hate speech. *Journal of Social Issues, 58*(2), 265–280.

Niven, D. (2002). *Tilt? The search for media bias*. Westport, CT: Praeger.

Nolan, D. (2009). Rethinking journalism culture and authority: Beyond 'professionalism.' In

References

T. Flew (Ed.) *Communication, Creativity and Global Citizenship: Refereed Proceedings of the Australian and New Zealand Communications Association Annual Conference*, Brisbane, July 8–10. Retrieved from https://www.anzca.net/documents/2009-conf-papers/61-rethinking-journalism-culture-and-authority-beyond-professionalism-1/file.html

Noor, M., Shnabel, N., Halabi, S., & Nadler, A. (2012). When suffering begets suffering: The psychology of competitive victimhood between adversarial groups in violent conflicts. *Personality and Social Psychology Review, 16*(4), 351–374.

North, L. (2009). Rejecting the 'f-word': How 'feminism' and 'feminists' are understood in the newsroom. *Journalism, 10*(6), 739–757.

Ohlander, J., Batalova, J., & Treas, J. (2005). Explaining educational influences on attitudes toward homosexual relations. *Social Science Research, 34*(4), 781–799.

Olasky, M., & Smith, W. C. (2013). *Prodigal press: Confronting the anti–Christian bias of the American news media.* Phillipsburg, NJ: P & R Publishing.

Omi, M., & Winant, H. (2014). *Racial formation in the United States.* New York: Routledge.

Oyewumi, O. (2001). Ties that (un)bind: Feminism, sisterhood and other foreign relations. *Jenda: A Journal of Culture and African Women Studies, 1*(1). Retrieved from https://www.africaknowledgeproject.org/index.php/jenda/article/view/25

Pager, D. (2003). The mark of a criminal record. *American Journal of Sociology, 108*(5), 937–975.

Pager, D. (2007). The use of field experiments for studies of employment discrimination: Contributions, critiques, and directions for the future. *Annals of the American Academy of Political and Social Sciences, 209*(January), 104–133.

Pager, D., & Shepard, H. (2008). The sociology of discrimination: Racial discrimination in employment, housing, credit, and consumer markets. *Annual Review of Sociology, 34,* 181–209.

Papacharissi, Z. (2002). The virtual sphere: The Internet as a public sphere. *New Media & Society, 4*(1), 9–27.

Parenti, M. (1996). *Dirty truths.* San Francisco, CA: City Lights.

Parillo, V. N. (1997). Strangers to these shores: Race and ethnic relationships in the United States (5th ed.). Boston: Allyn and Bacon.

Patterson, T., & Donsbach, W. (1996). News decisions: Journalists as partisan actors. *Political Communication, 13,* 455–468.

Pieper, A. L. (2011). Flouting faith? Religious hostility and the American left, 1977–2000. *American Politics Research, 39*(4), 754–778.

Pike, G. R. (2008). Weighting adjustments to compensate for survey nonresponse. *Research in Higher Education, 6*(49), 153–171.

Pitt, R. N., Jr. (2006). Downlow mountain? De/stigmatizing bisexuality through pitying and pejorative discourses in media. *Journal of Men's Studies, 14*(2), 254–258.

Pratto, F., & Stewart, A. L. (2012). Group dominance and the half-blindness of privilege. *Journal of Social Issues, 68*(1), 28–45.

Ramsey, E. M., & Santiago, G. (2004). The conflation of male homosexuality and femininity in Queer Eye for the Straight Guy. *Feminist Media Studies, 4*(3), 353–355.

Ranly, D. (1979). How religion editors of newspapers view their jobs and religion. *Journalism & Mass Communication Quarterly, 56*(4), 844–849.

Ribeiro, N. (2012). Objectivity versus 'toxic propaganda': The case of transborder broadcasts to Portugal during World War II. *Interactions: Studies in Communication & Culture, 3*(3), 275–287.

Richardson, A. (2011). Introduction: Essentialism in science and culture. *Critical Quarterly, 53* (4), 1–11.

Riesch, H. (2011). Changing news: Re-adjusting science studies to online newspapers. *Public Understanding of Science, 20*(6), 771–777.

Robinson, E. (2005, June 10). (White) women we love. *Washington Post.* Retrieved from http://www.washingtonpost.com/wp-dyn/content/article/2005/06/09/AR2005060901729.html?noredirect=on

References

Robinson, S., & Culver, K. B. (2016). When white reporters cover race: News media, objectivity and community (dis)trust. *Journalism*. Published online. doi 10.1177/1464884916663599

Roche, S. P., Pickett, J. T., & Gertz, M. (2016). The scary world of online news? Internet news exposure and public attitudes toward crime and justice. *Journal of Quantitative Criminology, 32*(2), 215–236.

Rodenberg, R. (2011). Perception? Reality: Analyzing specific allegations of NBA referee bias. *Journal of Quantitative Analysis in Sports, 7*(2). Published online. doi 10.2202/1559-0410.1326

Rodriguez, I. (2009). 'Diversity writing' and the liberal discourse on multiculturalism in mainstream newspapers. *The Howard Journal of Communications, 20*(2), 167–188.

Romer, D., Jamieson, K. H., & Aday, S. (2003). Television news and the cultivation of fear of crime. *Journal of Communication, 53*(1), 88–104.

Romer, D., Jamieson, K. H., & De Coteau, N. J. (1998). The treatment of persons of color in local television news: Ethnic blame discourse or realistic group conflict? *Communication Research, 25*(3), 286–305.

Roof, W. C., & McKinney, W. (1987). *American mainline religion: Its changing shape and future.* New Brunswick, NJ: Rutgers University Press.

Roszak, T. (1958). *The making of a counter culture: Reflections on the technocratic society and its youthful opposition.* Garden City, NY: Doubleday.

Rothman, S., & Lichter, S. R. (2008). *The vanishing conservative: Is there a glass ceiling?* In R. Maranto, R. E. Redding, & F. M. Hess (Eds.), *The Politically Correct University* (pp. 60–76). Washington, DC: The AEI Press.

Rowatt, W. C., Tsang, J. A., Kelly, J., LaMartina, B., McCullers, M., & McKinley, A. (2006). Associations between religious personality dimensions and implicit homosexual prejudice. *Journal for the Scientific Study of Religion, 45*(3), 397–406.

Ryan, C. S., Hunt, J. S., Weible, J. A., Peterson, C. R., & Casas, J. F. (2007). Multicultural and colorblind ideology, stereotypes, and ethnocentrism among black and white Americans. *Group Processes & Intergroup Relations, 10*(4), 617–637.

Samson, F. L. (2013). Altering public university admission standards to preserve white group position in the United States: Results from a laboratory experiment. *Comparative Education Review, 57*(3), 369–396.

Savali, K. (2015). Throw away the script: How media bias is killing black America. *The Root.* Retrieved from https://www.theroot.com/throw-away-the-script-how-media-bias-is-killing-black-1790860024

Schaefer, R. T. (1996). Presidential address—Education and prejudice: Unraveling the relationship. *The Sociological Quarterly, 37*(1), 1–16.

Schaffner, B. F., & Gadson, M. (2004). Reinforcing stereotypes? Race and local television news coverage of Congress. *Social Science Quarterly, 85*(3), 604–623.

Schiffer, A. J. (2006). Assessing partisan bias in political news: The case(s) of local Senate election coverage. *Political Communication, 23*, 23–39.

Schlosser, L. Z. (2003). Christian privilege: Breaking a sacred taboo. *Journal of Multicultural Counseling and Development, 31*(1), 44–51.

Schudson, M. (1981). *Discovering the news: A social history of American newspapers.* New York: Basic Books.

Schudson, M. (2001). The objectivity norm in American journalism. *Journalism, 2*(2), 149–170.

Schulte, L. J., & Battle, J. (2004). The relative importance of ethnicity and religion in predicting attitudes towards gays and lesbians. *Journal of Homosexuality, 47*(2), 127–142.

Seelye, K. Q. (2007, March 26). Drop in ad revenue raises tough question for newspapers. *The New York Times.* Retrieved from https://www.nytimes.com/2007/03/26/business/media/26paper.html

Semati, M. (2010). Islamophobia, culture and race in the age of empire. *Cultural Studies, 24*(2), 256–275.

References

Shandwick, W. (2011). Civility in America 2011. Published online. Retrieved from https://www.webershandwick.com/uploads/news/files/Civility_in_America_2011.pdf

Shapiro, B. (2011). *Primetime propaganda: The true Hollywood story of how the left took over your TV.* Northampton, MA: Broadside Books.

Sherkat, D. E., De Vries, K. M., & Creek, S. (2010). Race, religion, and opposition to same-sex marriage. *Social Science Quarterly, 91*(1), 80–98.

Shih, T.-H., & Fan, X. (2008). Comparing response rates from web and mail surveys: A meta-analysis. *Field Methods, 20*(3), 249–271.

Silk, M. (1998). *Unsecular media: Making news of religion in America.* Chicago: University of Illinois Press.

Singer, E., & Ye, C. (2013). The use and effects of incentive in surveys. *Annals of the American Academy of Political and Social Science, 645*(1), 112–141.

Skovsgaard, M., Albæk, E., Bro, P., & de Vreese, C. (2012). A reality check: How journalists' role perceptions impact their implementation of the objectivity norm. *Journalism.* Published online. doi 1464884912442286

Smedley, A., & Smedley, B. D. (2005). Race as biology is fiction, racism as a social problem is real: Anthropological and historical perspectives on the social construction of race. *American Psychologist, 60*(1), 16–26.

Smith, S. L., Choueiti, M., & Gall, S. (2011). *Gender inequality in popular films: Examining on screen portrayals and behind-the-scenes employment patterns in motion pictures released between 2007–2009.* Los Angeles: Annenberg School for Communication & Journalism. Retrieved from https://annenberg.usc.edu/sites/default/files/MDSCI_Gender_Inequality_in_300_Films.pdf

Snyder, D. (2015). One size does not fit all: A look at the disproportionate effects of federal mandatory minimum drug sentences on racial minorities and how they have contributed to the degradation of the underprivileged African–American family. *Hamline University's School of Law's Journal of Public Law and Policy, 36*(1), 77–118.

Sola, K. (2016). There are just 20 women CEOs of S&P 500 companies. Here's how much they make. *Forbes.* Retrieved from http://www.forbes.com/sites/katiesola/2016/05/06/there-are-just-20-women-ceos-in-sp-500-companies-heres-how-much-they-make/#4c4a9935420f

Somaiya, R. (2015, April 6). Rolling stone article on rape at University of Virginia failed all basics, report says. *New York Times.* Retrieved from https://www.nytimes.com/2015/04/06/business/media/rolling-stone-retracts-article-on-rape-at-university-of-virginia.html

Sreberny-Mohammadi, A., & Ross, K. (1996). Women MPs and the media: Representing the body politic. *Parliamentary Affairs, 49*(1), 103–115.

Stalsburg, B. L. (2015). The media's coverage of Hillary Clinton is downright irresponsible. Retrieved from http://www.huffingtonpost.com/brittany-l-stalsburg-phd/hillary-clintons-poll-num_b_8066832.html

Stamper, J., & Brants, K. (2011). A changing culture of political television journalism. In K. Brants & K. Voltmer (Eds.) *Political Communication in Postmodern Democracy: Challenging the Primacy of Politics.* (pp. 111–125). New York: Palgrave Macmillan.

Steele, J. E. (1997). Don't ask, don't tell, don't explain: Unofficial sources and television coverage of the dispute over gays in the military. *Political Communication, 14*(1), 83–96.

Stempel, G. H., III, & Windhauser, J. W. (1984). The prestige press revisited: Coverage of the 1980 presidential campaign. *Journalism Quarterly, 61,* 49–55.

Stossel, J. (2004). *Give me a break: How I exposed hucksters, cheats, and scam artists and became the scourge of the liberal media.* New York: Harper Perennial.

Streckfuss, R. (1990). Objectivity in journalism: A search and a reassessment. *Journalism Quarterly, 67*(4), 973–983.

Sullivan, D., Landau, M. J., Branscombe, N. R., & Rothschild, Z. K. (2012). Competitive victimhood as a response to accusations of ingroup harm doing. *Journal of Personality and Social Psychology, 102*(4), 778.

References

Sundar, S. S. (1999). Exploring receivers' criteria for perception of print and online news. *Journalism & Mass Communication Quarterly, 76*(2), 373–386.

Surette, R. (2014). *Media, crime, and criminal justice.* Stamford, CT: Cengage Learning.

Taylor, L. D., & Setters, T. (2011). Watching aggressive, attractive, female protagonists shapes gender roles for women among male and female undergraduate viewers. *Sex Roles, 65*(1–2), 35–46.

Tewksbury, D. (2003). What do Americans really want to know? Tracking the behavior of news readers on the Internet. *Journal of Communication, 53*(4), 694–710.

Tobin, G. A., & Weinberg, A. K. (2007). Profiles of the American university, Vol. 2: Religious beliefs and behaviors of college faculty. *Institute for Jewish and Community Research.* Retrieved from http://www.jewishresearch.org/PDFs2/FacultyReligion07.pdf

Tsesis, A. (2002). *Destructive messages: How hate speech paves the way for harmful social movements.* New York: NYU Press.

Twine, F. W. (1996). Brown skinned white girls: Class, culture and the construction of white identity in suburban communities. *Gender, place and culture: A journal of feminist geography, 3*(2), 205–224.

Underwood, D., & Stamm, K. (2001). Are journalists really irreligious? A multidimensional analysis. *Journalism & Mass Communication Quarterly, 78*(4), 771–786.

Viguerie, R. (2012). Newt exposes media's anti–Christian bias during non-debate in New Hampshire. Retrieved from http://conservativehq.com/article/6191-newt-exposes-media%E2%80%99s-anti-christian-bias-during-non-debate-new-hampshire

Vine, J. (2006). Does the lovable larrikin live? A comparative analysis of Australian journalism culture 1974 and 2003. *Australian Journalism Review, 28*(2), 67–78.

Visser, M., Lubbers, M., Kraaykamp, G., & Jaspers, E. (2014). Support for radical left ideologies in Europe. *European Journal of Political Research, 53*(3), 541–558.

Vos, T. P. (2012). 'Homo journalisticus': Journalism education's role in articulating the objectivity norm. *Journalism, 13*(4), 435–449.

Waldron, J. (2012). *The harm in hate speech.* Cambridge, MA: Harvard University Press.

Watts, M. D., Domke, D., Shah, D. V., & Fan, D. P. (1999). Elite cues and media bias in presidential campaigns: Explaining public perceptions of a liberal press. *Communication Research, 26*(2), 144–175.

Weaver, D. H., & Wilhoit, G. C. (1996). *The American journalist in the 1990s: US news people at the end of an era.* Mahwah, NJ: Lawrence Erlbaum.

Westerståhl, J., & Johansson, F. (1986). News ideologies as moulders of domestic news. *European Journal of Communication, 1*(2), 133–149.

Wilcox, C., & Jelen, T. G. (1991). The effects of employment and religion on women's feminist attitudes. *The International Journal for the Psychology of Religion, 1*(3), 161–171.

Wilder, D. A. (1984). Intergroup contact: The typical member and the exception to the rule. *Journal of Experimental Social Psychology, 20*(2), 177–194.

Wildman, S. M., & David, A. D. (1994). Language and silence: Making systems of privilege visible. *Santa Clara Law Review, 35*(3), 881–906.

Winant, H. (2004). Behind blue eyes: Whiteness and contemporary US racial politics. In M. Fine, L. Weis, L. P. Pruitt, & A. Burns (Eds.) *Off White: Readings on Power, Privilege, and Resistance* (2nd ed.; pp. 3–16). New York: Routledge.

Winship, C., & Radbill, L. (1994). Sampling weights and regression analysis. *Sociological Method and Research, 23*(2), 230–257.

Yancey, G. (2013). *Dehumanizing Christians: Cultural competition in a multicultural world.* Piscataway, NJ: Transaction Publishers.

Yancey, G., Reimer, S., & O'Connell, J. (2015). How academics view conservative Protestants. *Sociology of Religion, 76*(3), 315–336.

Yancey, G. A. (2010). *Neither Jew nor gentile: Exploring issues of racial diversity on Protestant college campuses.* Oxford, United Kingdom: Oxford University Press.

177

References

Yancey, G. A. (2011). *Compromising scholarship: Religious and political bias in American higher education.* Waco, TX: Baylor University Press.

Yancey, G. A., & Williamson, D. (2012). *What motivates cultural progressives: Understanding opposition to the political and Christian right.* Waco, TX: Baylor University Press.

Yancey, G. A., & Williamson, D. A. (2014). *So many Christians, so few lions: Is there Christianophobia in the United States?* Lanham, MD: Rowman & Littlefield.

Zilber, J., & Niven, D. (2000). *Racialized coverage of Congress: The news in black and white.* Westport, CT: Prager.

Index

www.ingramcontent.com/pod-product-compliance
Ingram Content Group UK Ltd.
Pitfield, Milton Keynes, MK11 3LW, UK
UKHW041355190726
13851UKWH00014B/125